D1482107

The Resurrection Effect

The Resurrection Effect

Transforming Christian Life and Thought

Anthony J. Kelly, CSsR

ORBIS BOOKS

Maryknoll, New York 10545

Founded in 1970, Orbis Books endeavors to publish works that enlighten the mind, nourish the spirit, and challenge the conscience. The publishing arm of the Maryknoll Fathers and Brothers, Orbis seeks to explore the global dimensions of the Christian faith and mission, to invite dialogue with diverse cultures and religious traditions, and to serve the cause of reconciliation and peace. The books published reflect the opinions of their authors and are not meant to represent the official position of the Maryknoll Society. To obtain more information about Maryknoll and Orbis Books, please visit our website at www.maryknoll.org.

Library of Congress Cataloging in Publication Data

Kelly, Anthony, 1938-
    The resurrection effect : transforming Christian life and thought / Anthony J. Kelly.
        p. cm.
    Includes bibliographical references and index.
    ISBN 978-1-57075-770-9
    1. Jesus Christ—Resurrection.   2. Theology, Doctrinal—History—20th century.   3. Theology, Doctrinal—History—21st century. I. Title.
    BT482.K45 2008
    232'.5—dc22
                                    2007038081

Contents

Preface

This book deals with the resurrection of the crucified Jesus as the focal event affecting all Christian faith and theology. With such a concentration, however, we intend neither to add another specialisation to an already over-specialised theological curriculum, nor are we trying to fit the resurrection more neatly into a theological system as one question, doctrine or scriptural theme among many. But we do intend to explore the focal character of the resurrection event for faith, and, as a consequence, the need for theology, in all its specialisations—biblical, fundamental, systematic, liturgical and moral—to be located "in the resurrection", so to speak, and to proceed in its light. With that end in mind, this is not "new theology" of the resurrection, building on, or in contrast to, the outstanding work of writers such as Durrwell, Pannenberg, O'Collins, von Balthasar, D. B. Hart, N. T. Wright, James Alison and so many others. Such a vast work of synthesis and systematic construction is surely a most desirable project for the future, even if beyond our present scope. On the other hand, this book can contribute to such a task, even if in a somewhat preliminary way, as it seeks to make theology more "resurrectional" in its method, mood and content. A fresh receptivity to the act of God in raising Jesus from the dead, along with a grateful appreciation of scholarship, past and present, will point in this direction. Consequently, we hope to make a contribution to the resurrection of theology as an assured, distinctive mode of Christian rationality.

Why such an exploration of the "resurrection effect" is timely will be explained in different ways as the book unfolds. Suffice it to say at the moment that the resurrectional focus of Christian life and thought is always in need of being refreshed and sharpened. Just as Sunday as "the Lord's Day" commemorating the resurrection can be lost in the modern secular weekend, or, for that matter, slip out of focus in the succession of liturgical seasons as, say, the first Sunday of Advent, or third Sunday of Lent, or the tenth Sunday of "ordinary time", and so forth, something similar can happen for theology. It came home to me after completing my recent *Eschatology and Hope* (Orbis, 2006) that all the various themes and questions treated in such a book depended, in the most elemental way, on the resurrection of Christ. Our present hope in the face of all the challenges of life, suffering and death, is an effect of the resurrection. Unless *that* had happened, hope would at best be a repressive optimism, or an accommodation to routine despair. But the effect of the resurrection is to see the world and to live in it otherwise. That is hardly an original insight. In fact it is so taken for granted that the originality of the resurrection's effect on the life of faith can be forgotten. What originally made all the difference gradually becomes a remote presupposition, only vaguely affecting the way we understand God, ourselves and the world itself. This book, then, aims to sharpen the focus and to assist readers to register the resurrection effect in all aspects of their lives.

To this end, the chapters converge in one aim—to refresh faith and theology in receptivity to the focal phenomenon of the resurrection. To some degree, such receptivity is always being presupposed in the quest for doctrinal clarity, systematic elaboration and moral theology. But there is room, we shall argue, for a more disciplined attentiveness to the ways in which this key Christian phenomenon is given or disclosed to faith. In short, a phenomenological phase precedes all theoretical or practical considerations. We must first attend to what is given in its own right and in its own light.

One way of elaborating a phenomenology of the resurrection is to appeal to a class of phenomena designated as "saturated phenomenona" (Jean-Luc Marion). However odd-sounding in current English, such a term suggests that the appearance, "given-ness", or self-disclosive impact of some phenomena, is so multi-dimensional, so inexhaustible in significance, so over-brimming and prodigal in its effect, that its special status must be recognised. In a word, these phenomena are recognised as "saturated". For instance, there is a kind of event—birth, death, a world war, falling in love—that overflows any fixed boundaries, and provokes endless interpretation. The same goes for a striking work of art: it eludes any one point of view. Da Vinci's *Mona Lisa* creates its own history of interpretation and imposes itself in an endless play of perspectives as succeeding generations view it through the centuries. Take another instance: our bodies or "flesh" are not something we simply possess and classify as a biological entity of a particular type. For the body is a field of incarnate communication with a whole world, especially in the intimate communications of love or parenthood. Another example is the "face" of another. It is no ordinary object, but, in a sense, a commanding presence. It calls one to a responsibility and an ethical co-existence with the other of limitless implications. All these phenomena have one thing in common: they occur as a kind of "revelation", for they are given from beyond the normal horizon of our perceptions. They are disclosed in a superabundant or over-brimming fashion. In the way they are given, they draw us into a field of an unobjectifiable and inexhaustible "excess". In this way, saturated phenomena affect us, not merely with the superabundance of their significance, but with the strange power to call us, individually or communally, to see the world within a different horizon. Each in its own way comes to mean the world to us—and our place within it. To a super-saturated degree, the resurrection of the Crucified is a singular instance of a phenomenon of this kind, while each of these particular instances, as we shall see, expresses some aspect of the manner in which the resurrection reveals itself to reflective faith.

Though phenomenological terminology may appear oddly technical or even exotic, the experience it appeals to is not unfamiliar. At the risk of being too literal in reference to "saturation", the following instance might be useful in emphasising what is at stake.

One may weary of reading about the wonders of the Great Barrier Reef and viewing documentaries on its marvels—and the present threats to it. We come to feel the need to go there, to dive into it, to be immersed in it, to be carried by its tides, to snorkel around its coral splendours and swim with its variegated marine life. Books and articles, photos and museum specimens are left behind for the sake of immersing oneself in the living reality, and so to have an immediate exposure to it at first hand. This does not demand leaving all scientific exploration behind, or forgetting ecological concerns. But it does mean letting the Reef reveal itself by drawing us into the immediacy of what is so overwhelmingly given. Receptivity to the character of the given tends to inspire energetic testimony to this natural wonder of the world. Moreover, unless people continue to experience and explore the Reef, all the words, policies, and programs would soon appear second-hand and paper-thin. Any number of concerns might lead the first-hand explorer to reflect on what has been so encompassingly experienced, and so inspire particular responses of a scientific, ecological, artistic or political character. But, in a profound sense, once it is immediately experienced, no one can get over what has been given by way of immersion in that exuberant world of marine wonders. Once "saturated" by it, immersed in it, it becomes significant in new ways. Awash with such experience, we may well see things differently in contrast to pages of scientific reports, the arresting photographs, the tourist brochures and so forth. For the Reef is not something disclosed by being catalogued as a national treasure, or treated as a resource for the local tourist industry, or made into a scientific object of marine biology—photographed, classified, catalogued, mapped and modelled with technical expertise. There is an original moment, might we say, when we can cease to possess or own it in such ways, and allow the Reef to possess us. As we float over its corals and swim amongst its schools of fish, we are no longer the centre. However fleetingly, its reality literally washes over us with a totality that makes us part of it. The Reef must be allowed to come to us in its uniqueness. And so we come to have an intimate familiarity with this particular natural wonder in a way that precedes, calls forth but ever eludes the

business of scientific analysis, ecological management, tourist development and so forth. Stealing a march on Marion and others, visitors may
speak of the Reef as an "event" that changed their perceptions of the
natural world forever: for they found themselves "faced" with nature in
its uncanny and enthralling otherness. Yet, at the same time, they feel
themselves newly "embodied" in a world of wonder and variety beyond
any normal range of contacts. They are met with the impact of a "beauty"
that overwhelms them. Something has "revealed" itself that words and
ideas can never capture.

All metaphors limp, and all experience of the totality is very limited;
but the point is there. The phenomenal given-ness of reality in the immediacy of experience precedes the questions, reflections and decisions
that might arise. The phenomenon is more than a reflection of our prior
concerns or previous experience. It exceeds expectations in a striking
way. In this and similar cases, it is as though the silvering which backs
the mirrors of our perception is stripped away and lets the light of a
larger world shine through—so that we see more than our own reflection. Some might prefer the more homely metaphor of not confusing the
woods with the trees—of a rain forest, for example. You can cut down
a particular tree for fuel or for timber, or even hunt out its flora and
fauna for some particular purpose, guided by any number of maps marking particular entry points. But, in the totality, you live in another key,
wandering through it, or lost in its wonders, alive to the prodigality of
its reality. No amount of records can ever "capture" what the explorer
has been through: the overall feel of the totality of the sounds, scents,
colours and profusion of forms is more than can be objectified in the
photographic records and mementos compared to what has been "given"
to those who have been there.

The point in making this rather literal reference to a saturated phenomenon in the natural world is to suggest how the resurrection of
Jesus is such a phenomenon, however uniquely, in the world of Christian experience. For, in ways yet to be discussed, the resurrection en-
compasses the life of faith with an inexhaustible significance. In recent
years, theology has been criticized for not clearly focusing on the specif-
ics of Christian revelation, and thereby being too influenced by dominant ideologies of the day.[1] All the more reason, then, to emphasise the
need for attentiveness to the concrete particular form of Christian revelation given in the cross and resurrection of Jesus. Moreover, if the

---

[1]For example, Michael J. Buckley, *At the Origins of Modern Atheism* (New Haven: Yale
University Press, 1987); Joseph S. O'Leary, *Questioning Back: The Overcoming of Metaphys-
ics in the Christian Tradition* (New York: Seabury, 1985); John Milbank, *Theology and Social
Theory: Beyond Secular Reason* (Oxford: Blackwell, 1993); William C. Placher, *The Domes-
tication of Transcendence: How Modern Thinking About God Went Wrong* (Louisville:
Westminster, 1996).

Christianity of this new millennium is to be increasingly in spiritual dialogue with the great religions of the East,[2] if it is to be a bearer of hope in the face of the horrendous evils of our time, it will be necessary to reclaim what is distinctive to Christian experience if the Christian contribution is to be authentic. Without a receptivity to what has been uniquely given, the doctrines of faith cannot but appear increasingly superficial, abstract and exotic, while theology will look like a more or less sophisticated distraction from the novelty at the heart of the New Testament itself. These pages aim to refine the sensibility of faith to "the fullness, the superabundance, the inexhaustible flowing forth . . . and encompassing flood of the divine attributes" (Newman)[3] as they are embodied in Christ risen from the dead: "for in him all the fullness of God was pleased to dwell" (Col 1:19). To this end, we structure our reflections into nine chapters followed by a brief conclusion.

Chapter One, " 'Placing' the Resurrection: A Theological Problem" is deliberately provocative. We point out the awkwardness of the place of the resurrection in theology, and attempt to suggest some of the reasons for this strange unevenness and even neglect. One of the humbler tasks of theology, if it is to proceed in good faith, is to affirm and explore the obvious. The resurrection is so obvious that it is too easily *taken for granted*, as a given, a *datum*, in the various theological specialisations. But what can be overlooked is the need to take the resurrection *as granted*, as the great presupposition in all theological systematic and moral discourse. It is not merely a *datum*, a given, but the *donum*, the gift *par excellence*, affecting the whole business of theology. Such critical remarks lead to the recognition of a need for a more phenomenological phase or space in which reflection on faith can recover a sense of the originality and uniqueness of the resurrection event as integral to every aspect of theology. We suggest, in fact, that the postmodern critique of philosophical and theological systems provides a fresh opportunity for Christian rationality to give a fuller and more vital recognition to the unique phenomenon of the resurrection as the focus of Christian life and thought.

Chapter Two, "A Phenomenological Approach to the Resurrection", moves into some more technical areas. It first pauses over the meaning of phenomenology in this theological context. We then move to a consideration of a special class of phenomena that can be designated as "saturated", because of the prodigality of their significance. By reflecting on such instances of these as "revelation", "the event", "the work

---

[2]The need to be attuned to the experiential dimensions of Christian truth is challengingly brought out by Joseph O'Leary, *La vérité chrétienne à l'âge du pluralisme religieux* (Paris: Cerf, 1994).

[3]John Henry Newman, *Discourses Addressed to Mixed Congregations* (London: Burns and Oates, 1881), 309.

of art", "the body" and "the face", we suggest a number of converging perspectives in which the unique phenomenon of the resurrection can be freshly appreciated as the mystery at the heart of Christian experience.

Chapter Three, "The Resurrection and the Phenomenon of the New Testament" is necessarily broad in scope. The basic point is that the New Testament in its entirety is a literary phenomenon arising out of the experience and proclamation of the resurrection. It reverses ingrained attitudes of seeking to find the resurrection "in the New Testament" by pointing to the need to appreciate the New Testament as a whole in the light of the resurrection. In that light, the rhetoric of these documents of faith is marked with a special creativity straining to express what has occurred, but can never be fully expressed in its excess and world-transforming effect.

Chapter Four, "The Resurrection Event", attempts a synthetic expression of the culminating event that gave rise to the New Testament—and to the life and mission of the Church. After a consideration of the multi-dimensionality of the resurrection event, we present some six aspects integral to it (paschal, paternal, filial, effusive, sacramental and eschatological). The chapter concludes with a remark on the kinds of rhetoric and dimension of meaning that the resurrection event inspires.

Chapter Five, "Paul and the Resurrection Effect", focuses on Paul as a primary witness to the resurrection effect in his life and thinking. After considering, with the aid of Eric Voegelin's analysis, the character of the Pauline experience of the risen Christ, we locate his conversion within the larger setting of his life and mission. We then examine how Paul's experience of the risen One determined the character of his hope and sense of God, with particular reference to 1 Corinthians and Philippians 2:5-11.

Chapter Six, "Resurrection: The Visual Phenomenon", addresses a basic question. From one point of view, the self-disclosures of the risen Christ to the vision of the early witnesses finish with Paul. Blessed are those who have not seen but believe (e.g., Jn 20:29). But this does not mean that the resurrection makes faith blind and renders it sightless. Are there other forms of "seeing" and sensing that are part of the resurrection effect in the ongoing life of the Church? The answer lies in the gift of the Holy Spirit, the first witness to Christ and the principal manifestation of the resurrection effect.

Chapter Seven, "Subjectivity, Objectivity and the Resurrection", is intended to answer some of the questions inherent in the previous chapters, and to lead into the account of "salvific realism" to follow. It recognises that a play of polarities between the subjective and the objective aspects of the resurrection is inevitable, but suggests such polarities are most fruitfully resolved in the field of communication introduced by the phenomenon of the resurrection event itself.

Chapter Eight, "The Salvific Realism of the Resurrection", is more systematic in style. It treats first the "salvific objectivity" encountered in the divine initiative, the "otherness" and humanity of Christ's presence, the offer of forgiveness, the witness of the empty tomb, and engagement with the wider world. Yet there is a correlative "salvific subjectivity" manifested in the experience of the disciples, in their sense of a new beginning and understanding, in their vocation to witness, in the universality of their mission, and in the sober acceptance of a reactive world.

Chapter Nine, "Extensions of the Resurrection Effect", restricts itself to just three theological considerations in which the resurrection does not usually figure in any significant manner. First is the resurrection in relation to the revelation of the Trinity. Secondly, we remark on the strange absence of the resurrection in moral theology and Christian ethics. Thirdly, in the context of interfaith dialogue, we reflect on the transcultural and universal significance of the resurrection for the mission of the Church.

A brief conclusion follows, both summarising the positions we have reached and pointing the way ahead.

Finally, my thanks go to my Redemptorist community who continue to support my theological activities, and to the colleagues and friends who commented so helpfully on the manuscript at different stages of its development. I must mention especially Anne Hunt, Mary Coloe, PBVM, and Tom Ryan, SM. When it came to French phenomenology, Shane Mackinlay, Robyn Horner and Kevin Hart were a source of information and guidance. Bill Burrows of Orbis deftly guided this whole project to its completion, and Peter Phan was his ever-encouraging self. With the resurrection of the Lord, we believe that we all have a place in the new creation; but one believes more firmly in the eschatological when he is supported by the goodness and wisdom of such friends and colleagues.

CHAPTER 1

"Placing" the Resurrection: A Theological Problem

There is nothing new in the observation that religions are reborn with each new day. Unless there is a continuing refreshment of religious experience, any religious phenomenon would vanish from history. Needless to say, this is true of Christianity. It proclaims salvation in Christ Jesus, crucified and risen. The salvific event of his rising from the tomb originally inspired the Christian celebration of Sunday as the Lord's Day (cf. Acts 20:7; 1 Cor 16:2; Rev 1:10)—before the development of the liturgical year as we now know it.[1] It remains, however, that the resurrection permeates the whole phenomenon of the Church—in its liturgy, sacraments, scriptures and communal witness: "If Christians as a whole ever stop believing in, and living from, his resurrection, that will be when the Church stops being the Church of Jesus Christ".[2]

This chapter, then, introduces the challenges and opportunities involved in re-aligning Christian theology to the resurrection. We group our reflections at this stage under six headings:

1. *The Awkwardness of the Resurrection for Theology*
2. *Reason and Resurrection*
3. *A Resurrectional Attitude*
4. *A Postmodern Opportunity?*
5. *The Resurrection and the Disturbance of Categories*
6. *Conclusion: A Phenomenological Standpoint*

The Awkwardness of the Resurrection for Theology

The resurrection of the crucified Jesus is, in effect, so embedded in Christian tradition as to having never required "definition" in the way that the mysteries of the incarnation and the Trinity eventually needed to be defined. Even if not defined—and inherently indefinable—the resurrection of the crucified Jesus reaches into every aspect of theology in all its Christological, trinitarian, ecclesial, sacramental and cosmic dimensions. The resurrection, however focal in this way, however pervasive in its effect on the whole of Christian life and experience, often, in fact, leaves theology tongue-tied. It would seem that theology on this topic suffers a certain embarrassment, compared to the assurance in which the supposedly meatier themes of Christian life and practice are treated. Perhaps it is inevitable that the resurrection must represent not only a peculiar difficulty, but also something of a frustration or even failure. In the history of Christian doctrines, the incarnation, from the third century on, attracted a major part of the Church's concern.

As far as theology was concerned, the incarnation was more adaptable to systematic presentation than the resurrection—even if, for both doctrine and theology, it is only in the light of the resurrection that the incarnation is appreciated as a mystery or encountered as a problem. Christian thought finds in the life, teaching and death of Jesus a clear point of departure. After all, the doctrine of the incarnation could call on quasi-universal notions concerning God and appeal to the experience of a common humanity. The Word incarnate, God-with-us in Jesus of Nazareth (Mt 1:23), not Christ apart from us in the resurrection, anchors theology more firmly in the world of human experience. Christ in his compassionate solidarity with the human race atones for its guilt on the cross and restores us to the Father's love. While ascribing to a thoroughly incarnational theology in the tradition of Chalcedon, one cannot but notice that its classic Christological doctrine does not mention the resurrection. Yet the confession of the "one and the same, our Lord Jesus Christ", acknowledged "in two natures, without confusion, change, division or separation" (DS 301), would have presented no problems and required no doctrinal definition if Jesus had not risen from the tomb.[3]

A fresh emphasis on that omission alone is surely in order. The mystery of the incarnation must extend to include Jesus rising from the dead, and be interpreted in that light.[4] It goes without saying that the resurrection is always implicit and, indeed, celebrated in the yearly cycle of the liturgy. But it was seldom made clear that the Word was made flesh, not only in being born, living, speaking and acting, suffering and dying as a human being, but also in his rising from the tomb. In the West, at least, the piety of the faithful accorded Christmas more importance than Easter. The Word and Son of God was born of Mary two thousand years ago in the stable at Bethlehem. His rising from the tomb did not have the same affective impact. The resurrection was intrinsically a far more awkward consideration. It was an event of another order; and imagination, in its efforts to depict it, could easily veer in the direction of fantasy. Despite the imaginative and affective importance loaded onto the birth of Jesus in the flesh, it needs be recognised that unless Christ had been raised, Christmas would lose its significance. Unless redemption had been realised in him, this Son, "descended from

David according to the flesh" is generated "Son of God with power . . . by resurrection from the dead" (Rom 1:3), there would be no theology of the incarnation, and no "merry Christmas".

We wish to draw attention, therefore, to what is most obvious. To bring into the light what is most taken for granted is surely a humble but often overlooked function of a theology. A reflective faith cannot overlook the revelatory event that originated the history of Christian faith itself. Yet the taken-for-granted "obviousness" of faith in the resurrection is also what has made it most vulnerable to a strange neglect. Decades ago, Karl Rahner lamented the dwindling theology of the resurrection.[5] Before him, F.-X. Durrwell expressed a similar concern:

> Not so long ago theologians used to study the Redemption without mentioning the Resurrection at all. The fact of Easter was made to yield its utmost value as a piece of apologetics . . . theologians stressed the note of reparation, of satisfaction, of meritoriousness in that life and death, and generally went no further. When the Resurrection was mentioned, it was not so much as to give it any part in our salvation as to show it as Christ's personal triumph over his enemies, and a kind of glorious counterblast to the years of humiliation he endured to redeem us.[6]

Even if there were more positive efforts, theologies of the incarnation, the Trinity, and of the Church in its sacraments, institutional structures and the moral life were far fuller, and more completely articulated. In all this, the resurrection of the crucified Jesus is not only taken for granted, but left to take care of itself amidst the more urgent doctrinal preoccupations of Church and its theology. The resurrection sounds perhaps as a bass chord in the larger symphonic arrangement of theology, but never particularly intrusive. It was heard only as an apologetic confirmation of something else—say, the reality of the incarnation, the wider claims of the Church, or the validity of hope in an afterlife.

To this degree, Christ's rising is thereby reduced to a probative fact. It did not figure as the pervasive source of meaning and value. When it could be defended with considerable success in the domain of critically established fact—and thus tidily located in the apologetic file—its full significance tended to get lost as a consideration preliminary to a variety of theological themes. Indeed, the very success of the apologetic claims in regard to, say, the empty tomb or the appearances of the risen Jesus, had the effect of isolating it as a probative fact. What was obscured was its status as the source from which the scriptures and the subsequent history of doctrine and theology derive. Even if its significance was not exhausted by its apologetic role, further consideration was deferred to a later treatment—perhaps as an addition to the incarnation to be treated as one of "the mysteries of Christ".

The problem did not go unnoticed. F.-X. Durrwell's *The Resurrection* appeared fifty years ago in its original French edition.[7] It stands out as a brave attempt to recall theology to its focal point. Yet it came and went, possibly because it was lost in the no-man's land of "biblical theology"— too biblical for theology, and too theological for the historico-critical styles of exegesis that were then developing. From both perspectives, Durrwell's presentation fell short of what was required in a theological method to give it a more lasting and critical effect. To a lesser extent, this is the case with N. T. Wright's monumental study, *The Resurrection of the Son of God*.[8] He presented this work as a "ground clearing task" to serve "a phenomenon so striking and remarkable that it demands a serious and well-grounded historical explanation".[9] Yet the reader of this splendid book cannot but notice how the author moves quickly from the phenomenon to a program of historical explanation with an explicit apologetic intent. I feel we must ask whether something is needed before that. This study suggests that there is. It consists in a renewed attention to "the phenomenon so striking and remarkable" that, before it demands "a serious and well-grounded historical explanation", it needs to be appreciated on its own terms—as the phenomenon that saturates the whole life of faith.

Yet at this point, theology seems to observe a strange silence. When it comes to speaking of what made all the difference, it is not only the women in Mark's Gospel who "said nothing for they were afraid" (Mk 16:8). Thinkers in every age can sympathise with the quandary felt by Festus concerning "a certain Jesus, who had died, but whom Paul asserted to be alive. Since I was at a loss how to investigate these questions, I asked whether he wished to go to Jerusalem, and be tried there on these charges" (Acts 25:19). That provincial governor is not the only voice of a cultural form of common sense confessing that it finds itself "at a loss" when it comes to the resurrection, and so willing to refer it to the adjudication of higher authorities.

However many centuries have passed since then, the puzzlement continues, and the stakes are still as high. Porcius Festus found that Paul was asserting the crucified Jesus "to be alive". How this is so poses many a question for pagan judge and Christian believer alike. Yet Paul was intimately convinced of the reality that had been revealed to him, understanding it to be central to the tradition he knew and handed on. In addressing a situation of confusion in the Christian community of Corinth, he expressed a vigorous logic: "if Christ has not been raised, your faith is futile, and you are still in your sins" (1 Cor 15:17). Paul presumes a knowledge of the life, death and words of Jesus, and even cites a saying of Jesus not recorded in the Gospels (Acts 20:35). It remains, however, that the resurrection of the crucified One is for him the event that made all the difference. Yet later theology inherits both the clarity of Paul's conviction and the complexity he experienced in trying to communicate it. When theology is busy about finding a hearing in the intellectual world in which it operates, it can seem oddly mythological to speak of the resurrection in a world in which the dead do not rise. Paul knew this then, and theology knows it now. Paul's experience of the mockery of the Areopagus when he attempted to tell his learned audience of "the good news about Jesus and the resurrection" (Acts 17:18) is nothing new. If the cross is a stumbling block to the Jews and foolishness to the Gentiles (1 Cor 1:23), to say nothing of subversive impact on Roman imperial claims, the resurrection only intensifies the problem.

For the Church itself, there are inevitable preoccupations occasioned by defending its rights to exist, especially in non-Christian or post-Christian societies. However urgent such concerns are, the energies of the Church's mission would be sapped if it began to so see itself as the guardian of ethical values, the promoter of human dignity, and the defender of its own institutional freedoms as to lose the sense of the resurrection effect pervading every aspect of its communal life and mission.

In terms of Christian ethics, the case is even more alarming, as Brian Johnstone has pointed out.[10] To emphasise the point: when Paul speaks of the new creation and conformity to Christ crucified and risen, or when John elaborates on "the life that has been revealed" (1 John 1:2), moral theology is most busy speaking of the "natural law" in a shared world in which the resurrection has made little difference. Likewise, in treatises on the sacraments, though sophisticated and helpful connections are made with the anthropology of ritual, symbols and signs, the resurrection effect can be oddly muted. Here, I have in mind two recent works of sacramentality in which the resurrection is barely mentioned![11] I would not for a moment indulge in an arrogant dismissal of such excellent works—especially since one of these authors has written a book on the resurrection[12]—but they do illustrate the problem: the resurrection is simply taken for granted. It is not appreciated *as granted*, as given within the inmost dynamics of God's self-giving love. As such, it determines every aspect of the life and mission of the Church.

An enduring theological temptation is to reduce the phenomenon of the resurrection to an experience of the new gift of the Spirit. The Spirit of Jesus indwells Christian consciousness. It animates the community of faith, and leads to a deeper appreciation of the life and message of Jesus. That is clear. Yet the event of the resurrection as something happening *to him* can be bypassed, a more or less mythic expression of the origin of new spiritual awareness.[13] Theology, especially in the West, has long felt the need for a refreshed theology of the Spirit. But this would be a doomed project if the gift of the Spirit is disconnected from the prior "given-ness" of the resurrection event. Put most simply, the risen Jesus is the source of the Spirit; and, in the resurrection of the crucified One, the transforming power of the Spirit is climactically manifested. What happened in Christ overflows from him into the lives of all believers, enabling them to share in the cosmic transformation that has been anticipated in his being raised from the tomb. The Spirit of new life animating believers has not left Jesus dead and buried.

The awkwardness for theology regarding the resurrection might be suggested in the following terms: if theology concentrates on the incarnation, the defining character of the resurrection is too easily presumed. If it highlights the post-resurrectional life in the Spirit unfolding in history, the resurrection of Jesus himself is easily relegated to a mythological past. If theology shoulders the responsibilities of liberating societies from oppressive political situations or dehumanising economic structures, the resurrection of Jesus can appear as a distraction from the human future that is still to be realised.[14] Though the Christian moral life is to be promoted in all its multiple demands, the resurrection seems to have no clear relevance in fact, if not in theory, within an increasingly complex world of pressing ethical problems. Even in von Balthasar's monumental theology, his dramatic treatment of the Paschal Mystery seems to exhaust its creativity in a rather operatic treatment of Holy Saturday.[15]

And then, there is the sphere of interfaith dialogue. Here, theology searches for points of contact with the great spiritualities and religious traditions of the world as, say, in the works of R. Panikkar and J. Dupuis. The resurrection so intensifies the particularity of Christ that it might appear as an obstacle in the desired dialogue, and so be best left unmentioned. Perhaps it might be given the status of an addendum to be considered at a later stage once points of possible agreement are clarified. But in the pressing agenda of the moment, it has no productive significance in its own right, and so is best deferred. It is certainly not to be used as the knock-down argument justifying Christian imperialism, thus making a genuine meeting of faiths impossible. On the other hand, when Christians engage in reverent dialogue with people of other faiths or spiritualities, the promise of such engagements must be compromised if the resurrection of the crucified Christ remains hidden in the realm of what cannot be mentioned—deemed by implication to be irrelevant to the sharing of hope.

Reason and Resurrection

The theological tendency to overlook the significance of the resurrection arises from more external considerations. It can be that theology is so much in the thrall of cultural forms of philosophy, and so intent on establishing its apologetic self-assurance, and so keen to gain a hearing in the wider worlds of philosophy, science and historical scholarship, that it sought its non-negotiable point in the mystery of the incarnation. In so doing, it reduced the resurrection to some kind of divine afterthought or optional extra. It is presumed that theology would have more anthropological bite and be more attuned to dialogue with science, philosophy and religion, if the resurrection were held in reserve. Its eschatological excess might end in being a distraction from a more broadly based human conversation.

Admittedly, the situation is more complex than the above provocative remarks suggest. One aspect of the problem that occurs is the precise meaning of "reason" itself. The singularity of the resurrection event must in some way leave some forms of reason, and even theological reason, at a loss. On the other hand, the resurrection of the Crucified so determines Christian consciousness that it provokes questions about the nature of reason itself, above all in systematic and universalizing pretensions.

The event of the resurrection is a singular phenomenon. It has had its effect in the historical phenomenon of the Church with its sacraments, its scriptures, its doctrines, and the way of life embodied in the cloud of witnesses, living and dead. Yet this singular event ruptures the natural phenomenality of human existence. The dead do not rise. His rising from the dead stupefies all forms of logical reason. It disorients, even to the point of disappointment, religious expectations of a messianic triumph and of worldly manifestation of the Reign of God—not only before the event (e.g., Lk 18:31-34; 22:67), but also after it (Acts 1:6-7). Jesus did not come down from the cross. Nor did he walk out of the tomb to confound his enemies and to reorganize his followers into an army of liberation for Israel. He did, however, appear to certain chosen witnesses, in a bodily existence which bore the marks of the cross and left the tomb empty. His appearances left the disciples amazed, in a manner that led to further questioning. Whatever the wonder and whatever the questioning, Christ's rising from the dead is an irreplaceable "given" in the life of Christian faith. Without this event, there would be no New Testament; and the life, teaching and death of Jesus would have been lost in the fragile particularities of past history. But because the resurrection is central to faith's perception of the saving action of God, it provokes, from its very particularity, endless reflection on its universal significance.[16] The resurrection may indeed seem irrational to the kind of reason that is intrinsically anti-resurrectional.

A Resurrectional Attitude

This study is not primarily intent on isolating the resurrection as a doctrine, or treating a topic in systematic theology. What we are about here is both more and less than either of these concerns. It is more, in that we wish to consider how the resurrection of Jesus, in its full-bodied totality, radically affects Christian awareness—of God and of creation itself. In this perspective, we wish to explore the phenomenon of the resurrection as the focal, refreshing point on which every aspect of Christian existence and its theoretic articulations converge. And yet, our aim is also less than a fully articulated "theology of the resurrection". Our concern is to attend to the experience of the resurrection in the consciousness of faith rather than to articulate its theological meaning in a full systematic sense. Our focus is, therefore, on the phenomenon which precedes, grounds, and endlessly provokes fresh theological formulations and practical applications.

I grant that some will find nothing particularly surprising in this attempt, and shrug it off as something that has all been done before. At the very least it can draw attention, from a particular perspective, to the work of previous writers, F.-X. Durrwell,[17] P. Perkins,[18] X. Léon-Dufour,[19] W. Pannenberg,[20] Gerald O'Collins,[21] Francis Fiorenza,[22] N. T. Wright[23] and others. While such authors have shown a strong theological emphasis, Richard Swinburne,[24] in contrast, has re-introduced a note of refined apologetic argument into this area. But this runs the risk of proving too much with its aims to demonstrate the occurrence of a transcendent event. The resurrection is presented as a miracle, or even a super-miracle in the world of rational thought and natural laws.[25] The idea of a new creation is not evident. On the other hand, it might prove too little, as though theology is now unburdened of the responsibility of looking further, now that its foundation is demonstrably secure. In another style, the theologies and biblical studies relying on the anthropological analyses of René Girard prove valuable in introducing into religious history a much-needed cultural critique in the light of the crucified and risen Christ. I draw attention here especially to the work of such writers as Raymund Schwager,[26] James Alison[27] and Gil Bailie.[28] Another kind of new beginning is exemplified in the reception of von Balthasar's The Glory of the Lord, as it is widely acclaimed and pondered, along with David Bentley Hart's theological aesthetics. All these works have influenced this present study and remain resources for a much fuller exploration than what we are attempting here. Each in its own way leads theology back to its focus on the resurrection.

A large factor in the blurring of resurrectional focus is the influence of an ever-narrowing and specialised rationality. At the level of popular culture, the myths of an all-explanatory science, along with the emphasis on individual experience, make any reference to resurrection at least odd, if not quaintly risible. On more sophisticated philosophical levels, entrenched forms of the hermeneutics of suspicion make the resurrection easy prey to any number of reductive explanations. In other words, faith on this central issue has to cope, now as always, with a world of thought and feeling for which the resurrection is impossibly fanciful. But no worldview is hospitable to what most calls it into question. Consequently, faith in the resurrection is faith at its most vulnerable to the defensive certainties of any culture and most irrational to its "rational" criteria.

If, in this regard, faith is at its most vulnerable, theology is embarrassed. It is understandable that theology, especially in dialogue or in confrontation with the unbeliever, feels uneasy in making the singularity of the resurrection the focus of systematic thought. There is not enough of the phenomenon to work on, might we say, in a world in which patently the dead do not rise, and when, given the social mission of the Church, commitment to the world must not be "distracted" by this ostensibly other-worldly event. The objections of non-believers are intensified by the misgivings of believers.

Of course, that is not the end of the issue, nor even a properly critical assessment of what is involved. The challenge remains of pointing the way forward. Paradoxically, it is also a question of leading the way back, in the sense of a *reductio in mysterium*, "bringing everything back" to the original and final mystery. To the degree that the hitherto dominant, excessively rationalistic metaphysics are called into question, there is an opportunity of reconsidering, in a fresh way, the resurrection as the focal phenomenon in the Christian tradition. For example, the hermeneutic of suspicion can be questioned. It can be countered by a hermeneutic of receptivity and gratitude. Then, things begin to look different. Openness to the given, thankfulness for it, participation in it, all stand in contrast to an ideological suspicion of the phenomena. The data, the "givens" of love and life, are a new point of departure. The intimations of wonder and astonishment in the face of the uncanny gift of existence in all its forms call forth another kind of disciplined awareness. It is not a matter of taking everything naively for granted.

There is, however, a more critically nuanced receptivity appropriate to the unobjectifiable particularity of persons, things and events of things. It means not taking them *for* granted, but *as* granted, as being given into consciousness in their originality.[29] This disciplined receptivity is not preceded or subsumed by a prior ontology which would pretend to establish the limits of the possible. Pannenberg, as already mentioned, is notable for a powerfully systematic, future-oriented ontology which is already anticipated in the historical fact of the resurrection—even if, to some degree, his system, as it develops, seems to overwhelm the particularity and uniqueness of the phenomenon. Whatever the case, the creativity of the human response to the given is not reduced to a kind of passive attentiveness that would disallow critical questions as to reality and the demands of what has been revealed. It would be an absurd mutilation of the phenomenon of human consciousness itself if explorations of meaning, truth, value and reality were discouraged. Indeed, what is given in the particularity of experience provokes critical thinking on such data—the givens and the gifts involved—not to replace the experience, but to illuminate it in the full dimensions of its meaning.

Hans Urs von Balthasar, along with David Bentley Hart, sought to elaborate a "theological aesthetics" in order to allow the phenomenon of revelation to be appreciated first of all on its own terms. Von Balthasar considers this experience by exploiting the metaphor of a "journey". The radiance of what has been revealed can be experienced only by surrendering oneself to the movement inherent in faith itself.[30] He writes,

> In faith and through it, rather, I am made open and dispossessed of self . . . The important thing is the movement away from my self, the preference of what is other and greater, and precisely the person who has been expropriated for God does not want to become fully secure with regard to this Other and Greater.[31]

The revealed phenomenon is not contained in some subjective horizon of the self, but destablilises it with the excess of the attractiveness and demands of what is given. As will appear, this is equivalent to what we will term the "saturated phenomenon" of revelation. The multi-faceted character of Christian experience can never be reduced to this or that aspect. Von Balthasar goes on to describe this "saturation" in reference to the Johannine pattern of experience:

> Christian experience, rather, implies a progressive entrance of the believing person into the total reality of faith and the progressive "realization" of this reality . . . The best justification for this are the criteria of experience that in John continually circle around each other, always pointing one to the other. And the impossibility of ordering John's different aspects at the theoretico-theological level into a manageable system . . . points us in the direction of another level of synthesis, that of Christian experience as the fruit of a faith lived in obedience to God.[32]

We must explore, then, how the resurrection of Jesus is the door inviting the "progressive entrance" of the believer into the "total reality of faith". It is to that "other level of synthesis" eluding every "manageable system" that faith—with the transcendent originality of what has been so given—offers entrée. It provokes humility, wonder and self-surrender— features of a fresh and more genuine sense of mystery, not as something to be analysed, solved, reduced to a system, but a gift to be lived. Newman contrasts the phenomenon of mystery with its opposite:

> Instead of looking out of ourselves . . . throwing ourselves forward upon Him and waiting for Him, we sit at home bringing everything to ourselves . . . Nothing is considered to have an existence so far forth as our minds discern it . . . in a word, the idea of Mystery is discarded.[33]

Karl Rahner, in the mystagogic and pastoral emphasis of his vast oeuvre, repeatedly points to the often unnamed experience of God as "the Mystery" intimated in the depths of life, love and even death. In a key article,[34] he writes,

> Today it is becoming clearer, and that too within Christianity at the doctrinal and institutional level, that this experience of God ... really constitutes the very heart and centre of Christianity itself and also the ever living source of that conscious manifestation which we call "revelation".[35]

Rahner draws out an implication: "It is, therefore, a task precisely for Christianity itself to point ever anew to this basic experience of God, to induce man to discover it within himself, to accept it and also to avow his allegiance to it in its verbal and historical objectification".[36] Questions arise: how is this experience of mystery related to the resurrection? Is there not a sense in which God's act in raising the crucified Jesus from the tomb is an excess overflowing any "verbal or historical objectification"? Has the "basic experience of God" been somewhat displaced into a generalised transcendent realm so as to diminish the particularity of the New Testament experience? Such questions are not easily answered, but it would seem that a more phenomenologically attuned approach might well contribute to a fuller response which would allow for the different kinds of communication, both within the Church and beyond it.

Bernard Lonergan's magisterial *Method in Theology*[37] raises similar questions. His phenomenology of human consciousness and its self-transcending dynamism is undoubtedly a remarkable achievement. It not only grounds and connects the variety of theological operations ("specialties"), but also locates theological activity at the heart of intercultural and interfaith dialogue. A key aspect of this is his description of religious experience as a radical, all-transcending and unreserved "being in love", underpinning all religious and theological objectifications, the phenomenological equivalent of "the state of grace".[38] As this gift of love animates and subsumes all other forms of loving, it gives intelligence a clouded awareness of a mystery, to provoke its own kind of questions and to lead to its own kind of answers.[39] The gift of God's love occurs as something of a holy disruption in the routine flow of life, with religious, moral and intellectual consequences.[40] Lonergan writes,

> That fulfilment is not the product of our knowledge and choice. On the contrary, it dismantles and abolishes the horizon in which our knowing and choosing went on and it sets up a new horizon in which the love of God will transvalue our values and the eyes of that love will transform our knowing ... Though not a product of our knowing and choosing, it is a conscious dynamic state of love, joy and peace that manifests itself in acts of kindness, goodness, fidelity, gentleness and self-control.[41]

Without prejudice to Lonergan's wider methodological concerns, a question must be posed: how does the resurrection of the crucified Jesus occur, "not as the product of our knowledge and choice", but so as to set up "a new horizon" in which the love of God is climactically manifested in its transforming effect? Lonergan has given telling expression to what Christian theology would term the gift of the Spirit. It can appear that the phenomenon of the resurrection is somehow extrinsic to his approach, an "outward word",[42] merely declaratory of inner reality of the gift of God. A full discussion of this question would need a careful consideration of the relation between "inner" and "outer" aspects of the resurrection event. Likewise, derivation of general and particular categories of theological systematics would need examination.[43]

Here, we simply note the problem: without receptivity to the key phenomenon of the resurrection as determining the horizon of Christian reflection, it will be deferred to some later consideration in Christology—with a consequent loss of its original and universal significance. Though no theological method or system can say everything all at once, there are genuine concerns when the resurrection event does not seem to affect the horizon in which theological questions unfold. What Lonergan means by the "constitutive"[44] role of the word of God's revelation in history needs to be unpacked along the lines of what we are here presenting. In our emphasis on the phenomenality of the resurrection as foundational to theological method we are in fact bringing out the point made by Lonergan when he writes, "the word of the gospel that announces that God has loved us first and, in the fullness of time, has revealed that love in Christ crucified, dead, and risen"[45] introduces "a radically new situation of being in love and that begins the unfolding of its life-long implications".[46]

We would argue, then, that a basic attentiveness to the unique datum or, better, *donum*, is demanded. The particularity of the "gift" embodied in the resurrection and its effect is more fundamental than the efforts of theology to reduce it to a topic, a theme, or even to a basic systematic principle. If that were to happen, theology would be pale, like a plant without sunlight. On the other hand, with a more experiential and phenomenological awareness, theology recovers its original freshness, and overcomes the threat of boredom and stagnation. The resurrection of Christ thus saturates doctrinal positions on the Trinity and the Church, sacraments and moral life, and so forth. When these long-crystallised doctrinal elements are washed over with the stream of living water, their life-giving elements shine more brightly, purified and renewed.

A Postmodern Opportunity?

The "postmodern" context and style of thought presents a special opportunity. For it is more hospitable to the particular, and less inclined to accept settled generalisations. Admittedly the fluidity of this new context can be disconcerting to the classical theological tradition. The theoretical apparatus of this long-standing systematising tradition employs a number of metaphysical categories. Its analogical form of exposition and argument appeals to the principle of cause and effect in grounding its account of the vestiges, images, and likenesses of God represented in the world of creation. In contrast, postmodern styles of philosophical and theological thinking seek to disencumber themselves of such metaphysical assumptions. They are more sensitive to the indefinable "traces" of historic phenomena, as with "the God effect"[47] that Kevin Hart has described. To this degree, postmodernism is generally more hospitable to the phenomena rather than traditional forms of conceptualisation. It favours the mystical over the metaphysical. It is more inclined to the evocatively negative rather than to the traditional affirmative, and more attuned to existential witness, in the open-endedness of the pluralistic world. Traditional "negative theology" is not enough, if, for instance, "God" is presupposed as known in a manner prior to the negations that come into play. In that case, the postmodern critic would point out, classic forms of negative theology are not nearly as negative as they claim to be.[48]

Kevin Hart concludes an influential study of deconstruction in philosophy and theology with the following summary:

> God is possible, says the positive theologian, meaning that the divine is revealed if only we would see (and the terms of seeing are then spelled out). God is impossible, says the negative theologian, meaning that God always exceeds the concept of God. Each theology claims priority: without negative theology God talk would decay into idolatry, yet without positive theology there would be no God talk in the first place. It is the permanent task of religious thought to keep the negative and the positive in play, to demonstrate that the impossible is not in contradiction with the possible.[49]

Influenced by Derrida, Kevin Hart contends that these positive and negative possibilities offer no theoretical solution, but peter out in an *aporia* that demands an act of decision and commitment on the part of believers. As he explains, these positive and negative possibilities

> are not to be resolved dialectically or logically: they arrange and rearrange themselves in the negative form of an aporia. Religious experience pulls a person in different directions at the same time, demanding we attend both to the possible and the impossible; and in negotiating this aporia one's conscience is never satisfied. This experience of desire, dissatisfaction, insufficiency and uncertainty is a part of the God-effect.[50]

What is given, be it in the wonder of life and love, or in the beauty of art or in the arresting witness of saints and martyrs, of mystics and great thinkers, is not nothing. If the concretely "given" is not to be abstracted into a generalised metaphysical system, neither is it to be ruled out of consideration by an ideology of negativity and suspicion. The "given" is perceived as all important, and to be appreciated as such, even when concepts and words fail. In the religious realm, there may be a self-disclosure of such a kind as to call forth the special receptivity we name "faith", even while reducing to folly all efforts to master it in terms of human reason and control—as Paul, for instance, would contend (1 Cor 1:25-29). In that case, God is self-defined, in and through the negations that are experienced, as the absolute "otherness", experienced and known only in its drawing near.

I believe such is the case with the resurrection of Jesus. It remains a matter of faith, yet the evidence it provides is not a once-and-for-all solution to all life's negativities. On the other hand, it is given to faith in a way that summons the believer to decision and service of the world. Where Hart speaks of the "God effect", we prefer to speak of Christian experience in terms of the "resurrection effect". From one point of view, the resurrection represents the most intense point of a positive theology. From another perspective, it inspires a demanding negative theology, for the resurrection, even though it "means the world" to Christian faith, is "out of the world"—in terms of any analogies, concepts or symbols that pretend to depict it. Positivity and negativity are intertwined. Each aspect impels toward the other, and both look beyond themselves to the singularity of the resurrection-phenomenon itself. Aquinas, for all his systematic coherence and precision of expression, suggests the indefinable character of the resurrection in what reads as a disconcertingly modest and open-ended description: "Christ in his rising has not returned to life as it is perceived in common human experience, but to a kind of deathless life which is conformed to God".[51] Thus, the resurrection occupies a point beyond human perception, beyond the limits of death, ultimately definable only by the form or character of the mystery of God itself.

The current philosophical turn to the phenomenological categories at the expense of the metaphysical presents a fresh opportunity for theology to revaluate the place of the resurrection in Christian experience and in theological reflection on it. If the phenomenality of the experience of faith is lacking, the philosophical categories and systems supporting doctrinal positions cannot but appear as ice-sculptures needing the controlled atmosphere of a protective metaphysical system, now threatened by the hot winds and the changing seasons of historical experience. Phenomenological vigilance is needed if what is given is to be received on its own terms.

Without such receptivity, theology tends to be confined defensively within the atmosphere of a locked room of firm floors and ceilings, allowing for a certain number of doors and windows, but when, all along, letting in the light and atmosphere of an eschatological event is at stake. Just as the risen Jesus entered the locked rooms to the surprise of his fearful disciples, a more phenomenological approach makes any theological space more hospitable to the light of Christ and the fresh air of his Spirit. The conclusion of John's Gospel remains a healthy reminder: the risen Jesus is not contained within the linear print of any book—or all the books of the world (Jn 21:25). The phenomenon exceeds all efforts to express it. In a more contemporary vein, theology is not engaged in a video replay of the highlights of the game, passively assured of the outcome, once one's team has won. For beyond the play of images, there is the risk of openness to the "given". It is not a matter of reproducing impressions or trying to capture a dwindling after-effect. The challenge is otherwise: to enter into an involvement with what causes everything to be seen anew—the resurrection effect.

The Resurrection and the Disturbance of Categories

The singularity of the resurrection disturbs a number of settled philosophical and theological notions. Take, as a first instance, the notion of the "physical". In its most ancient understanding, the task of philosophy was described as "metaphysical"—*meta ta physika*, going beyond the physical data of experience into the realm of being and ultimate meaning. The resultant tendency is to dissolve the *physika* and the experiential, along with the particular phenomena of Christian tradition, into abstract generalisations. This is a special problem for Christianity. The range of its faith essentially includes the incarnation, the resurrection of the body (of Christ and all), the sacramentality of the Church's liturgy and the concreteness of loving our neighbour. Rather than de-physicalising, dis-incarnating or spiritualising the body and the material world, the phenomenon of the resurrection of Christ points in another direction, namely to a transformed physicality. This is the point of N.T. Wright's neologism, "transphysicality", in his notable study of the resurrection.[52]

Then there are the polarities of subject and object which we shall treat more fully later. For the moment, let us note that the event of the resurrection disturbs any facile correlation of subject and object. For instance, the subject is not already established in self-possession, already constituted and anticipating what is given. What is disclosed is not a missing element designed to fit into a complete prior worldview. Nor, on the other hand, is the resurrection (or the appearances of the risen Christ associated with it) an objectively classifiable type of event, an instance of similar events within our experience of the world. Any horizon of prior philosophy with its catalogue of categories is called into question. In an obvious sense, as far as routine experience or thought patterns are concerned, the risen Jesus makes himself present more like an attractive absence—as a non-experience within the world of accessible experience. This paradoxical mode of presence-in-absence calls forth the commitment of faith, and summons the believer into a life of self-surrender: "when he is revealed, we shall be like him . . . all who have this hope in him purify themselves as he is pure" (1 John 3:2-3). It occurs as a singularity, causing all the generalities of language to strain. The Gospel of Matthew, for instance, records the promise of the risen Lord, "Remember, I am with you always, to the end of the age" (Mt 28:20). A play of paradoxes results: in an obvious sense, Jesus is absent; he was crucified, dead and buried in terms of previous modes of presence. Yet he is now declared to be present, in a new mode of existence. But it is a presence of an odd kind, eluding any precise location in the previous world of mundane or even religious experience.

Another problem stirs in what appears to be a lack of first-hand experience in the believer's relationship to the risen Lord. The singularity of the resurrection event is intensified in that the risen Jesus discloses himself only to privileged witnesses. Christian faith relies on what they once saw, not on what believers now see for themselves. For a theology locked in its own self-referential procedures, the mediating role of past witnesses is disconcerting.[53] It would appear that the focal event of Christian faith is accessible only in a second-hand fashion, much removed from the experience of the original witnesses. Does faith then mean having no first-hand experience of Christ's resurrection?

In response, we might note first of all that the interpersonal situation of our social experience and understanding is not necessarily some kind of defect. There is something grotesque in thinking that all truth must be immanently generated only within the isolated critical individual if it is to be regarded as valid. In contrast, the path to truth is usually opened only through an encounter with others. We transcend our own limits and sense what transcends them when the monadic ego is confronted with the testimony of other people. For instance, their wisdom and dedication, their love and forgiveness, can have an unsettling impact on any egocentric world. The drama of their lives and the deaths they die, leave us changed. This is all very unsettling for the self that egocentrically pretends to occupy centre-stage in the universe of truth and goodness. For the self-centred ego, it must be humbly acknowledged, is a self embroiled in some measure in the patterns of envy, violence and depression that infect the culture it lives and breathes. Such a self cannot be fully transparent to itself. No doubt, a genuine intellectual, a true lover, an artist or a mystic, will contribute a precious testimony in the interpersonal exchanges of social life. But this is not despite others; it is with, for, and influenced by them—all that "cloud of witnesses" which calls us forth, beyond ourselves, to what is outside the horizons of our projections. A generalised account of the dynamics of human consciousness as self-transcendence is undeniably valid, as we would find this expressed, say, in writings of Bernard Lonergan.[54] Still, it is ever a self-transcendence in the making. We are summoned out of ourselves through the self-transcendence incarnate in others. The truths they embody and the values they live by radiate a summons to do likewise. Any failure to note the basic interpersonal phenomenon of witnessing cannot but diminish the value of witnesses to the resurrection. They are relegated to a mythological past, while later ages are limited to a self-contained present, armed with its prejudices against both the possibility and meaningfulness of the decisive event to which they have witnessed. Yet their particular testimony is woven into the texture of Christian tradition. Their witness gives the "non-seeing" of faith in the ages that follow a peculiar focus and assurance.[55] A later chapter will deal with this point in more detail.

Another aspect of the problem confronts us when we find ourselves claiming too easily that, though we do not have direct evidence of the reality of the resurrection, we can represent it in various ways, through word, sign and sacrament. There is a general problem with such a claim. Are we implying that we already have a clear grasp of the reality in question, say, an event or a person, so as to represent it by employing an endless series of signs? The habitual logic of philosophical thinking tends to focus on the reality before considering the way it is signified, with a similar emphasis on the cause prior to its effects. The thing in itself precedes our apprehension of it, the *in se* comes before the *quoad nos*, to use scholastic parlance. But this inevitable philosophical logic must attend to something prior to itself. Phenomenologically speaking, we must respect the priority of the "effect", "sign" or "trace" over the realities they disclose. In our time-bound mode of consciousness, we can perceive what is given in the past only though its continuing effects carrying over into the present.

The originating given, the actual event, cannot be captured or recaptured in a way that makes it immediately present, even as it continues to generate its present effect. Though the realities of events or persons given into our past form life now, they are revealed only to the measure of a receptive openness. But the manner of this reception is contingent upon the variable capacities of the recipient. Here we note the pertinence of the scholastic axiom: "whatever is received is received according to the manner of the receiver"—*quidquid recipitur, recipitur per modum recipientis*. This is, of course, a biblical principle, as we find in the Gospel of Luke, as the seed of the Word of God falls by the wayside, or on stony ground, or among thorns—or on good soil with a happy outcome (Lk 8:4-15).

Let me add immediately that this emphasis placed on receptivity does not preclude an exploration of the "ontological reality" of what has been and is being given. Though the scattered seed is subject to differing conditions, it can still be understood as good seed. Its ontological reality is not diminished, but appreciated more fully in the abundance of the harvest. There is no suppression of wonder at the fertility of the seed, nor is there a prohibition against asking questions as to the variety of the seed that has been sown, nor the character of the sower. What it does mean, however, is that such ontological questions are provoked, in effect, from what is given. There is no prior assurance and systematic hold on what is already possessed. Attention, then, to the given is a first condition for all genuine thinking. It demands receptivity, wonder, and self-commitment—in those who "hear the word, hold it fast in an honest and good heart, and bear fruit with patient endurance" (Lk 8:15).

And so, a question: if the resurrection is the sign or trace of God *par excellence*, how is it perceived in its effect, and what questions does it generate? If, for instance, the risen Christ is disclosed as the divinely-wrought transformation, how does this singularity and extra-mundane "otherness" register in our sense of human existence and its destiny? How does it dismantle particular cultural standpoints and create a trans-cultural space within the unconditioned horizon of the reign of God?

There is a further basic problem. This occurs when "being" is understood as a generic concept, somehow including every instance of what exists, whether we speak of God or finite created being. Thus, God, friends, and the flowers and frill-necked lizard basking in midday sunshine in the garden are "beings". Such a generalised, abstract concept of being would reduce all differences, and render impossible the recognition of the Other, whether infinite or finite. The hemorrhaging of the sense of "Other-ness" gives rise to a neuralgic reaction to any application of the concept of "being" to God, as though God were one being among the many "beings" of the world. In this regard, Marion attained a certain notoriety in his book entitled *God without Being*.[56] In the self-communication of love from that beyond-ness, the divine mystery can never be represented in a finite concept. It must be adored in the possibilities—and actuality—of the divinely free self-revelation and self-giving, in terms of love, mercy and judgment. God is not a metaphysical idea, but a self-communicating mystery of love.

The analogical notion of being, understood in a more Thomistic manner, can indeed clear the ground, as it were, for an ever greater sense of God as Be-ing without restriction, the Being-in-Love from which all gifts derive. The transcendence of God from the world opens the way for a deeper appreciation of divine communication to the world, in which God is revealed in the giving, as both gift and giver. Self-giving love is the primary colour vividly outshining the grey abstraction of divine "being". We do note, nonetheless, that in the Thomist tradition, God's Being is not subsumed under a generic concept. Nor, for that matter, was "being" an idea at all. It is more the attractive goal pulling intelligence beyond sense impressions, beyond imaginative figurations, even beyond thinking itself, to a reverent objectivity before what is given in its uniqueness. In this regard, the Thomist tradition sees the universe of what is as an original gift. There is a radical giving inscribed into all existence: for God does not look at the universe of being and decide to love it, but by loving it, brings it into existence: "The love of God is ever inpouring and creating the goodness of things" (*amor Dei infundens et creans bonitatem in rebus*).[57]

Faith does not diminish or replace the notion of the "One Who Is", even if it seeks understanding in metaphysical and analogical terms. In this sense, the notion of God as sheer Be-ing, far from replacing the freedom and grandeur of the gift, or being simply an extrinsic support for the self-surrender demanded of faith, is in fact the hermeneutical space in which the freedom and unreserved character of love can be more fully appreciated. Theology does not divinise love or idolise the gift, but trembles at the point of acknowledging that the infinite, eternal abyss of divine Be-ing is freely imparting itself to creation: *amor Dei . . . creans bonitatem in rebus*.[58]

Aquinas expresses a basic phenomenological grounding of his theological metaphysics in a striking manner. He is responding to an objection arising from Psuedo-Dionysius. While accepting the more intimate relationship with God that comes about through revelation, the objector supposes that our knowledge of God does not rise above the limits of natural reason.[59] Aquinas' reply is instructive for the "resurrection effect" we are here considering:

> Although through the revelation of grace in this life we may not know the essence of God (*quid est*), and so are united to him as one unknown, nonetheless we know God more fully in as much many and more excellent his effects disclose him to us; and, in so far as we attribute to him from divine revelation things that natural reason cannot attain, as that God is both one and three.[60]

There are four points to be especially noted in this response. (1) God, though remaining radically unknown, is a self-revealing subject; (2) this self-revelation brings about union of love with the God who has so acted, even if his radically unknown character remains; (3) yet despite the divine unknowability, various God-wrought effects disclose God more fully than the scope of natural reason would allow; (4) this fuller knowledge results from the many and more excellent effects, and through attributing to God what can be known only from the divine self-disclosure, the pre-eminent example being the trinitarian constitution of the divine mystery.

Aquinas' words suggest a valuable lead for our exploration of the "resurrection effect". The four points listed above can be further specified. The God who acts in the resurrection remains unknown, and, in a sense, more "unknown" to the natural scope of reason limited to a world of death in which the resurrection is not a possibility. On the other hand, it points to a more intimate participation in the life of God through the personal and cosmic effects of Christ's rising from the tomb. Moreover, it offers possibilities of a further graced mode of knowing through the light that emanates from it. Amongst "the more excellent effects", the resurrection has a focal status in that it illuminates the whole climactic movement of divine self-disclosure. Implicit in this more outstanding effect is that of the witness of the tradition to which the events of revelation give rise, above all the testimony of the chosen witnesses to whom the risen Christ has disclosed himself as the process of divine revelation is unfolded in history.

In short, any rigid correlation of subject and object, cause and effect, presence and representation, limitless being and self-giving love has to be recast in the light of the phenomenality of the resurrection. Words like revelation, grace, faith, wonder and receptivity take on fresh meaning. Indeed, it is hoped that a return to the focal phenomenon of the resurrection will have a purgative effect on theology, expelling the waste material of misplaced rationalism that has long accumulated. It will be no unhealthy outcome if the resurrection is to be allowed to shock theology to its foundations with the immeasurable, original "excess" embodied in the risen Jesus.

What is required is a continuing conversion to the data. St. Thomas, reacting to the objection that his employment of the psychological analogy amounted to proving the mystery of the Trinity, significantly remarked, *posita trinitate, congruunt huiusmodi rationes*,[61]—translatable as, "once given the Trinity, an analogical manner of elucidating it is appropriate". This raises the question of how the mystery of the Trinity is first "given" or "assumed" or "posited", and the sense of congruence or "fittingness" in the theological manner of thinking about it. We could think of this given-ness in a purely propositional fashion—as in the words of scripture or doctrinal definitions. But while Thomas certainly assumed this, he also speaks of the quasi-experiential knowledge of the Trinity through the mission of the divine persons in the gift of grace.[62] In other words, there is a gift experienced before it is objectified in propositional form: "the act of the believer does not reach its end in the proposition, but in the revealed reality itself".[63] He goes on to say that "we form propositions only for the purpose of coming to a knowledge of the [given] realities, as is the case both in science and faith".[64] In recognition of this point, a further theological conversion can occur. It is taking seriously the first of Lonergan's imperatives which precedes those expressing the need for questions and reflection: "Be attentive!"[65] From attending to the initial experience, the sense of "fittingness" and analogical congruence in theological reasoning derives.

Instructive for the theologian is an incident described in the life of the composer Berlioz. One evening during a visit to Rome, while returning to his lodgings after what we must assume was a very satisfactory dinner, he fell into the Tiber. The anxiety of his companions turned to amazement when he surfaced, singing a refrain that had long eluded him.[66] The dripping composer is an image of our present challenge: to re-immerse ourselves in the shock of the phenomenon in order to recover the full symphonic effect of what is given from beyond the limits of any world.

By attending to the resurrection as the original datum of faith, theology is invited to re-focus its attention precisely on what originally collapsed all categories, and left tongue-tied the original disciples who witnessed it, namely, the resurrection of the crucified One. It is this which, quite literally, must be allowed to shock theology to its foundations and dazzle its systematic clarity. The strong wind of the Spirit shakes the whole house of our thinking. The no-longer controlled atmosphere makes the ice sculptures melt. The freedom of the living One interrupts the linear format of our books and disturbs the locked doors of our previous security: something else is in play, involving believers in a way that no replay of highlights can satisfy.

Here, I suggest that theological method in general, and in regard to the resurrection in particular, can take advantage of the fluid open-endedness of the postmodern landscape if it learns the requisite adroitness. When postmodernity is such an elusive term, one must be hesitant to proclaim one's approach to the resurrection as postmodern, as though the indefinable singularity of this event can be better served by what appears to be similarly indefinable. Yet some points are clear. In a general sense, the postmodern era allows for a radical critique of that Enlightenment form of rationality which was most intensely antagonistic to the claims of revealed religion. More particularly, the postmodern era is uncomfortable with the traditional forms and categories of metaphysical thinking or any superintending philosophical tradition in this regard. An appropriate critical theological realism is not diminished but assisted by a more phenomenological receptivity.[67] Indeed, it presents a long overdue opportunity for theology to attend to Christian experience, and to the resurrection which is at its heart. Even if such an effort proves to be too ambitious, any attempt, however defective, to refocus theology in its primary datum can be no bad thing.[68] Perhaps an enlightenment of the Enlightenment will be possible—from a distinctively Christian perspective. The postmodern situation can create more space for the uniqueness of the Christian phenomenon, and of the various forms of witness to it.

Further, it seems to me that, if it is to guard and refine the great doctrinal tradition, contemporary theology cannot refuse to move within a postmodern landscape.[69] The breakdown of ideologies means that any

comprehensive system or synthesis or overarching narrative is regarded
with suspicion, to say the least. Traditional theological approaches provoke impatience because of their claim to metaphysical objectivity. The
postmodern mood is notoriously uncomfortable with canons of ortho-
doxy in any area, and more alert to what had been previously pushed to
the margins. It delights in alternative possibilities, and to pursue ways
not taken. It is prepared to give a hearing to voices forgotten or never
heard. It is vividly aware of the "otherness" of what is given, and resists
all efforts to homogenise it into more of the same. Heterogeneity is the
primary stress.

But there are considerations, larger and more demanding than a change
of theological or philosophical procedures. We note, for instance, that
the hermeneutical place of the victim, at least in the history of the West
is highly—and mysteriously—valued. There are many factors at work—
the influence of a new humanism, the imperatives of democratic gov-
ernment, the political breakdown of old empires, and the gospel itself
quietly permeating human cultures, even at this post-Christian phase of
history. Whatever weight one might place on each of these, singly or
taken together, voices "from the underside" are given a hearing as never
before; and the histories written by the victors are called into question.
Postmodernity to this extent has a political and social form.

On the other hand, the standpoint is important. Dispassionate intel-
lectuality is one thing, but the experience of solidarity in elemental suffering, guilt and threat, to say nothing of the intimations of love, is
another. The resurrection is an event addressed to hope and love, not a
cure for agnosticism or the denial of God. The philosopher Wittgenstein,
in the following intriguing remark, ponders on what inclines him to
believe in the resurrection. His words point to the peculiar status of the
phenomenon of the resurrection and the manner in which it is perceived:

> What inclines even me to believe in Christ's Resurrection? . . . If he
> did not rise from the dead, then he decomposed in the grave like
> another man . . . but if I am to be REALLY saved—what I need is
> certainty—not wisdom, dreams or speculation—and this certainty
> is faith. And faith is faith in what is needed by my *heart*, my *soul*,
> not my speculative intelligence. For it is my soul with its passions,
> as it were with its flesh and blood, that has to be saved, not my
> abstract mind. Perhaps we can say: only *love* can believe in the
> Resurrection. Or: it is *love* that believes the Resurrection . . . what
> combats doubt is, as it were, *redemption* . . . so this can come about
> only if you no longer rest your weight on the earth but suspend
> yourself from heaven. Then *everything* will be different and it will
> be "no wonder" if you can do things you cannot do now. [Emphasis
> original][70]

Receptivity to the phenomenon of the resurrection on its own terms is not unlike Wittgenstein's figure of no longer resting "your weight on earth"—the world of routine phenomena and rational analysis. On the other hand, being "suspended from heaven" and the experience of the world "otherwise" is to allow for the prodigality or overbrimming "saturation" of what is disclosed to the eye and heart of faith, in ways to be clarified in the next chapter.

Conclusion: A Phenomenological Standpoint

We aim, then, to discern the uniquely self-giving character of the resurrection to Christian faith. Even in apologetic terms, it seems wiser for theology to risk rejection of Christian claims for the right reason—and not because of a truncated or excessively abstract intellectual position. If that phenomenological account can be properly inclusive of the basic human dimensions of bodiliness, love, death, and moral responsibility for our neighbour, it will communicate more tellingly what is being given and what is at stake. In other words, it means working not so much with the doctrine as with the experience in its multiple mediations of presence and absence. The relevance of all this to the event of the resurrection needs a fuller exposition. We will move on to consider the multi-dimensioned "given-ness" that marks the experience of paschal faith. It is not as though theology needs to relocate the resurrection in the arrangement of its system, but must allow its systematising intelligence to be in some measure dislocated—if it is to be true to what has been so given to faith in Jesus' rising from the tomb.

To hurry past the phenomenon in order to impose a systematic form on the data may arise from a fear of fundamentalism or fideism. However, as I will contend, a new phenomenological perception of the resurrection in the community of the Church can bring forth its own theological realism by generating a narrative and systematic language appropriate to what is originally given and disclosed. In other words, there is no reason why the phenomenon—or the experience—cannot give rise to critically realist positions appropriate to *philosophia*, a critical and salvific realism, as the genuine search for wisdom.

In the chapter to follow, we will take up some elements of a phenomenological approach bearing on the focal phenomenon of the resurrection.

CHAPTER 2

A Phenomenological Approach
to the Resurrection

Faith seeks to understand what has been revealed, and to explore its implications for the conduct of Christian existence in the world. In addressing this task, theology, with greater or less success, calls on the tradition formed by scripture, Christian experience, Church doctrines, liturgical practice, scholarly exploration and moral responsibility. It aims to come up with a critically realistic account of what is believed, and why. Given the diversity of historical epochs, cultures and concerns, the task is unending. For a past age, Melchior Cano's ten *Loci Theologici* (1543-50) indicate the extent of the data.[1] In a general sense, at least, theology begins with a receptivity to what has been God-given and revealed, on terms and conditions not limited by any mundane horizon of possibility or expectation. To this degree, there is an implicit phenomenological recognition of what is being considered. We can take this further under the following four headings:

1. *The Phenomenological Turn*
2. *The Resurrection as Saturated Phenomenon*
3. *Five Aspects of the Resurrection-Phenomenon*
4. *Conclusion: Saturated Phenomenon or Mystery?*

The Phenomenological Turn[2]

Husserl, long recognised as a seminal figure in the development of phenomenological methods, recalled an abstract and ego-centred philosophy to return to "the things themselves" (*zu den Sachen selbst*). This was in large measure a reaction to jaded and generalised systems of thought that had lost their persuasive power. The alternatives are stark: either return to the phenomena and recover the wonder of experience in all its particularities, or end with a deracinated nihilism, unable to free itself from its own self-imposed limits. A new centre of gravity had to be sought to serve the genuineness of thinking. It would contest the nega-

tive bias inherent in the pretensions and projections of the omni-compe-
tent thinking subject. In such a setting, the self is the starting point; and
the "given", the data, tends to be a mirror-image of the rational ego.
But when the given phenomenon begins to be appreciated in its own
right and in the conditions of its appearance, the intentionality of the
all-competent rational subject is reversed. The centre of gravity shifts. A
critical and even contemplative reverence for the given phenomenon
becomes primary, thus allowing it first of all to be received on its own
terms. The preconceptions and fixed points of our routine perceptions
and representations are called into question, and our whole mode of
perceiving is reordered. In this sense, what is given to consciousness
may be metaphorically described as "iconic", for it shines with light
from beyond the limited world of our habitual vision, even as it allows
an endless play of perspectives.

An "idolic" mode of thinking stands in contrast to the "iconic" mode
of disciplined receptivity to what is given. Grammatically speaking, this
idolic form privileges the nominative case—as when "I" am always the
subject of the sentence, or the accusative—as it affects "me", or the
ablative—it is what is done "by me". By contrast, the iconic character
of the phenomenon, in resistance to any reduction to a pre-established,
all-governing ego, privileges the dative case.[3] It is what is given, in its
own terms, "to me". In its uniqueness, it presents a surplus and an excess of significance in the face of all abstract ideas and systems. "I" am
not the all-comprehending ego, but the one to whom things have been
given, appearing in their arresting and particular otherness. Predictably,
we will be arguing that the event of the resurrection will be best described in this manner, for it is disclosed as a disruptive occurrence for
the earliest witnesses and for believers in every age.

But before making this theological application, let us emphasise the
general point: receptivity to the given and the mode of its given-ness is
the necessary fundamental attitude. Admittedly, as expressed in the scholastic adage, *quidquid recipitur, recipitur per modum recipientis*, receptivity allows for different modes and capacities. There are different attitudes, moods, preoccupations and perspectives. This plurality of
possibilities affects not only an endless variety of individuals, but also
cultures, societies, historical epochs and the Church itself. Differing or
contrasting modes of receptivity can conflict. The viewpoint of a
reductively secular method constricts everything within its own self-
limited horizon. To such an outlook, the resurrection is an impossibility,
or at best a mythic expression of something more real and familiar. Such
an attitude is dialectically opposed to that of faith. For the Christian
believer, the resurrection is the focal phenomenon. Its significance affects every aspect of one's interpretation of the world. At the same time,
it demands patience and inspires hope against the day when it will be
revealed in its full evidence. Despite this irresolvable conflict, the histo-

rian can hardly deny the phenomenon of the Christian fact in world history, even if it is received only as already interpreted within the world already mapped out by secular rationality. Phenomenology, it might be presumed, is designed only for secular, not for religious, experience, let alone for the particularity of Christian experience. Theology, for its part, can pass over the phenomenality of faith by limiting itself to the demands of a doctrinal clarification or systematic coherence or moral praxis, and so abandon the field to secular phenomenology as inhospitable to unique events of revelation and the moral stance they inspire. Ideally, the Church would be an organised receptivity to the gift that called it into existence. But such an attitude can appear too insubstantial compared to the demands of doctrine, theological rationality, and of a clear communication of the Christian tradition of faith and morals.

Phenomenological methods and Christian faith, despite different intentionalities and modes of receptivity, share, to some degree, a common attitude. Phenomenology insists on attending to the given-ness and appearance as a necessary basis for all thought and analysis. Christianity, for its part, speaks of a special kind of given-ness, namely the self-giving of God in grace, and of a special kind of appearance, namely God's self-revelation in Christ. This likewise grounds all subsequent doctrine and theoretical analysis and self-referential concerns. For instance, grace does not presuppose human merit. In this reverse intentionality common to both phenomenology and Christianity, the subject does not possess what is other by drawing it to itself, but by being subjected to it. What is given or appears allows itself to be so given or so appear. The rational subject is not in possession of, but is possessed by, the demands of what is other—even to be constituted by it, at least on a new level of intentionality. The philosophical and theological attitude can, therefore, be analogically related, precisely in the domain of the given, and in the manner it is revealed. Both approaches converge in their sense of the extravagance at the heart of reality, a prodigality of the given that outwits the rational mind.

We may go further. A phenomenological attitude must be for reflective faith a "first theology". We are not speaking of a preamble to faith in a rational or logical sense, but of a standpoint on the level of receptivity and attitude. Moreover, the resurrection of the crucified One is the first moment in this "first theology". For it is the culminating gift of God in which all else is interpreted. It is a self-giving disclosure that saturates the meaning of revelation and the tradition that serves it. We are not so much asserting the primacy of experience over thought or belief. For, along with the variety of experiential elements in the signs, symbols, analogies and sacraments of faith, there is an experience of "non-experience". The risen One is no longer seen as once he was. There is a rupture in experience—a void, an emptiness and an ending in the fabric of experience. But it is a void and a death that only Christ can fill. Only he can be the non-experienceable plenitude saturating all possible experience. Where astrophysics has found it necessary to postulate "dark matter" and even "dark energy" to account for the mass and expansion of the cosmos, the risen body of Christ and the gift of his Spirit alone can account for faith's vision of the new creation and its energies, along with the demand for continuing conversion and hope for what is not seen: "Now hope that is seen is not hope" (Rom 8:24).

To focus on the phenomenon of the resurrection is to gather together many dimensions of receptivity to it. Believers hearken to the Word and ponder the inspired text. They celebrate the sacraments, and participate in a community of faith and witness, as they are carried forward, giving and receiving, within the cumulative tradition of doctrine, theological reflection, mystical experience, moral responsibility, and so on. The phenomenon of the resurrection of the crucified Jesus saturates all else with its significance: "in him all things hold together" (Col 1:17).

As a bridge between this section and the following, Newman's words are vividly relevant: referring to the prodigality of God's self-giving, he writes,

> We all confess that He is infinite . . . but, we ask, what is infinity? . . . The outward exhibition of infinitude is mystery; and the mysteries of nature and of grace are nothing else than the mode in which His infinitude encounters us and is brought home to our minds. Men confess that He is infinite, yet they start and object, as soon as His infinitude comes in contact with their imagination and acts upon their reason. They cannot bear the fullness, the super-abundance, the inexhaustible flowing forth, and "vehement rushing," and encompassing flood of the divine attributes. They restrain and limit them to their own comprehension, they measure them by their own standard, they fashion them by their own model.[4]

The phenomenological attitude involves being receptive "to the super-abundance, the inexhaustible flowing forth" of the gift of God, beyond the limits of human comprehension. We are now in a position to be more specific in applying this to the resurrection, the better to appreciate its unique significance. The writings of Jean-Luc Marion[5] and others are a special resource in this regard.

The Resurrection as Saturated Phenomenon

A critically elaborated account of the radically "given" quality of what is disclosed is found in Jean-Luc Marion's influential trilogy, *Reduction and Givenness* (1989), *Being Given* (1997) and *In Excess* (2001).[6]

The overflowing or "saturated" significance of the phenomenon imposes itself on the subject. It is given to such an extent that the subject is more like a witness to an event than an agent of its construction.[7] To make this point, Marion coins a word to highlight the passivity and receptivity of the subject in regard to what is given, namely, *l'adonné*, "the one to whom it is given", the recipient of the self-giving in question.

As was remarked above, "Grace", the gift of God in all its forms, is most expressed in the grammar of the dative case. The gift is given to the believer; it is not simply "there" to be inspected or possessed, as something taken for granted. It gives itself, communicates itself, to the subject, and re-constitutes it in a new awareness: "for those who are in Christ, there is a new creation" (2 Cor 5:17). In this instance, as in others more generally, what is given is primary—not the preconditions laid down by our rational capacities. In this regard, true thinking must be aware of the modes of given-ness at its foundations. It is less thinking "about" something, and more thinking from *within* what is given, by responding to it, and by allowing to appear what is arrestingly "other". This phenomenological return or "reduction" to the given provokes a kind of theological conversion in its method and style. It understands itself first of all as a "theology of disclosure",[8] beholden, humbly and reverently, to what is given. It is marked by contemplative receptivity to the data of faith. As I suggested in the previous chapter, present developments in a phenomenological philosophy can be a rich resource for theology—especially as it regards the event of the resurrection, the culminating gift that illumines the whole trajectory of God's self-giving in Christ.

Understandably, there will be some theological uneasiness over such an approach. There is the danger of collapsing everything into a fideistic subjectivism which would be an obstacle to the full development of the theological intelligence and wisdom. At the other extreme, some may be rightly wary of an objectivism that overwhelms the role of the believing and thinking subject. Admittedly, a disclosive theology inverts habitual patterns of intentionality that presume the subject is in possession before anything appears to it, as previously mentioned. A phenomenological style puts the emphasis on the self-giving "object". As a result, any activity on the part of the subject is conceived in terms of receptivity and responsiveness so that rationalistic pretensions no longer occupy centre-stage. What is vigorously precluded is a notion of the subject as a detached monad projecting itself onto what is other.[9] For the subject is the one who is "subjected" to what is overwhelmingly other, and made a witness to it by being stripped of all pretensions to comprehend or constitute what is given.[10] In its receptive role, the subject becomes a luminous indicator of what is given, to function as a screen on which the phenomenon is registered in its originality.[11] In this manner, the subject is reconstituted, as it were, by being drawn into the saturated field of the phenomenon. Its role is to disclose the "visibility" of what has been given from beyond its vision.

Yet intelligence and further exploration are not thereby put to sleep. Take, for example, the phenomenon of one's own birth. A response of gratitude is called forth, as is an endless effort of interpretation of the personal and communal meaning of such an unobjectifiable event.[12] It provokes an exploration of both the past that preceded it, of the present as it occurs, and of the future it gives rise to—even though the event of my "being born" fits into no prior project on my part—and perhaps not on the part of my parents!

As we shall see later in regard to the resurrection, the subject-object polarity is an inevitable point of reference. Yet, as we shall argue, the extremes of both objectivism and subjectivism are spurious totalities. Each of these rigid categorisations is incapable of appreciating what is given or the manner in which it provokes the response of thought or action. In an earlier and perhaps more obvious sense of "saturation", an approach to the given can be so "saturated" by preconceptions and concerns that the given is immediately subjected to one's own interests. In that case, it would be merely raw material to be transformed into an acceptable conceptual and rational form by the self-contained subject. In the sense of Marion and others, however, the phenomenon is "saturated", not by one's prior attitudes, notions and tastes, but in its overbrimming significance. Its inexhaustible freshness leaves thought ever at a loss to objectify what has so disclosed itself. The prior dominance of any philosophical ordering principle—either in an empiricist, subjectivist or idealist sense—is thus radically called into question by the excess of the "saturated phenomenon".

Five Aspects of the Resurrection-Phenomenon

To return to our main point: theology can serve the mystery of the resurrection by calling on the resources of phenomenology. Here, we are limiting ourselves mainly to the writings of Marion.[13] He makes his point in reference to five especially saturated phenomena: an event, a painting, the flesh, the face, and, in a way that tends to combine all four, revelation.[14] All five such instances have this in common, namely, a primordial self-giving.[15] None of them is constituted by the subject, but each appears in its original and self-imposing impact. Thus, the subject comes to itself in a new consciousness only through the self-giving otherness of the phenomenon concerned.

Janicaud has objected to an unwarranted intrusion of theological perspectives into phenomenological methods.[16] But that is not our problem. In fact, Marion has conveniently posed the question:

Could not theology, in virtue of its own demands, and solely in view of formulating them, suggest certain modifications of method and operations to phenomenology? . . . Could not theology's demands allow phenomenology to transgress its own limits, so as finally to attain the free possibility at which, from its origin, it claims to aim?[17]

I think so.[18] Theology can only be enriched by a more phenomenological method. And, in its turn, it can enrich that method with possibilities deriving from attentiveness to the singularity of positive revelation.[19] Still, the general phenomenological principle stands. The saturated phenomenon shows itself by giving itself, and in a more intense and saturated manner in the case of theology.[20] Let us then apply some instances of Marion's saturated phenomena to the resurrection.

The Resurrection as Revelation

For our theological purposes, it is best to start with the phenomenon of revelation,[21] and then offer a brief exposition of the phenomena of event, art, flesh and face. Philosophy's difficulties in dealing with religion, let alone divine revelation in history and the singularities it contains, are well known and understandable. Though metaphysical perspectives can accommodate mythic and symbolic expressions, the historic particular is off the page. The speculative impossibility of anything being God-given is often entrenched in philosophical systems and the ideologies they support.[22] An idealist, subjectivist or empiricist system must have difficulty with the singular phenomenon of any self-revelation of a transcendent Other.[23] With some theological abandon, Marion focuses on Christ as the phenomenon saturating the whole of the New Testament and Christian life.[24] For Christ is given in a way that exceeds all expectations. He gives himself by way of an excess. The density and expansiveness of the resurrection of the crucified One outstrips quantitative assessment of any kind. Moreover, there is a qualitative intensity inherent in the Christ-event that makes it "unbearable" (Jn 16:12). The resurrection appearances are a troubling irruption.[25] The whole frame of previous relationships is radically rearranged: the Word becomes flesh, and in that flesh he is crucified and raised from the dead.[26] A plurality of horizons converge and collide in the inexhaustible excess confronting any human expression of the event (cf. Jn 21:25). The singularity of Christ's appearances overflows the expressive range of all the terms, genres, symbols, concepts, testimonies and descriptions related to time and place and form.[27]

The self-revealing phenomenon is presented to faith, not to theoretic understanding. What is perceived in the excess of the given phenomenon leaves the believer tongue-tied. Because intelligence is at a loss to frame what has been received in faith into any conceptual system, it is a sense dazzled and rendered sightless:

> Standing before Christ in glory, in agony or resurrected, it is always words (and therefore concepts) that we lack in order to say what we see, in short to see that with which intuition floods our eyes . . . God does not measure out his intuitive manifestation stingily, as though he wanted to mask himself at the moment of showing himself. But we, we do not offer concepts capable of handling a gift without measure and, overwhelmed, dazzled and submerged by his glory, we no longer see anything. [28]

Marion is making a point. Still, the event of revelation, with its form revealed on the face and in the flesh of the risen One, does not so stun and overwhelm contemplative intelligence that understanding necessarily atrophies. Insights, judgments, artistic expression and verbal forms, however limited in their respective contexts, can positively nourish and direct the contemplation of faith. An appropriately critical realism is governed by the imperative to allow the Christian phenomenon to disclose itself in its own evidence and on its own terms. For Christ is encountered as the revelation of a love and the source of life, at once within the world and beyond it. The excess of light overbrims the capacities of meaning.[29] There is a play of appearance and disappearance, of presence and absence, of self-revelation and concealment.

Yet this saturated phenomenon *par excellence* continues to give itself through its manifold effect in the life and mission of the Church.[30] The self-disclosure of Christ that once enabled a privileged seeing on the part of chosen witnesses has passed into the tradition. Compared to their "seeing", faith is the experience of "not seeing", but believing—to that degree, an experience of non-experience. But faith is neither a form of blindness nor a surrender to nothing or to no one. The self-giving of the risen One saturates all the "senses" of faith. Faith hearkens to the Word.[31] It breathes the Holy Spirit. It is strengthened by the testimony of privileged "eye witnesses" and the cumulative evidence of transformed lives. It sacramentally eats the body and drinks the blood of the risen Christ. It tastes with the savor of mystical wisdom. It enjoys the flickering illuminations of theology itself. Through all this, the self-giving phenomenon of Christ draws believers into its field. It summons to a conversion that is never fully attained. It amounts to a rebirth in a new world of praise, thanksgiving, communion, compassionate intercession and confident prayer.

This self-revealing phenomenon of the resurrection implies levels of manifold self-giving. It affects the life of the Church in its every aspect. In this respect, the revelatory impact of the resurrection event is such

that it is not one act of divine self-revelation among many, but the culminating act of self-revelation that defines the meaning of revelation
itself. To that degree, the resurrection is not a particular instance of a
general notion of revelation, but the particular self-disclosure of God
that defines what Christian revelation might mean. A full account of
this would need to include the following aspects of the phenomenon of
the resurrection:

- Jesus gives himself by appearing to the chosen disciples
- He is given in his full-bodied, but transformed physicality, marked by
  his empty tomb
- He is given as the one who has given himself for the life of the world
- He is given as one given by the Father out of love for the world
- He is given as the Son who has received all things from the Father
- He is given as one who has unconditionally given himself unto death
  on the cross
- He is given as the source of the Spirit
- He is given in the word of scripture and in the celebration of the
  sacraments
- He is given so as to draw all who receive him into his own self-giving
  existence
- He is given as the one who is to appear in eschatological evidence

With the resurrection in mind, we now turn to other kinds of saturated phenomena,[32] namely, the event, the aesthetic form, the flesh and
the face.

The Resurrection as Event

In its singular and expanding impact, a phenomenal event is not circumscribed by any concept of reality or anticipation. Needless to say, it
bears little resemblance to the mass production of "events" for any limited purpose (e.g., entertainment, sport, religious gatherings, political
rallies and so forth). For an event in the saturated sense is inexpressible
in its scope and implications. It occurs outside any calculus of cause and
effect. The origins and effect of such events can never be fully grasped,
despite their expanding impact.[33] In its "excess" and unrepeatable particularity, the event disrupts any metaphysical theory or comprehensive
explanation.[34] For example, the tragedy of the First World War is still
largely inexplicable in destructiveness. It overflowed the bounds of any
horizon of rationality.[35] More positively, the historical emergence of
Christianity, and, indeed, other world religions, are events of world-
shaping proportions. Attempts to reduce such events to a circumscribable
object serve only to blind rationality to the overwhelming character of
what has taken place. Claude Romano helpfully distinguishes a mere

event from a far more significant happening.[36] A factually-recorded event is impersonal in its objectivity. It has no existential import. It is datable as a *fait accompli*—an innerworldly empirical fact. In contrast, there is an event of another kind. This happens beyond all previous calculations and intimately involves those caught up in it. Its impact leads to world-changing decisions. For the world of one's previous life is reconfigured, and made newly meaningful and significant, outside the logic of cause and effect. Obvious examples would be, say, religious or moral conversion, a devastating grief or failure, or falling in love, or even a deeply significant friendship. Events in this sense give rise to a certain "anarchy", as the fixed points of previous horizons are dramatically shifted. As a result, the full significance of the event in question can only emerge with time, as it awaits a future to unfold.[37] The self is caught up in an incalculable existential venture, not as a passive recipient, but as an active participant, and as inspired to a new level of action. In this respect, it is not a matter of projecting new possibilities on an already established world, but of being involved in a new register of existence—within a world newly understood. Something has occurred from outside any previous individual horizon. A convenient example, again, is one's own birth—or that of others. For each birth is an event that occurs as given from beyond, yet at the same time it opens possibilities that are not predetermined against any settled horizon.[38]

The resurrection of the Crucified is pre-eminently such an event. By any showing, it is a world-changing occurrence. It radically shifts the death-bound horizon of existence to open it to the promise of eternal life already anticipated in the act of God's raising Jesus from the tomb. The origin and outcome of the resurrection transcends the world of previous calculations. Yet it "saturates" with Easter significance the lives of Christian believers to affect their sense of the universe itself: "if anyone is in Christ, there is a new creation: everything old has passed away; see, everything has become new" (2 Cor 5:17). This "new creation" is presented in various ways as a new spiritual birth, the beginning of a life that looks to an eschatological fulfilment (1 John 3:2). The Christian, to accommodate Romano's usage, is an *advenant*, one caught up and carried forward in an adventure of life, to a degree unimaginable within the horizon of previous existence.

The Resurrection as Aesthetic Form

The phenomenon of art adds a further dimension. A great painting, for example, saturates our perceptions in an especially intense fashion. It cannot be merely a tasteful adornment to the décor of a room or a dwelling. Its aesthetic impact causes everything to be re-arranged in the living-space of our mundane experience. If the art-work is regarded as an item of decoration, something owned and catalogued as property, it simply reflects one's own criteria of taste or status. A great work of art overflows any individual mode of appreciation because of its universal appeal. The painting dazzles the viewers' limited perceptions with a peculiar and inexhaustible excess, and so invites an endless contemplation that exceeds the flat manner of looking at an object.[39] Viewers, with their varying sensitivities and appreciative capacities, are drawn to behold what is framed to see the world anew. In this regard, a great painting possesses an iconic quality. It presents itself not so much as an arresting object within the routine scope of our vision, but is luminous with a light beyond the familiar.[40]

Theology is indebted to Hans Urs von Balthasar for attempting to restore an aesthetic dimension into the heart of faith. The first volume of his *Herrlichkeit, The Glory of the Lord, Seeing the Form*, appeals to the aesthetic form of divine revelation itself. Before God's self-revelation is taken into various systematic expositions, it is first of all a glory, a beauty, and with its own attractive force. It comes as a *Gestalt*, an irreducibly concrete, whole and complete form. Beholding this form does not stop short at the limits of vision. It invites participation. Its radiance sweeps up the beholder into an *eros* and rapture, under the attraction of what is revealed in Christ.[41] Von Balthasar writes,

> The Gospel presents Christ's form in such a way that "flesh" and "spirit", incarnation to the point of suffering and death, and resurrected life, are all interrelated down to the smallest details. If the Resurrection is excised, then not only certain things but simply everything about Jesus' earthly life becomes incomprehensible . . . [his] death and resurrection . . . are comprehensible only if they are understood as the transformation of this earthly form by God's power, and not as the form's spiritualisation or apotheosis.[42]

David Bentley Hart's theological aesthetics[43] is closely related to von Balthasar's approach.[44] The self-revealing phenomenon of beauty comes on its own terms and transfigures the world of our experience. The beautiful makes its own space, and keeps its own distance, for it eludes any fixed structure of apprehension or control.[45] The beautiful form gives itself, not as a pleasurable satisfaction, but as a summoning to self-transcendence in the light of the truth and value it represents. The beautiful crosses all boundaries, all types of being. It permeates creation in such a way as to subvert totalising ideologies, be they in mythic, conceptual or pragmatic form.

Hart's theological aesthetics are focused in the resurrection. The rhetoric celebrating the form of the risen One possesses "an infinite power of expression" eluding all efforts to silence it.[46] In reference to Luke 24:13-35, Hart remarks:

As the disciples who encountered the risen Christ on the road to Emmaus discover, Christ can now no longer be recognised as an available and objective datum, a simple given, but must be received entirely as a *donum*, as gift in the breaking of the bread, in the offer of fellowship given anew even when all hope of fellowship seems to have been extinguished.[47]

For David Hart, as for von Balthasar, the resurrection does not figure simply as an aesthetic principle. It radically subverts all totalitarian pretensions, be they political, cultural or intellectual. The dehumanising forces of culture appear triumphant in the crucifixion. The cross is the final word in their effort to determine the form of the world.[48] Yet at that very point, the Word of God is definitively and inexhaustibly pronounced: Christ is risen.

I note, in passing, that the phenomenality of the resurrection has a bearing on a theology of Christian art. I would suggest that artistic creativity is not simply an illustration of faith in an extrinsic sense, but more an inner dimension of resurrection-faith itself. Artists speak generally of "inspiration" in some manner guiding their creative imagination of the form and its realisation in the work of art, be it figurative, literary or musical, or expressive in other modes. In terms of depictions of the resurrection, there are innumerable examples of great power (e.g, from Matthias Grünewald to, say, the contemporary Chinese paintings of He Qi). But there is a deeper aspect when it comes to the resurrection, where a phenomenologically attuned theology and contemplative Christian art meet. For when faith is met with the phenomenon of this world-transforming event, however depicted or expressed, only an artistically conscious faith can appropriately respond to it by devising a form expressive of what originally disrupted all mundane forms of expression. Art is, at it were, an inner moment in the phenomenality of the resurrection, be it in music, painting or even poetic expression.

The Resurrection as "Flesh"

The phenomenon of "my body" or "flesh" is saturated with a special sense of immediacy and unobjectifiable intimacy. While it is "mine", it is the field of communication with the other. The body or "flesh", so intimately constituting the subject, gives the possibilities of intimate self-giving and self-disclosure, as in the case of erotic or maternal love. In this sense, the flesh is a field of mutual indwelling, a being with and for the other. In the eros and generativity of love, my bodily being is re-experienced in the flesh of the other.[49] Embodied existence transcends the status of being simply a physical body in a material world. The human body is the zone of incarnated relationships.[50] For the body of my conscious being is affected by and affecting the larger phenomenon of the world. It is at once my "natal bond" with the world, an immediate exposure to it, an immediate participation in it and a primal communication within it.[51]

In this respect, the phenomenon of the resurrection is a communication of the "body" of Christ in the Pauline sense, or "flesh" of the risen One in a more Johannine expression. In the Pauline vocabulary, of course, the "flesh" has negative connotations. Nonetheless, Paul envisages a transformed physicality in a bodily sense: "For just as the body is one and has many members, and all the members of the body, though many, are one body, so it is with Christ" (1 Cor 12:12). With the diversity of the many spiritual gifts, ". . . you are the body of Christ and individually members of it" (1 Cor 12:27). The shared breath or living atmosphere of the body is the Holy Spirit, the one Spirit manifested in the diversity of gifts. In this one Spirit, "we are all baptised into one body . . . and made to drink of the one Spirit" (1 Cor 12:13). To change the metaphor, with some reliance on Merleau-Ponty, the Spirit of Christ is the "inspiration" and "expiration" of the risen One invigorating the whole body of Christ.

The body or flesh of the risen Lord, transformed itself, is also transformative in its effect. The Word became flesh; and in that flesh he is crucified, and raised from the dead.[52] The flesh, with all its implied organic and social limitation, is still, after the resurrection, God's chosen field of communication. For the Christian phenomenon is not accessible to the order of thought alone. It is disclosed only in the phenomenality of body, flesh and "incarnation". Ps. Dionysius speaks of *pati divina*, "to experience the things of God" as transcending all thought and imagination. This venerable phrase has a strongly mystical overtone, and figures as such in the elaboration of negative theology. Nonetheless, the tradition it represents must never be separated from the bodily event of the resurrection of the crucified One.[53] Experiencing "the things of God" revealed in the death and resurrection of the incarnate Word presupposes the mediation of the flesh of Jesus and his risen bodily form. The primary Christian import of the mystical phrase, *pati divina*, suggests the possibility of interpreting it also as *pati humana et carnalia*—the experience of God in the flesh and body of Jesus Christ. In Tertullian's cryptic wordplay, *caro est salutis cardo*, the flesh (*caro*) of Christ is the turning point (*cardo*) of our salvation of our embodied existence. Christ is the form and source of incarnate, bodily communication. The risen Lord is, therefore, not simply the source of a new theology. Nor does Christian faith mean being involved in any ongoing theological seminar. It does mean being drawn into a new form of bodily existence, since God has made him "the head of all things for the church which is his body, the fullness of him who fills all in all" (Eph 1:22-23).

The phenomenology of the body inevitably strains against excessively spiritual interpretations. Yet the Church is the body of Christ. He is the head, and we the members. In the Johannine idiom, he is the vine and we the branches, as his flesh is given for the life of the world. His flesh/body is the field of Christ's relationship to the world, as both affected by and affecting the manifold phenomena of our incarnate co-existence. Though now transformed, his risen body continues to be his "natal bond" with the world. It expresses the immediacy of his exposure to the world in the process of its transformation in him. Through the body, he, the Word incarnate, is constituted in a primal communication with all incarnate beings, and continues to affect the material universe. In that transformed bodily being, he breathes his Spirit into all his members, so that there is one Spirit-vitalised body—even if Jesus himself is risen and his members are on the way to being transformed as he is.

Through incorporation into that subjective-body of Christ, his living flesh, the world is disclosed to his members in its original and eschatological significance. Consciousness is illumined with the "light of life" (Jn 8:12). Though Christ has come and remains in the flesh, his vitality emanates from the very life of God: "What came into being in him was life and the life was the light of all people" (Jn 1:3-4). The primordial generative mystery of the Father is thus revealed in the flesh: "Just as the Father has life in himself, so he has granted the Son to have life in himself" (Jn 5:26). In answer to Philip's request, "Lord, show us the Father, and we shall be satisfied" (Jn 14:8), Jesus replies, "Whoever has seen me has seen the Father . . . Do you not believe that I am in the Father and Father is in me?" (Jn 14:10). Life flows from a source beyond time and space into the living flesh of Christ and those united to him. It constitutes the phenomenological condition of Christian corporate existence. In this regard, there results an extraordinary sense of inter-subjectivity and mutual indwelling within the incarnational field of communication. Jesus prays, ". . . that they may all be one. As you, Father, are in me, and I in you, may they also be in us" (Jn 17:21).[54] The incarnate "Word of Life" (1 John 1:1) takes the form of a communal existence:

> This life was revealed, and we have seen it and testify to it, and declare to you the eternal life that was with the Father and was revealed to us . . . so that you may have fellowship with us; and truly our fellowship is with the Father and with his Son Jesus Christ (1 John 1:2-3).

The life of the vine flows into the branches (Jn 15:5), just as the head of the body governs the activity of each of its members. The incarnation, already reaching its fulfilment in him, is extended into a living corporate form of the Church. It determines a form of self-giving love for those who are "members, one of another" (Eph 4:25), "for no man hates his own flesh, but nourishes and cherishes it, as Christ does the Church because we are members of his body" (Eph 5:30). The Letter to the Ephesians does not hesitate to appeal to the most intimate, ecstatic and generative human experience of the body in sponsal love to express Christ's relationship to the ecclesial body. Just as man and woman become "one flesh" (Gen 2:23; Mt 19:6; Mk 10:8), the risen One is one flesh with the community of believers.

Though Jesus is glorified in the flesh, he is still marked by the wounds of the cross, thus representing his compassionate involvement with humanity in its sufferings and with the whole groaning reality of creation (cf. Rom 8:18-25). The power of his resurrection reaches into the alienated and mortal sphere of our corporate existence, for "even when we were dead through our trespasses, [God] has made us alive together with Christ . . . and raised us up with him" (Eph 2:5-6). A new field of incarnate relationship is disclosed in the phenomenon of the resurrection, so that Christ's rising from the dead does not mean disincarnation, but a new form of incarnation. The former sphere of fleshly divisions is now relocated, as it were, in a new form of incarnate existence (Eph 2:14-22). Its vitality derives from Christ's self-giving love, in order that "we are to grow up in every way into him who is the head, into Christ, from whom the whole body, joined and knit together by every joint with which it is supplied, when each part is working properly, makes bodily growth and upbuilds itself in love" (Eph 4:15-16). Physical existence is transformed—a bodily "mutation" has occurred, the life-blood of which is the love that possessed the head and conforms his members to him. His giving is embodied: "the bread that I will give for the life of the world is my flesh" (Jn 6:51). By sacramentally assimilating his flesh and blood, given and outpoured for the life of the world, believers are conformed to his risen life: "Those who eat my flesh and drink my blood have eternal life, and I will raise them up on the last day; for my flesh is true food and my blood is true drink" (Jn 6:55).

In the risen Christ, communication in the flesh does not cease, but opens out to an unimaginable fulfilment. The mutual indwelling and openness to the other characterising the earthly experience of the flesh is now actualised in a new mode of mutual co-inherence: "Those who eat my flesh and drink my blood, abide in me and I in them" (Jn 6:56; cf. 15:4, 6). In this paschal realm, believers "abide in the Son and in the Father" (1 John 2:24; cf. 3:24), and so inhabit a field of love in which earthly *eros* is subsumed into the *agape* of the divine self-giving: "God is love, and those who abide in love, abide in God, and God abides in them" (1 John 4:16). To the degree faith assimilates his flesh and blood and Spirit, there is new sight, hearing, touching, tasting, eating and drinking, feeling and indwelling—the new senses of faith, as Origen recognised so clearly.[55] Because of its unobjectifiable immediacy, the phenomenon of the flesh earths and embodies faith in the risen One with fresh directness. There is less risk of rising to a level of abstraction, either in thought or symbol, that ill serves what has been uniquely given.

The Resurrection and the Face of Christ

The phenomenon of the face is saturated with significance, in a more distanced manner compared to the intimacy of the flesh. George Orwell saw something of this experience in his verse tribute to the "crystal spirit" on the face of the young Italian militiamen with whom he served in Spain—and also in the terrifying emptiness written on the face of "Big Brother". Whenever he read a moving piece of writing, Orwell found himself conscious of "the face somewhere behind the page, which is not necessarily the actual face of the writer", but as he put it, "the face that the writer *ought* to have". Here he had Charles Dickens especially in mind.[56] This leads into the elusive but ever arresting phenomenon we here consider.

When "faced" with the other, I am not looking at something amongst other objects in the world, or at a "somebody" in the crowd. When someone looks at me, I am confronted with a striking otherness. It lays claim to my attention and concern. Here Marion is indebted to Levinas's widely influential account of the other, especially in his/ her suffering. To be faced with this other is to feel the force of the question, Where were you, given what you now see?[57] The face paradoxically makes visible the invisible totality of the other. It resists objectification. At the same time, this "you" calls for a respect and regard, in such a way as to render inhuman any gaze that is just a mere "looking at", as in the inspection of objects. The centre of gravity is shifted—not *here*, in the perception of the self-contained ego, but *there*, in the other, whose look stops us in our tracks. In this sense, the face of the other is a commanding presence.[58] The face of the other does not reflect back to me what I desire to possess or dominate. It takes me out of myself, into the disturbing world of responsibility, respect and love. The face is not a mirror in which I see myself, but more a window through which the light of arresting otherness breaks through. It calls forth a self-transcendence that goes beyond any symmetries of an "I and Thou" relationship. For this other who confronts me, face to face, breaks into my awareness as inviolable uniqueness: "thou shalt not kill"—despite the disruption of the secure world of the ego.

As regards the face of Christ, we have to admit that the New Testament, neither when speaking of the risen Jesus, nor at any stage in his earthly life, shows no interest in describing a face in any conventional terms. Icons, of course, and the long tradition of Christian art already referred to, have sought to serve revelation and faith by expressing, in Orwell's terms, the face somewhere behind the biblical accounts of Jesus deeds and words. But at its best, faith, seeking to find its best artistic expression, is intent on the phenomenon of the face of Christ, the icon of the self-revealing God. Paul speaks expansively of Christ, "the image of the invisible God" (Col 1:15). But the otherness of the transcendent must be allowed to appear on its own terms—looking us in the face, rather than being a projection of our look.[59] The only appropriate attitude when faced by the icon is prayer, adoration and self-surrender. The unenvisageable is rendered visible only to faith, hope and love. Surrender to this kind of evidence exceeds a full cognitive or conceptual comprehension. It enjoins a waiting and longing for its final appearance, typified in the earliest recorded Christian prayer, Maranatha, "Come, Lord!" (1 Cor 16:22; Rev 22:20).[60] The face of Christ as the one who is to come allows for a deferral and delay, filled with an endless diversity of significations through the course of history.

The face of Christ is not merely the face of any other that would call forth the biblical prohibition against killing, and so demand the reverence and care due to anyone bearing the image of God. For Christian faith looks upon the Jesus who has in fact been killed by human agencies. He has been raised up, as the embodiment of God's self-giving love: "They shall look upon the one whom they have pierced" (Jn 19:37). In this kind of gaze, faith lives in the world of dim reflections of the future "face to face" vision (1 Cor 13:12). Yet, in the bold Pauline idiom, there is already a kind of experience of the face of Christ who is turned toward us in a light from beyond this world: "For it is the God who said, 'Let light shine forth out of darkness', who has shone in our hearts to give the light of the knowledge of the glory of God in the face of Christ" (2 Cor 4:6). The most striking aspect of the face of Christ is not so much our seeing, but that of "being seen through". In its apocalyptic rhetoric, the Book of Revelation gives a visionary description of the face of Jesus with "eyes like a flame of fire" (Rev 1:14; 2:18), who declares, "I know your works", "your affliction and your poverty", and "where you live" (Rev 2:2, 9, 12, 19; 3:1, 8, 15). He identifies himself as "the living one, I was dead, and see, I am alive for evermore" (Rev 1:18). The transparency of all who encounter him pervades the Gospel accounts (e.g., Lk 9:47; 11:17; Jn 1:48). Before there are any "resurrection appearances", before the chosen witnesses see him, he sees them (e.g., Jn 20:27-29). They experience themselves as being "seen through", and so faced with him as the truth of who they are and what they are now called to be. For faith to be faced by the crucified and risen One means to "lose face" in terms of world glory, and to be faced with glory of what is not of this world.

Conclusion: Saturated Phenomenon or Mystery?

In the foregoing pages, we have attempted to present the resurrection as a saturated phenomenon, by exploiting the approaches opened up by

Marion, Henry and others. As a phenomenon of revelation, the resurrection represents a culminating moment in the self-revelation of God. As an event it saturates in its intensity and expansiveness our view of the world and of the universe itself. As the manifestation of divine beauty and art, the resurrection contests the world made ugly by despair and evil. In the flesh of the risen One, our own enfleshed or incarnate lives have already entered the realm of an eternal life of communion. On the face of the risen Jesus, we discern, in a clouded way, God's glory and our true selves.

This has all meant perceiving in the risen Jesus a phenomenon that saturates our perceptions of the world in any number of respects. We realise that a phenomenology restricted to clearly determined philosophical limits will contest this theological extension of what are otherwise regarded as mundane phenomena. On the other hand, the Church is a phenomenon in world history, and it would seem unrealistic not to appreciate it as such, and to explore what has called it into being. We appreciate too that a theology, more habituated to a propositional and systematic exposition, may find this exposition too primitive. Yet what is at stake is not only the distinctiveness of the focal Christian phenomenon, but also its salvific efficacy and impact. Our procedure has not been designed to bypass the demands of systematic theology, but to awaken it to a new freshness. For example, in the humble form of its "givenness" as a phenomenon to Christian experience, the resurrection has a trinitarian density. It cannot be located outside the self-giving of Jesus unto death, and his self-disclosure to his chosen witnesses. Nor can it ignore the originating dynamic of the Father's giving and glorification of his Son for the world's salvation. Finally, and most obviously, it can never be appreciated at all unless the Spirit had been poured out as its primary witness, forming Christian consciousness into an ever new awareness of the Resurrection and the Life.

As was said in the preface to this book, our efforts to attend to the resurrection effect for theology are not simply a matter of making room for the resurrection in an already overburdened theological curriculum. We are not trying to fit it more neatly into a theological system or even to come up with a new theology of the resurrection. Rather than trying to locate the resurrection in some specific area of theology, we are suggesting that theology, in all its endeavours, needs to be located "within the resurrection" and be suffused with its light, to become, in a word, more "resurrectional" in mood and methods. Admittedly, the more phenomenologically specific it is, the more Christian faith is likely to experience itself as the "foolishness" that Paul speaks of (1 Cor 1:18-25). The erudite "scribe" or the rationalist "debator of this age" (v. 20) will find that the actuality or possibility of the resurrection event cannot be rationally entertained. But a genuine Christian apologetics must not apologise for the particularity of what has been given to faith. Nor must it concede that it is "irrational"—when it is only such to a rationality that cannot allow God to act in the scandalous bodiliness of raising the crucified Jesus from the dead.

This understanding of the saturated phenomenon is not unrelated to the polyvalent and originally biblical word "mystery". In current common usage, it refers to a puzzling phenomenon that demands investigation and, for the adept investigator, the detection of an eventual solution. When all questions are answered, the puzzle is solved, and the book ends when the "mystery" is no more. In contrast, and in a completely different context, Paul can speak of "the mystery that has been hidden throughout the ages and generations but has now been revealed to his [God's] saints . . . Christ in you, the hope of glory" (Col 1:26-27). The language of Christian doctrine refers to the "mysteries of faith"—the Trinity, incarnation, grace and the beatific vision. These are the revealed objects of faith; for reason unaided could not deduce them. On a more devotional level, there are the "mysteries" of the life of our Lord, or the once fifteen and now twenty mysteries of the Rosary, as various aspects of Christian revelation have become the subject of contemplation. On a more theological plane, say in the theology of Karl Rahner, "mystery" is a fundamental notion expressive of God's self-communication to the human spirit.[61] The mystery in this sense is not something to be solved, but something so given, and so self-giving, that it constitutes the basic horizon of life and existence itself. The many "mysteries" of faith are aspects of the one self-giving mystery of God, which, even as it communicates itself in the Word and Spirit, remains ever beyond any finite grasp. To see God is to be given a vision of the inexhaustible infinities of the divine reality: even though the blessed participate in the life of God, the divine mystery is not lessened, but more positively appreciated in its boundless excess.

Why not speak more simply, then, of the "mystery" of the resurrection rather than make this phenomenological detour? Would not that word say more than any quasi-philosophical term could suggest and say it better? In response, I would simply suggest that that the term "mystery" and its specific Christian and theological meaning is best recovered and even intensified by the approach we are taking. To the degree we treat the phenomenonality of the resurrection, it will be less likely to be reduced to a particular truth of faith that transcends the limits of reason, or be located outside the consciousness of the believer (and theologian) as an object of some kind to be inspected at will and be assigned a place in some larger scheme. In a sense, a genuine phenomenology is about restoring a sense of mystery, and more so in the instance of saturated phenomena, but most of all in the case of the resurrection of the Crucified.

Finally, different kinds of phenomenality need to be recognized. In the scriptural texts, as in the four Gospels, the letters of Paul and so forth, there are different kinds of disclosure. In the celebration of the liturgy and its sacraments, in mystical experience and other modes of Christian life, the mystery of Christ reveals itself in a variety of ways.

CHAPTER 3

The Resurrection and the Phenomenon
of the New Testament

We now turn to the New Testament as a literary phenomenon. Libraries of remarkable contemporary scholarship and any number of splendid commentaries are an irreplaceable resource. In what follows, I pretend to no mastery of such erudition, even while profiting from this or that aspect of it. Our aim is quite simple, as we seek to recover a sense of wonder at this literary phenomenon. It finds its source and coherence in the all-saturating phenomenon of Christ's resurrection. In the previous chapter, following Marion, we referred to this phenomenon as revelation, event, aesthetic form, flesh and face. These aspects of the resurrection brim over into the confessional writings of the early Christian community. They share in the revelatory phenomenon as its written form. What is written by and for the community of faith is also a literary event in its own right. What is so expressed has the impact of a work of art. These writings communicate in the phenomenality of both flesh and face. In the saturated phenomenon of the flesh, the words, images, literary genres and techniques are incarnated in Christian experience. What is written "words" the body of Christ, and gives its members the capacities to write, read, speak and imagine in ways proper to the resurrection event. As face, too, for the written word carries the experience of being faced by the risen Lord as the source, content and object of this form of literary expression.

The modesty of our aims suggests a limited number of perspectives, presented under the following four headings, leading to a brief conclusion:

1. *Receptivity to the Divinely Given*—for faith is openness to the gift of God
2. *Interpretation in the Light of Christ*—for Christ is the fundamental hermeneutical principle and agent
3. *Rhetorics of Receptivity and Excess*—for a special creativity is needed when language stutters and ideas strain to express what can never be fully expressed

4. *Light in Darkness*—for what is given is beyond any human control or calculation

Receptivity to the Divinely Given

The New Testament writings derive from the paschal event of the resurrection of the crucified Jesus. It saturates the unique literary phenomenon foundational to Christian tradition. To approach such writings with the receptivity due to them entails both a scholarly receptivity to the literary data and also a contemplative openness of faith to the gift. The *data*, the givens, in this case emanate from the *donum*, the gift, of the actuality and extent of God's self-gift in Christ. Outside the resurrection event, Christian speech or sacred scripture would lack their essential focus. This is simply to restate the Christian tradition that the canon of the New Testament is a collection of "inspired" writings (i.e., inspired by an event that gave rise to them in the first place, to permeate them with its un-objectifiable excess in every word).

Any theological interpretation of this literary phenomenon must not set its sights too low. Certainly, the New Testament is the product and record of conversion. Indeed, there are multiple evidences of conversion arising from an encounter with the crucified and risen Jesus. But conversion, in whatever sense and intensity, does not cause Jesus to rise from the tomb. Nor does it engender faith in the resurrection in some purely psychological sense. Moreover, the resurrection initiates a profound and far-reaching process of "remembering Jesus". But the act of remembering alone does not supply evidence of the resurrection. However much the early disciples retained a living memory of the dead Jesus, it does not cause him to rise. Rather, the particular kind of remembering expressed in the New Testament arises from the resurrection itself. Indeed, it is a way of remembering initiated by the risen Jesus himself. Having returned to his disciples from death and defeat, he unlocks the capacities of memory to understand in a definitive manner what the past traditions of the faith of Israel were pointing to. The risen Lord himself reshapes the manner in which his life and shameful death are recollected. The phenomenon of the resurrection, and the testimony of the witnesses inherent in it, inspire the creation of a literature designed to form faith in the living Christ throughout history. Event, witness and expression are each a facet of the identity of him who, in his life and death, words, deeds and mission, has been vindicated by God as the form and source of eternal life. In short, the New Testament expresses forms of conversion and memory after the event, not as constituting it.

James D. G. Dunn concludes his recent monumental study, *Jesus Remembered*, by referring to four clear elements within the tradition, namely the empty tomb, the appearances of the risen Christ, the mission of the disciples and the temporal reference to the third day and the first day of the week.[1] Each of these must be recognised, but always in the context of a fifth and most obvious feature, present from the earliest to the latest writings of the New Testament. It is the praise of God identified as "the one who raised the Lord Jesus" (2 Cor 4:14).[2] In this doxological current pervading the scriptural witness, God is not the *mysterium tremendum et fascinosum* of a generalised phenomenology of religion. Rather the God who has acted by raising Jesus from the tomb is identified and praised as the generative mystery of love. The divinely engendering love has been at work through the whole of creation. It has inspired the faith and hopes of Israel, and is revealed at a culminating moment. This God is to be praised as the Father of our Lord Jesus Christ, adored and thanked in his free act of raising his Son from the dead (Acts 17:31). Yet this God who has freely acted in the resurrection has opened a free space of response. History has not been stopped, but opened to an unimaginable fulfilment. A universal transformation has been already anticipated in Christ. Yet the life of faith, hope and love, passing through all the unpredictable contingencies of history, must press on to the goal. Forms of this authentic response are expressed in the witness and literary creativity of the early Christian writings.

Interpretation in the Light of Christ

Paul's use of the traditional phrase, "according to scriptures" (e.g., 1 Cor 15:3, 4) is linked to a reference to the resurrection. The mystery of God's saving will is inextricably connected to the horizon of hope attested in the sacred writings of Israel. Yet the varied expressions of promise inscribed in them are now interpreted anew in what has taken place. In Lukan terms, the risen Christ himself explains the scriptures, introducing himself as the new, the final and the utterly Other around whom the totality of the biblical witness is refigured (Lk 24:25-27, 44-47). Jesus does not present God by showing himself as a particular image of the divine, but as the living "synthesis" or embodiment of the mystery hidden in the whole history of salvation.[3] In this Christ-centred and Christ-instigated exegesis, no single aspect of the biblical witness by itself expresses the totality. Each aspect has to be interpreted on the basis of the whole. Jesus' teaching does not stand apart from his suffering. His miracles have no meaning apart from his message. Neither his teaching, message, miracles nor suffering attain their universal salvific relevance apart from the resurrection.[4] Moreover, with the formation of the New Testament writings, the Christ-inspired interpretation of the scriptures of Israel carries over into a new form of scriptures, specifically witnessing to Christ. In this regard, D. Moody Smith has asked the question, when did the Gospels become scripture?[5] F. J. Moloney has given a detailed answer with specific reference to the Gospel of John.[6] Biblical scholarship thus points to an early sense of the New Testament as the guide and nourishment of faith, completing and specifying the writings of Israel.

Neither the content of the New Testament narratives nor an interpretation of them is possible outside the Easter event.[7] The resurrection so affected the consciousness of the early disciples that, in their witness to the full significance of Jesus Christ, they came to admit their resistance and misunderstanding in regard to what Jesus was revealing to them all along. After the resurrection, they understood Jesus precisely in terms of what they had previously resisted (Mk 8:29, 31ff.).[8] Admittedly, something was at work, hidden in their previous forms of attachment to Jesus, even if this defied any adequate expression on their part. However the first followers of Jesus perceived his identity and mission, despite the confusion and incomprehension they experienced, it constrained their discipleship. In the aftermath of Easter they were enabled to admit to an embarrassing ignorance and failure. But with Jesus' return from the dead everything was made clear—in the sense that they now understood, where before they had constantly missed the point. Despite the clarity of this admission on their part, it was only with difficulty that they could later describe their previous conflicted experience of what had been going on all along. They had indeed sensed in him the overwhelming attractiveness that had drawn them out of their former lives into the precarious and vulnerable discipleship involved in following him. They had been drawn to Jesus and listened to his teaching. They had even received a more personal form of instruction over and above his more public communications to his hearers as a whole. The original followers of Jesus could recall only in approximate terms a phenomenon, at once involving them, but all the while remaining elusive or even incomprehensible. What had drawn them to follow the Jesus who had called them to leave all for his sake had now been made manifest in his rising from the dead, as one singularly vindicated by God.[9] Brendan Byrne[10] states a key principle of interpretation:

> . . . the Gospels are not primarily biographies. From beginning to end they are replete with the deeper awareness of Jesus' identity, status and function that came to the disciples along with faith in the resurrection. We never meet in the Gospels the purely "pre-resurrection" Jesus. The light of the resurrection shines through all; not even in Mark is it entirely dimmed (1:1; 1:10-11; 4:41; 6:45-52; 9:2-12:35-37) . . . it is always the risen Lord that one encounters in the Gospels.[11]

Amid the many factors behind the development of the New Testament, the impact of the resurrection remains the central factor. The post-Easter community called on the tradition inspired by the early witnesses. What had previously been hidden was now clearly grasped. Inevitably, the foundational writings of faith retrojected aspects of the risen Christ into its account of what had taken place in the course of the earthly life of Jesus. In their corporate recollection of the life, death and teachings of Jesus of Nazareth in the light of Easter, the followers of Christ expressed their new understanding of the risen One. He is now understood as the embodiment of all that he had previously stood for, by proclaiming unto death the Kingdom of God. When faith recognises that the crucified One is raised from the dead, the words and deeds of his earthly life shine with existential significance for those who follow his way.[12] With his resurrection, the full meaning of who Jesus was, the significance of his words and deeds, and all that he stood for in life and in death are brought into focus. All the past of Jesus' birth, deeds, teaching and death are sealed into the present condition of the risen Jesus, so as to be grasped as successive "mysteries" of the life of Jesus as narrated in the Gospel and celebrated in the liturgy. For Jesus is risen as the one who was born of the Virgin Mary, and baptised by John. He is risen as the one who performed works of healing and forgiveness, and in all his relationships to those he encountered. He is risen as the proclaimer of the Kingdom of God and as the one who was condemned and executed because of it.

Rhetorics of Receptivity and Excess

Being open to the New Testament witness on its own terms necessarily demands attending to the complex and often creative rhetoric of its expression. We catch in the totality of the written testimony the attempts of faith to make some sense of the revelatory, yet ever unrepresentable "excess", embodied in the risen Jesus as the object of faith.[13] In order to give a creative and relevant expression to the universal meaning of Christ, the New Testament came into being. These texts must speak for themselves. They witness to the originating character of the event that provoked their emergence.

The receptivity demanded by the New Testament phenomenon can be short-circuited by the otherwise laudable attempts to describe the "Jesus of History". Here we must continually recall what is most obvious: only in the light of the resurrection does the "Jesus of history" become a scholarly problem. For Christian faith—and the scholarship that serves it—the transforming event of the resurrection and the historical life and death of Jesus of Nazareth are interwoven. For example, the typical Pauline designation, "Christ Jesus", is a condensed expression of how the resurrection is the light in which the life and death of Jesus of Nazareth is newly apprehended in the God-wrought event of his rising from the dead. And yet the risen Christ is the crucified Jesus of Nazareth. As such, he enters into the larger memory of faith as it extends to every aspect of his earthly life as recorded in the Gospel narratives. The Jesus who rose is identified as born of Mary, baptised by John, who proclaimed the Kingdom, and suffered the consequences.

Here, a special question emerges concerning the Jesus of history project. Though this quest has yielded valuable results in terms of the history, geography, cultural, linguistic and social setting of the life of Jesus, the foundational narrowness of its methodology suggests a rather uncritical disjunction between the Jesus of history and the Christ of faith.[14] In this narrow methodology, the religious consciousness of faith is straightjacketed into a perception of ever-receding "facts" in the past. What is most evident is the emphasis on facts to the neglect of the meaning of the underlying phenomenon, along with a certain abstraction from the living experience of the communities of faith from which the New Testaments arose. The work of recent scholars has restored a more genuinely theological perspective.[15] Yet, we must ask whether, given the disciples' post-resurrectional recognition of the identity of Jesus, the historical quest has been as focused as it might have been. Because of the awkward opposition of the Jesus of history to the Christ of faith, something more crucial was bypassed, namely, the difference between the historical post-resurrectional understanding of the early disciples and their witness to the historical awareness of Jesus himself. There is room to refocus this whole question, and it is worth pointing this out, if theology is to be more keenly focused on the resurrection.

The condensed kerygmatic proclamation of "Christ Jesus" cannot be divorced from the variety of narrative expansions instanced in the four versions of the Gospel of "Jesus Christ". While both designations of the crucified and risen One—"Christ Jesus" and "Jesus Christ"—occur in the light of the resurrection, the Pauline "Christ Jesus" is more cryptic, in its concentration on the end point: "If Christ has not been raised, your faith is futile, and you are still in your sins" (1 Cor 15:17). The Gospels crystallise the tradition some decades later, at a stage when the details of the words and deeds of Jesus are appreciated in their existential significance for Christian life in all its varied contexts. For instance, Luke introduces his Gospel with the words: "Since many have undertaken to set down an orderly account of the events that have been fulfilled amongst us" (Lk 1:1). He promises to offer his own account for the benefit of the excellent Theophilus, "so that you may know the truth concerning the things about which you have been instructed" (Lk 1:4). In contrast, Paul, though presuming all or much of this (see next chapter), was not concerned with presenting any "orderly account", overwhelmed as he is by the revelation of the risen One that had been made to him. That singular truth was not to be lost in the details of times, places, characters, teaching and events that had significance only in terms of Jesus being raised by God. It would seem that Paul is implicitly taking for granted the various traditions of the logia, miracles and exemplary actions recollected from the earthly life of Jesus, and to some degree deliberately refocusing the emerging tradition on its central point. For him, such details were not the place to start, even if as a teacher in Antioch he would have been familiar with all elements that were forming the tradition (Acts 13:1). The radical moment of truth was not knowing Jesus "in the flesh" (2 Cor 5:16). That, by itself, would not raise Christian existence above an improved Jewish ethics or Greek wisdom or, for that matter, beyond an overheated apocalyptic vision. For him, everything must be centred, and continually re-centred, on the resurrection of the Crucified, in anticipation of a completely new creation (2 Cor 5:17).[16] It was not a matter of looking back, but of looking forward and outward to a creation transformed.

In the literary phenomenon of New Testament witness to the risen Jesus, there is evidence of a remarkable creativity and diversity of expression, given the supra-categorical "excess" of the event that had made all the difference. This creativity is often of a highly literary and artistic form. It came up against the limited capacities of human language to express the singularity of what could never be fully expressed. The inexhaustible density of the event of God's self-revelation caused all language to stutter and all expression to grope.[17] The original—or better, originating—event provoked the creativity of a variety of rhetorics and images employed in the earliest preaching, instruction and writings that came to be distilled in the New Testament canon. In view of what exceeded all language, any effort to reconcile all such varied forms of expression reaches an impasse. Even images, chosen for the sake of vivid communication, move around a centre of attraction that can never be imagined or described. Narratives and kerygmatic expressions were formed out of this creative tradition in order to put into words what escaped all expectation and powers of expression. They show evidence of drawing together various aspects that can never settle into a stable synthesis or even narrative form. For they tell of how Jesus is recognised and not of how he becomes present and disappears; of how he is touched, and yet refuses contact; of how he is humanly corporeal, but exists now in another form. In all this he is the glorified Lord, yet never more related to the disciples as "my brothers" (Jn 20:17); he is "in them" (Col 1:27), but "above" them (Col 3:1). The phenomenon resists any harmonisation on the mundane level of experience—as Paul's different accounts of his encounter with the risen Christ make clear.

The original simple confessions embedded in the tradition are subject to various forms of development as the meaning of faith is proclaimed in the ongoing experience of the Church and crystallised into narrative forms. For example, the fact that God had vindicated Jesus against his executioners by raising him from the dead (Acts 2:36) overflows into a vindication of the faith and ministry of his followers (Rom 4:25; Lk 24:46ff.). In the light of the resurrection, the salvific "for-us" of Jesus' death on the cross was soon elaborated with reference to the Suffering

Servant of Isaiah 53. The Son freely takes our sins on himself (Gal 2:20; 3:13; Col 2:13). The divine initiative is present at every stage (Acts 3:18ff.; Lk 24:7, 26, 45). The primary agent is always God (Rom 8:32; 2 Cor 5:21), the creator of the world (Acts 3:15), the Father who has wrought the resurrection of Jesus, in power, glory and Spirit (Rom 8:11; 2 Cor 4:14; Gal 1:1; Eph 1:20; Col 2:12). Within this divine agency, the Father and the Son are one, so that in the mature theological Johannine account, the pre-existent status of Jesus is evident. From here develops a reinterpretation of the life and words of Jesus, not only as the revelation of the Father, but also in its widest anthropological and cosmic reach as the Spirit of the risen One guides the perceptions of faith "into all truth" (Jn 16:13).

Exegetes must ponder the different configurations of elements in the tradition, (e.g., Lk 24:13-49), and the process of enrichment that takes place (e.g., details like the presence of Joseph of Arimathea, the much larger issue of the increasing role of the women witnesses, the exoneration of disciples, the role of Peter)[18] as the conditions of time and space enter into the narrative totality formed in the light of the one decisive event. Is there a gradual "physicalisation" of the risen Jesus in evidence—especially in Luke? What is the true ending of Mark's Gospel? Is the location of the appearances in Jerusalem or Galilee? What is the significance of angelic figures at the empty tomb? All such questions and the temporal references to the third day and to the Ascension after forty days resist any synthetic account.

The hermeneutical situation is complex. In the light of the resurrection, the words and deeds of the earthly Jesus are recalled as on the way to their fulfilment. Furthermore, in the experience of the early communities, Jesus' life, words and deeds, death and resurrection are re-appropriated in different existential, religious and cultural situations. Moreover, the religious mentality of Israel was shocked by both the cross and the resurrection: on the one hand, no servant of God could be so manifestly cursed; and, on the other, even though the Pharisees admitted a final resurrection, it did not allow for its anticipation in this way. The philosophical mentality of the ancient world was not hospitable to the physical and cosmic significance of the resurrection, just as it was politically dangerous to proclaim God's exaltation of the condemned and crucified Jesus within the Roman imperium. Indeed, the new wine burst the old wineskins.

N. T. Wright has deftly pointed out a number of surprising aspects of the Gospel accounts of the appearances of the risen Jesus.[19] First, while the scriptures of Israel figure pervasively in a Christ-inspired hermeneutics of the cross and resurrection, the event of the resurrection and the related self-disclosures of Jesus are in no sense deduced from this biblical background. It is the foreground of the event that reshapes the interpretation of the scriptures, and forms them into the presupposition of

Christian faith, despite the more general scriptural presuppositions of the Gospel of John—". . . for as yet they did not understand the scripture, that he must rise from the dead" (Jn 20:9)—and 1 Corinthians stating that Christ both died and rose "according to the scriptures" (1 Cor 15:3-4). Secondly, in contrast to 1 Corinthians 15, there is no expression of an existential carry-over into the life of the disciples, beyond commissioning them as witnesses to what has happened. Thirdly, no glorious light or radiance of any kind is associated with Jesus' self-disclosure, as is the case in Luke's description of Paul's experience in Acts. In fact, the encounters with Jesus are almost a let-down. There is no glorious radiance or voice from heaven as he walks, converses, eats and relates to the disciples in a familiar fashion. Fourthly, as the tradition develops, the role of the women witnesses begins to predominate, even if their legal recognition as witnesses was scarcely acceptable in the culture of the time. Yet these differing accounts presuppose a unique event before any tradition of interpretation developed. Even if the later synoptic narratives work up the most primitive oral testimony, and thus may be taken as "putting the icing on the cake", Wright pointedly argues that this presumes that there was "an original cake".[20]

As to the literary creativity evident in the Gospels, von Balthasar cites the following words of A. Schlatter:

> The coming into existence of a poetry which is concerned with the image of Christ is as old as evangelisation itself, and we find in many passages of the Gospels brilliant achievements of early Christian poetry, through the clarity of graphic power contained in the narratives and simultaneously through the delicacy of the drawing, which knows how to direct the eye to the aspect of the event which has value for its beholder. In some cases there are no precise boundaries to mark off the point at which remembrance became poetry and the graphic forming and narrative became remote from the real course of events. But the greatness of Christian poetry is essentially due to the fact that its imagination . . . remains subjected to a powerful discipline which has its *raison d'être* in the fact that the presentation of Christ never separated from the faith, and for this reason never forgot the difference between myth and reality.[21]

Different forms of rhetoric employed are readily discernible. The oldest form is the liturgical and doxological language of praise and thanksgiving, referring to God who had acted in raising Jesus from the dead. Then, there are more articulated creedal forms shaping the tradition—best exemplified in 1 Corinthians 15. Later still, there are the four Gospel narratives. Though each is inspired by the Spirit of the crucified and risen Christ, together they serve to indicate the different perspectives that the expression of faith allows. Each Gospel narrative concludes with an account of the discovery of the empty tomb. With the exception of Mark (at least in the form of its apparently truncated ending), the discovery of the tomb is the prelude to the variously depicted "appearance narratives". These are not designed simply to illustrate a message of some kind from which they can be detached. Nor do they figuratively express, as inspirational legends, the experience of a conviction that is focused elsewhere, as in some other and deeper reality. The opposite is the case, as Paul crisply points out in 1 Corinthians 15. The appearances of the risen Lord are clearly taken as guarantees of the realism of the fact—without which faith would be in vain.

Then, interweaving these writings, there are the great panoramic hymns (Jn 1:1-18; Phil 2:6-11; Col 1:15-20; 1 Tim 3:16; Rom 11:33-36, and throughout the Book of Revelation). Such literary expressions reach beyond the poetry and prose of any literary genre. They are permeated with the present sense of victory of Christ over death, and of its universal, eschatological significance. The utterance of praise and thanksgiving issues forth into the expressions of hope and prayer for the collective fulfilment of what has been anticipated in Christ's rising from the tomb.[22]

Light in Darkness

Yet there is insistent recognition of the reality of the pressing historical situation. Though the light has shone, the darkness of evil, often in monstrous forms, threatens it. Indeed, the resurrection of Jesus in some ways intensifies the experience of the powers of evil reacting to what most threatens them. History continues in a dramatic form, and the conflicts born of acceptance or rejection of Christ become more extreme. The resurrection of Jesus did not bring history to a close. Life goes on, with its experience of suffering, death, persecution and violence. At such moments, an exultant poetic form is not enough, neither to defend the believer from evil nor to express the indescribable fact of the resurrection and its bearing on the future. In the collision between faith in the risen Lord and the virulence of evil, the more vivid apocalyptic imagery of the Book of Revelation is mined from the Old Testament to make its point in the desperate situations in which the Christian community finds itself. Even though the forces of evil have been cast down to earth in the heavenly war (Rev 12:7-9), the world still remains a battleground. The great dragon seeks to devour the offspring of the woman (Rev 12:3-6, 13-17), and the beast rises from the abyss, drawing the world to worship it, and to make war on the elect (cf. Rev 13:1-10). These, and other luridly imaginative representations of the power of evil, are born out of crisis. They are inspired by the terminal experiences of struggle, persecution and judgment. The world, or better, perhaps, the world that is in its death-throes, is ending, and proving implacably hostile to Christian existence. And yet even here, the englobing image is that of Jesus, the Alpha and the Omega, the source of eternal life (Rev 1:17-18; 22:12-17). In him all the forces of the creation are concentrated (Rev 1:12-16). He is the Lord of history, but as the Lamb who was slain (Rev 5:6-12). The terrible travail that is described throughout the subsequent appalling visions culminates in a new heaven, a new earth and a new Jerusalem (Rev 21:1-5)—the luminous dwelling place of God and the Lamb (Rev 21:22-22:5). In its "patient endurance" (e.g., Rev 1:9; 2:2-3; 2:19; 3:10), the prayer of the Church is condensed into the cry of confident longing, "Come, Lord Jesus" (Rev 22:20). The Jesus that has come and gone, and returned from the dead, is still the Jesus that must come in his power to transform all things. All this is far from what we previously referred to as a video-replay of highlights after one's team has won.

Along with this apocalyptic style of imagination and expression, there is, in contrast to the lurid expressiveness of apocalyptic, a pervasive "negative theology" discernible in the New Testament. The cumulative force of this can be easily overlooked, for the New Testament witnesses to the revelatory shock of the resurrection. This shock is notably registered in the peculiar negativity of the New Testament rhetoric. At heart, it remains the language of excess, given the nature of the gift: "Christ, in you, your hope of glory" (Col 1:27). Yet the excess of the gift precludes any complete grasp or possession of it. The breadth and length and height and depth of the immeasurable greatness of what has been given surpasses knowledge (cf. Eph 1:19; 3:18-19). It is not subjected to the limitations of human knowledge or desire, but transforms all expectation. Its otherness is not a totality comprehended by any act of theological thought, but something twice removed from any such comprehension. For there are two all-encompassing kinds of totality—namely, the totality of Christ's subjection of all things to himself, and the totality of the Father's final action: "When all things are subjected to him, then the Son himself will also be subjected to the one who put all things in subjection under him, so that God may be all in all" (1 Cor 15:27-28). Any human comprehension lives in humble expectation of the eschatological completion of God's own giving.

The negativity typical of the New Testament, however much it witnesses to the light, is not afraid of admitting to the deepening shadows in which the vision of faith operates. The experience of the risen One throws into relief the darkness of the present experience of and in the world. The stone rejected by the builders has become the chief cornerstone (Ps 117:22; Mt 21:42; Mk 12:11; Acts 4:11; 1 Pet 2:4-8), introducing a radical new alignment in the constructions of culture. Even if rejection is followed by the acceptance of faith, even if the stumbling block has now become the cornerstone, even though darkness has yielded to light, no steady all-surveying gaze is permitted. The excess of light is too much. It can be expressed only in a negative fashion.

The biblical witness to the crucified and risen One emerges out of a double silence. There is the dark silence of the dead body of Jesus on the cross. And there is the even deeper silence of the resurrection. Faith, trembling at the brink of the new creation, is at a loss for words. The intentionality of Christian consciousness does not bring old wineskins to the fresh wine of revelation (Mt 9:16-17; Mk 2:21-22; Lk 5: 36-39). Nor is it a matter of putting new patches on old garments. The new and the utterly other have rent the fabric of any previous world.

Take the case of the earliest witnesses to Christ. After his crucifixion and death, Christ "had presented himself alive to them by many convincing proofs" (Acts 1:3). Yet they could still ask, "Lord, is this the time when you will restore the kingdom to Israel?" (Acts 1:6). Jesus' answer is instructive: "It is not for you to know the times or the periods that the Father has set by his own authority" (Acts 1:7). Judgments based on time or place or culture—that is, anything less than God's salvific freedom—are precluded; the disciples are commissioned to witness to Christ, "in Jerusalem, in all Judea and Samaria, and to the ends of the earth" (Acts 1:8). Faith in every age is subject to the dimensions of God's saving design, never to possess it as a clear blueprint.

Though Paul is clear that the resurrection of Jesus is the focus of Christian existence, he implies no end to waiting and darkness. For all the intensity of his own experience, he emphasizes the darkness of the surrender of hope, rather than the evidence of sight. There is no all-controlling vision of what is to come, only a patient openness to what is coming to be. Paul writes, "Now hope that is seen is not hope. For who hopes for what is seen? But if we hope for what we do not see, we wait for it in patience" (Rom 8:24-25). In reference to Isaiah, he writes, "What eye has not seen, nor ear heard, nor the heart of man conceived what God has prepared for those who love him" (1 Cor 2:9). Compared to human perceptions, the ways of God remain inscrutable and divine judgments are unsearchable (Rom 11:33). Paul alludes to the oldest recorded prayer in the New Testament, "Maranatha! Our Lord, come!" (1 Cor 16:22; cf. Rev 22:20). The coming of the risen Christ has not yet reached its term. Paul's references to the future are more like descriptions of what is being left behind. A rear-vision mirror does not map what lies ahead. Paul's impatient reply to a Corinthian query is noteworthy: "How are the dead raised? With what kind of body do they come?" (1 Cor 15:35). He answers in predominantly negative terms. The risen body is contrasted to what is "perishable, dishonourable, weak, physical" (1 Cor 15:35) in our present experience. Yet in the light of Christ's resurrection, he anticipates that the risen body of each one will become "imperishable", "glorious", "powerful", "spiritual" (1 Cor 15:42-44). Hope for a risen existence reaches beyond any capacity to determine or even to represent the future. It awaits a fulfilment in the God who, "by the power at work within us is able to do far more abundantly than all we ask or think" (Eph 3:20). Paul contrasts straining after a controlling knowledge of the future with the transcendence of God's wisdom. Here, he quotes both the prophet (Isa 29:14) and the psalmist (Ps 33:10) alike: "I will destroy the wisdom of the wise and the discernment of the discerning I will thwart" (1 Cor 1:19). He goes on to say, "For since in the wisdom of God, the world did not know God through wisdom, God decided through the foolishness of our proclamation to save those who believe" (1 Cor 1:21). He points to the source of true wisdom beyond all human measure and control: "And we speak of these things in words not taught by human wisdom but taught by the Spirit, interpreting spiritual things to those who are spiritual" (1 Cor 2:13).

A certain negation or "deconstruction"—at least in a general sense— is demanded. The ever-new gift is not a simple *datum*, but an incalculable *donum*. It cannot be represented in accord with the calculations and categories of present experience. If "the Jews demand signs and the Greeks desire wisdom" (1 Cor 1:22), the cross of Christ will be a stumbling block to the expectations of the traditional religion, just as it will appear to the philosophers and to any imperial ideology as an extravagant or subversive folly: "For God's foolishness is wiser than human wisdom, and God's weakness is stronger than human strength" (1 Cor 1:25). Even though Paul himself is justified in invoking the riches of the tradition of Israel as his own—"a Hebrew born of Hebrews, as to the law, a Pharisee . . ." (Phil 3:4-6), he has come to regard all this as "loss" (Phil 3:7; cf. Mt 10) and "refuse" (Phil 3:8), so that he might gain Christ and find justification in him alone (cf. Phil 3:7-11). Hope in Christ has meant for him a "deconstructed" life, intent on the ways of God, rather than any intellectual or traditionally religious assurance. When the faith of any age is focused on the resurrection of the Crucified as its luminous centre, something like such a vertiginous "loss" is a sign of its health and authenticity.

Though Paul is unconditional in his witness to the resurrection, and to its universal significance, and to the fact that the risen Jesus was seen by him, the last of the list of chosen witnesses, it remains that faith must express itself as a hope in what is not yet "seen". The Christian imagination must not be allowed to rest in any image drawn from the present sphere of human experience: "hope that is seen is not hope" (Rom 8:24). It expands to its proper proportions only by yielding to what only God can bring about. Even praying for the fulfilment of hope must not be confined to the limitations of human desire. Our desiring needs the guidance and direction of the Spirit: "for we do not know how to pray as we ought, but the Spirit himself intercedes for us with sighs too deep for words" (Rom 8:26). An extraordinary paradox runs through the whole of Christian experience that comes to expression in the writings of the New Testament. Despite the clarity of its faith in the risen One, hope must learn to live not only with not-understanding and not-representing, but also with a certain not-willing. It must yield its mundane desires and expectations to the incalculable dimensions of the Spirit. The mundane ego of the ancient world, even in its most religious expressions, is radically disturbed in its desires and projections.

The Synoptic Gospels do nothing to lessen this distinctive Christian sense of negativity and provisionality. Despite the evidence that the Gospel writers were dead-sure of the all-deciding event that has occurred in Christ, they left plenty of room for what is yet to be revealed, even though the light of the resurrection illumines all that has gone before, in the birth, life and death of Jesus. The growth and seasons of the Kingdom are not in human hands, nor subject to human law or prediction (Mk 4:26-29). Moreover, the scope of God's reign allows for wild aspects of undecidability. It nets fish of all kinds and qualities (Mt 13:47-50), and permits the weeds to grow alongside good grain (Mt 13: 24-30). To enter into this Kingdom is to treasure new things and old in a proportion that remains unclear (Mt 13:51-52). For Luke especially, it means refraining from judgments and the condemnation of others, if one is to be included in the incalculable field of God's mercy (Lk 6:37-42). The true relatives of Jesus are not those represented by blood relationships, but those who do the will of God (Lk 8:19-21). Most notably, the separation of the sheep and goats in Matthew 25 is disconcerting to all believers—and non-believers too—who have allowed a cultural form of religion to obfuscate the inclusiveness of God's Kingdom (Mt 25:31-46).

From the Johannine perspective, even though Jesus encourages his disciples to accept his word, he allows that they cannot yet bear the full reality of what he has to say: "I still have many things to say to you, but you cannot bear them now" (Jn 16:12). His followers must go beyond their present apprehension to await an as yet incalculable future: "When the Spirit of truth comes, he will guide you into all truth . . . and will declare to you the things that are to come" (Jn 16:13). Earlier in the Gospel, Jesus declared to the Samaritan woman that "you will worship the Father neither on this mountain nor in Jerusalem" (Jn 4:22). The true worship of God is not tied to sacred sites marking the particularities of religion and culture, but must be conducted in the space proportioned "in spirit and in truth" (Jn 4:23-24). Neither geographically nor ethnically nor conceptually bounded, the only horizon that remains is the indefinable reality of the Father himself who is seeking out such worshipers.

The Johannine confidence in the continuing revelatory power of the Spirit is compatible with a warning against believing every kind of spirit. The First Letter of John advises such caution. That early community, undergoing the conflicts and temptations inherent in its special and apparently isolated history, is advised: "Beloved, do not believe every spirit, but test the spirits to see if they are from God . . . By this you know the

Spirit of God: every spirit that confesses that Jesus Christ has come in the flesh is from God" (1 John 4:1-2).[23] Such a demand for discernment is not without its difficulty. It entails holding together in some way the truth of God's self-giving love, and the human character of its revelation. But once intelligence tries to come to grips with the elusive and opaque human reality of "the flesh" in which Jesus has come, discernment becomes complex. Only to a lofty Gnostic system is everything clear, pure and untroubled by the presence of the utterly other. But the true discernment points in another direction: "We know love by this, that he laid down his life for us—and we ought to lay down our lives for one another" (1 John 3:16). This demand is insistent: "for those who do not love a brother or sister whom they have seen, cannot love God whom they have not seen" (1 John 4:20). John's letter has a stark, but not altogether surprising, conclusion: "Little children, keep yourselves from idols" (1 John 5:21). Some kind of orientation beyond neat religious notions or consoling interpretations seems to have been envisaged all along: "Let us love, not in word and speech, but in truth and action" (1 John 3:18). This is the original emphasis of the Gospel itself. To know God is not a matter of "seeing" the divinity in some immediate gaze. A commitment to following the other-directed "way" of Jesus (Jn 14:6) is the essential point, for "no one has ever seen God; it is the only Son, who is turned toward the Father, he has made him known" (Jn 1:18). Believers are reminded not to settle for any provisional version of human identity, no matter how secure the promise of eternal life, for "it has not yet appeared what we shall be" (1 John 3:2). Though Jesus is "the Resurrection and the Life" (Jn 11:25), the risen Lord is never an object of matter-of-fact description. Experiences of his presence and absence interweave in the lives of these early witnesses to faith (cf. Jn 20:29-31).

More radically still, the demand for a complete self-dispossession pervades the New Testament. Only by losing one's life for the sake of the gospel can one truly save it (Mt 16:24-25; Mk 8:35; Lk 9:24; Jn 12:25). The moral and spiritual implications of this radical demand, rightly enough, point to the character of Christian conversion. But there are also implications of a more cognitive character. Faith-inspired thinking seeks to go beyond the pretensions of all theoretical systems. In their inability to allow for "God's foolishness", the productions of human wisdom tend easily to become idolatrous. In contrast, the biblical authors show an eschatological reserve. They defer to a fulfilment and justification that only God can give. In doing so, they also exhibit a deliberate "unknowing". It is embedded in its most confident testimony. Paradoxically, the very confidence of their witness calls forth the expressions of negation, dispossession, reserve and waiting we have summarily cited. The various theological and spiritual traditions of "negative theology" in, say, the mystical writings of Pseudo-Dionysius or John of the Cross, clearly stem from the New Testament itself.

It is not as though no category is sufficient to comprehend the resurrection. Neither "negative theology" nor wordless mysticism is at issue. The challenge is more direct. The cross reveals the terminal resistance arising in the defensive heart of any culture that uses its ideology or even its religion to dehumanise itself. Though the one true God is a sanctuary for Israel, Isaiah recognises that who God is and the way God acts can also be a stumbling block and a scandal (Is 8:13; cf. 53:1-12 and Ps 117:22) in the world of human calculations. In the New Testament, the resurrection of the Crucified is not merely incomprehensible. The scandalous character is intensified as "the stone that makes them stumble, and a rock that makes them fall" (1 Pet 2:8). This stone, rejected by the builders of the world, has become the cornerstone of the edifice that God is building (1 Pet 2:4-8; Mt 21:42; Mk 12:11; Acts 4:11). The First Letter of Peter summons its readers: "Come to him, a living stone, though rejected by mortals, yet chosen and precious in God's sight, and like living stones, let yourselves be built into a spiritual house, to be a holy priesthood, to offer spiritual sacrifices, acceptable to God through Jesus Christ" (1 Pet 2:4-5). Against any anodyne interpretation of "spiritual", the spirituality in question is of scandalous proportions.[24] For the followers of Christ as "living stones" are called to collaborate in the construction of the new temple of humanity built on this hitherto rejected cornerstone. As the construction proceeds, the more grotesque features of former dwellings appear. Likewise, the architects of the palaces and fortresses of the former world are disclosed as benighted. They have chosen not to build on solid rock but on ever-shifting sand.

The vigour of this rhetoric of negation draws on the unique event which had taken place in the resurrection of the crucified Jesus. All previous categories are questioned, negated or relativised in the light of the overwhelmingly positive phenomenon. From within it, the distinctive rhetoric of New Testament witness is formed. While this is entirely positive in its intent, it works on many fronts to resist any totalising system of interpretation or control. The singular illuminating phenomenon of the resurrection does not allow its meaning to be reduced to an instance or example of something else.[25] And yet it is endlessly productive of meaning. In the light of Christ, notions of God, the self, relationship to the other and responsibility within human history are recast. The more significant the event, the greater the play of possible meanings, and the continuing need of interpretation as it affects the course of life. The greater the gift, the more it overbrims with excess whether the giver of the gift or its recipients are considered.[26] In every genuine gift there is an inherent indefinability that breaks out of the calculations of mere exchange or manipulation. In this regard, Christian faith must attend to the indefinable and incalculable otherness of God's self-giving in Christ. It comes from God who remains invisible, and comes to human subjects whose destiny is not yet realised. It would seem that the more hope is focused on the risen Christ, the more it moves in a certain darkness and limitless distance. The future of "what God has prepared for those who love him" is not a simple, homogenous extension of our present limited understandings or expectations. Faith must work through hope, relying on God alone to reveal the final evidence of the saving love at work. In this it defers to the unimaginable "otherness" of what cannot be comprehended. It deconstructs any repetitious sameness or incremental extension of either our notions of God, or of ourselves. There is no all-clarifying horizon of interpretation, no systematic grasp of the whole. John's First Letter makes the point: "what we shall be has not yet been revealed. What we do know is this: when he is revealed we shall be like him, for we shall see him as he is" (1 John 3:2).

A full exploration of the inherent darkness of the experience of faith would need to be related to the experience of Israel, even if we cannot here pursue this background. The chosen People always maintained a sense of the uniquely gifted origins at the key points of their history (Gen 12-36; Exod 1-15; Ps 78:67-71).[27] Each saving event leads to an ever-larger sense of the universal activity of God working in all times and in all peoples (Jer 30-31; Ezek 33-48, especially Ezek 37:1-14; Is 40-55).[28] These antecedents in the history of Israel's hope are not forgotten in the witness of the New Testament. They serve to remind Christian faith that the ways of God are never designed to fit into human calculation. The resurrection of the crucified Jesus comes from beyond every human horizon. And in this regard, the scriptures offer their witness in rhetoric formed within the unimaginable excess of the event that has occurred.

Conclusion

We may say, therefore, that the phenomenon of Christ's rising from the dead is found "in" the New Testament writings, saturating their every expression. On the other hand, these writings have their origin "within" the disciples' experience of the risen One, and their varied witness to it. Their faith in the glorified Jesus constitutes the matrix out of which the New Testament emerges. As a literary response to what has occurred, these writings emanating from the early witnesses to Christ are "inspired"—to serve the faith of others, then as in later generations. These others in the unfolding history of faith no longer "see" Christ, either in his earthly life, or as privileged witnesses to his resurrection. Yet what has been written continues to shape the life of faith, a blessing for those who have not seen, but believe (Jn 20:29; 1 Pet 1:8).

CHAPTER 4

The Resurrection Event

James D. G. Dunn is clear in his judgment: "No Christianity without the resurrection of Jesus. As Jesus is the single great 'presupposition' of Christianity, so also is the resurrection of Jesus".[1] In the same vein, Pheme Perkins considered that the resurrection is "the condition for the emergence of Christian speech itself".[2] Without this event, there would be no New Testament. The resurrection of the crucified proclaimer of the reign of God provokes a literary witness to everything Jesus was and continues to be. In its light, all the words, deeds and events of Jesus' life are brought together, to be interpreted in their salvific significance. Without the event of the resurrection, the life, teaching and death of Jesus would have been lost in the fragile particularities of past history. But because the resurrection is the radiant centre of faith's perception of the saving action of God, its all-encompassing effect is being continually disclosed. It extends to all nations and cultures, to include the whole of creation.

Clearly, our focus on the phenomenon of the resurrection requires something of a spiralling mode of investigation. After discussing in chapter 1 the need for a more phenomenological approach, the second chapter moved to a suggestion of how this might be implemented—with reference to Marion and others. We followed this with a reflection on how the New Testament itself was a literary phenomenon deriving from the resurrection and saturated with its significance. In this present chapter we move to a consideration of various aspects of the resurrection event itself. The chapter following this will bring together the New Testament text, the resurrection event and Paul's experience of it under the title of "The Pauline Phenomenon". After that, we will be in a position to examine the underlying question of the resurrection as a visual phenomenon. Further chapters will be more synthetic in character as we consider the objective and subjective polarities involved. Hence, the metaphor of spiralling movement can be usefully kept in mind.

This chapter treats of four related topics:

1. *The Multi-Dimensional Phenomenon*
2. *Six Dimensions of the Resurrection Event*

3. *The Light of the Resurrection*
4. *The Light and Its Meaning: Patterns of Rhetoric*

The Multi-Dimensional Phenomenon

Jesus is in person "the resurrection and the life" (Jn 11:25). The life, embodied and given in him, is at the heart of the Christian phenomenon. Apart from him, there can be no "accounting for the hope that is within you" (1 Pet 3:15). Yet this accounting is necessarily multi-dimensional.[3] Faith and hope attempt to express what is given in him in a variety of ways, with different themes and points of reference. Despite these varied expressions, they are unanimous in confessing him who is "the first and the last, and the living one" (Rev 1:17-18). Centred in him, the horizon of faith and hope is unbounded in its scope. It is determined only by the "excess" of God's action in Christ, "who by the power at work within us is able to accomplish abundantly far more than all we can ask or imagine" (Eph 3:20-21). Although a divine generativity already constitutes believers as "children of God", they must anticipate an indefinable excess (1 John 3:2). Hope finds no fixed place to stand outside further surrender to God revealed in Christ, crucified and risen. The uniqueness of the resurrection event provokes its own form of "way of negation", as we outlined in the previous chapter. Words fail and concepts fall short in response to what has been given. The searching intelligence of faith presses on, not to replace the excess of the resurrection event with its own concepts and systems, but to serve its further disclosure. Faith seeks understanding within the overwhelmingly positive character of what is given in the concrete, holographic uniqueness of Jesus rising from the dead.[4]

"Resurrection" is a metaphor, with its connotations of "waking up", "raising up", "being raised", "lifted up", "exalted", and so on—a play of meanings bound up with how God has acted in this case.[5] A theology of disclosure must let the metaphor do its work. It is the only way of saying what could not otherwise be said. There is no better-known experience that can serve as an analogy or a symbol. This master-metaphor draws theology back to the inexpressible phenomenon of how God has acted in this unique instance. That event is the unspent source of further metaphors, symbols and linguistic and artistic forms that direct the vital energies of Christian existence.[6] The singular metaphor of resurrection works within the excess of a primordial communication. It demands the receptivity of faith and its creative expression in a disciplined intelligence and in all the arts. The past, present and future Christ-centred sweep of God's action finds its compact interpretation in the event of the resurrection of Jesus.[7] Its overbrimming excess has a peculiar density that eludes all attempts to reduce it to something else. It evokes the horizon in which the many parables of the Kingdom of God that came from the lips of Jesus made his hearers see their ordinary world turned upside-down. His way of imagining the world and its God was different. He called into question the hitherto invincible systems of worldly power and status. As raised from the dead, he embodies the supreme parable of the way God is acting in the world—the parable behind all the parables he uttered—the ultimate upturning and disruption of the ways things are.

In the hearing of faith, "resurrection" is a primordial word, an *Ur-Wort*, in Rahner's sense.[8] No derivative language of symbol or translation can render it adequately. The affirmations and confessions of Christian tradition would be empty gesticulations without the prior receptive openness of faith to what is given. Both receptivity and response are shaped by the scriptures—the sacred writings of Israel freshly understood, and now focused and further amplified in the literary creativity that is now called the New Testament. In the light of the resurrection, these writings were composed to be read by later ages of faith, above all in the setting of the paschal sacraments of baptism and Eucharist. All ecclesial charisms and offices conspire to keep faith intent on what has been originally given and revealed. The prayer of faith, be it praise of the giver, thanksgiving for the given, or the asking, seeking and knocking at the door for what is still to be received from the limitless store of original gift, move mind, heart and imagination on to further limits of attentiveness, thankfulness and surrender.

The response of theological reflection employs a suite of the techniques—by making analogical correlations, interconnecting all themes and dimensions of faith within the primordial mystery of God's self-revelation, and by deferring all this to a future fulfilment that only such a God can give. The task of theology is not to subject the given to a rational system, but to disclose the gift and lead more deeply into its reception. In all this, the steady ecstasies of hope and love keep faith receptive and intelligence restless. The imperatives of the moral life are never exhausted. The Christian vocation keeps on being a vocation until the world is made new in the light of the risen One. The cloud of witnesses, saints, martyrs, mystics and reformers, those who have been transformed in varying degrees by what has been revealed, accompany all believers in their experience of the resurrection effect.

Without this multi-dimensional receptivity, Christian tradition would be an endless regression into hear-say. The "more blessed" state of believing without seeing (Jn 20:29) would lack the historic witness of those early disciples to whom Jesus had "presented himself alive by many convincing proofs, appearing to them during forty days and speaking about the Kingdom of God" (Acts 1:3). When, and to the degree, this witnessing to the resurrection is part of the fabric of the tradition, that tradition retains its inexhaustible novelty. It lives with the assurance of its capacities to mediate to all believers the manner in which God has entered into our world and met it at the sharpest edges of the problem of evil, typified in suffering, death, guilt and meaninglessness. The tradition of faith becomes a womb of life, forming the followers of Christ into agents of a new humanity through the power of his Spirit. After the resurrection of the crucified One, the world can never be the same. It is always timely, then, for theology to re-immerse itself in the phenomenon of the resurrection, and to focus its energies explicitly on the most radical and transforming moment of Christian faith.

Six Dimensions of the Resurrection Event

Within the expanding and saturating phenomenality of the resurrection, there are six irreplaceable and interweaving dimensions. These can be named, however inadequately, as the paschal, paternal, filial, effusive, sacramental, and eschatological aspects of the phenomenon.

The Paschal Aspect: The Resurrection of the Crucified

Most obviously, the phenomenon of the resurrection includes within it the reality of the cross. It is the crucified Jesus who is raised. His resurrection cannot be disclosed apart from the cross, nor distanced from the corpse of this executed criminal lying in the tomb of death, disgrace and defeat. God has acted to raise this man from the tomb, to be the light shining in otherwise impenetrable darkness. The brute reality of his crucifixion, the terminal moment of his death, the long day of his being dead and buried, are all sealed into the resurrection event. This Jesus is raised up, glorified in the death he died and vindicated in all that he lived for.

The cross, then, must be seen as an inner moment in the resurrection, constituting its paschal character. But Jesus is not resuscitated so as to return to the inconclusiveness of his previous earthly life. He lives now in the definitive, "conclusive" character of his self-offering to the Father for the sake of the world's salvation. Hence, the resurrection saturates with novel significance the terminal extreme of Jesus' crucifixion and the excess enacted in his self-giving unto death. At the point where death cancels out the human presence of Jesus and brings to an end his earthly witness, he is given back to his disciples in another order of existence, glorified in the cruciform character of his love.

The resurrection of the crucified Jesus means that love is not frustrated. It is not diminished or changed into something else in its lethal encounter with evil. Despite its exposure to rejection, betrayal, condemnation, torture and death, love keeps on being love, "to the end" (Jn 13:1b). Love is not altered into violence or vengefulness, but is manifested in its own excess: "the light shines in the darkness, and the darkness did not overcome it" (Jn 1:5). Not only is the radiance of this light contrary to the darkness of evil, but it also unmasks evil for what it is, namely, the negation of God, humanity, life and love.

There is more. The paschal light of Easter is not simply the divine contradiction of the power of evil, nor even its unmasking as finally impotent and futile. For through the resurrection of the crucified Jesus, love makes death its own and occupies its place. It absorbs the destructive menace of death into itself. Death no longer appears as a dread limit blocking any human relationship with God, as though our mortality were the terminal evil enclosing human existence in ultimate sterility and isolating defeat. Christ's death is now the very form of surrendering to the God who is the giver of life: "unless a grain of wheat falls into the earth and dies, it remains just a single grain; but if it dies it bears much fruit . . . those who hate their life in this world will keep it for eternal life" (Jn 12:24-25). In the light of the resurrection, death is, therefore, not the defeat of God's communication with the world. It neither reduces the power of the creator to impotence nor the divine Word to silence. For death, in the most brutal guise of the crucifixion, is the extreme to which God's love has gone, to occupy and take possession of it. At the dark point of death, love is revealed in its excess, saturating all Christian life: "We know love by this, that he laid down his life for us— and we ought to lay down our lives for one another" (1 John 3:16). In his exposure to the power of evil and in not being overcome by it, Jesus is the "Lamb of God who takes away the sin of the world" (Jn 1:29). The Lamb who was slain (Rev 5:7) has become the "atoning sacrifice for our sins . . . but also for the sins of the whole world" (1 John 2:2). The excess of evil is met with the always greater excess of love.

With Jesus glorified in his self-giving death, a great reversal to the vicious circle of self-destruction begins in human history: "If anyone does sin, we have an advocate with the Father, Jesus Christ the righteous" (1 John 2:1b). Through its intimate familiarity with the conflict between an ever-vulnerable love and the violence of human self-assertion, a sober realism is woven into the texture of Christian experience. Still, the love manifested in the "lifting up" of the Son on the cross remains an immeasurable excess. Unconditional love swallows up all human conditions: ". . . we will reassure our hearts before him whenever our hearts condemn us; for God is greater than our hearts . . ." (1 John 3:19-20). Love remains; it keeps on being love even at this darkest point. The "weakness of God" is the refusal of the love that God is (1 John 4:8) to be anything but itself when confronted with the most violent form of rejection. A divine folly of unconditional self-giving is at work, to undermine the self-centred calculations of the human wisdom which prove incapable of coping with either the cross or the resurrection (1 Cor 1:21).

The Paternal, Generative Source

Inscribed into the phenomenonality of the resurrection is a dimension of primordial and transcendent self-giving. It is given from a source beyond itself to reveal a divine self-giving and disclosure. Within the event of the resurrection, God is invocable in the generative capacity of "the Father" who has so raised up his Son. Where apologetics once appealed to the resurrection as a proof for the divinity of Jesus, what is here first "proved" or disclosed to faith is the life-giving power of the Father as the God of the living (Lk 20:38). The risen Jesus is God's self-utterance as "the word of life", of the "life [that] was revealed", "of the eternal life that was with the Father and was revealed to us" (1 John 1:1-2).

God appears as the source of the resurrection. It is the Father who exalts Jesus as his Son, to bear the divine name and receive the obeisance of all creation: "Jesus Christ is Lord, to the glory of the Father" (Phil 2:11). As the form and source of eternal life, Jesus rises as the living anticipation of a universal resurrection. The God who raised him is, in the words of Jesus, now made known as "my Father and your Father" (Jn 20:17). He is the fount of an expanding communion of life: "As you, Father, are in me, and I in you, may they also be in us, so that the world may believe that you have sent me" (Jn 17:21). From the Father's giving comes "the gift of God" (Jn 4:10), the gift of the one who "is love" (1 John 4:8). The originality of this giving precedes all human response: "In this is love, not that we loved God but that he loved us and sent his Son . . ." (1 John 4:10).

Thus the Father is the loving and generative source of all that has been given, and continues to be offered. As the absolute "beginning", the Father of love precedes all creation, all time and all human action. His generative initiative is involved throughout the life, action, speech and mission of Jesus himself.[9] In the Gospel of John, Jesus speaks of himself as light (Jn 8:12; 12:46), life (Jn 11:25; 14:6), and the truth (Jn 14:6). The First Letter of John, attentive to the logic of the gospel, refers everything that Jesus embodies back to the Father, the source from which all gifts flow: God is love as the light (1 John 1:5), and as "true God and eternal life" (1 John 5:20). The absolute originality and initiative of the Father can be appreciated only through a faith that transcends everything that restricts or diminishes its confidence. Whatever the fearful frontiers of human perception, God remains "greater than our hearts" (1 John 3:20; 4:4, 18; 5:4, 9).

The generative, life-giving action of the Father in raising his Son from death opens up an horizon of unreserved giving. The God who so loved the world as to give his only Son (Jn 3:16) has glorified this Son in his self-giving death for the life of the world. In this horizon, the life, death and resurrection of Jesus incarnate the originating love that God is.

Turning to the Father, Jesus prays for his disciples that they may see his glory—which the Father had given him "because you loved me before the foundation of the world" (Jn 17:24).

In the Pauline idiom, the "Father of our Lord Jesus Christ has blessed us in Christ with every spiritual blessing, just as he chose us in Christ before the foundation of the world" (Eph 1:3-4). This "God, who is rich in mercy, out of the great love with which he loved us even when we were dead through our trespasses, made us alive together with Christ . . ." (Eph 2:4-5). For "we are what he has made us, created in Christ Jesus for good works, which God prepared beforehand to be our way of life" (Eph 2:10). The Father originates the phenomenon of revelation. He is the source of the creative and redemptive love that precedes all creation, to be its goal, in order that "God may be all in all" (1 Cor 15:28).

The resurrection, therefore, is the disclosure of God entering the world as pure gift. The love that is the source of this giving is not compromised by human lovelessness and despair: "God showed his love for us, in that while we were yet sinners, Christ died for us" (Rom 5:8). Within this all-originating gift, God is invoked as both Father and love. For the gift that is given wells up out of the innermost depths of divine freedom, in the Father's eternal self-determination to be "our God". Paul exults, "O the depths of the riches and knowledge of God. How unsearchable are his judgments and inscrutable his ways . . ." (Rom 11:33-34). A consciousness receptive to the phenomenon of the resurrection unfolds in praise and in thanksgiving to the Father. He is revealed as the original and engendering love that has brought the universe into existence, and fulfilled it in the resurrection of the Son.

Filial Identity

However expansive the significance of the resurrection event, it is focused on the singular identity of risen One. Closely related to the "generative" aspect above, the identity of Christ is expressed in a paschal and filial *Gestalt*. The Word that is with God from the beginning has been given as incarnate within the world. Though God remains invisible, God is turned to the world: "It is God the only Son, who is close to the Father's heart, who has made him known" (Jn 1:18). In his incarnate existence, Jesus is the revelation of the Father, not as an idol to replace him, but as an icon through which the engendering light and love of God shine. For Jesus has come in the transcendent otherness of an identity that the cross cannot nail down. By raising Jesus from the dead, the Father identifies Jesus as his unique Son, and displays his "face" and the original uniqueness of his relationship to the Father: Jesus is "declared to be Son of God with power according to the Spirit of holiness by resurrection from the dead" (Rom 1:4). Paul announces the "gospel of God" (Rom 1:1) as the "gospel of his Son" (Rom 1:9). The originating, engendering love of God is unreservedly self-giving in the sending of this Son.[10] The Father gives what is most intimate to himself, his "only Son", into the darkness and disgrace of the world: "In these last days he has spoken to us by his Son" (Heb 1:1-2). This unique, intimate and unreserved communication, is summed up in the Johannine statement, "God loved the world so much as to give his only Son . . . that the world might be saved through him" (Jn 3:16). The sending of this only Son discloses the excess of the Father's gift.[11] So intimately connected is the Son to the Father's self-revelation, that 1 John can state: "No one who denies the Son has the Father; everyone who confesses the Son has the Father also" (1 John 2:23). God's self-communication in the Son draws the believer into the inter-subjective communion that exists between the Father and the Son. It enfolds the Christian community into a divine realm of unity (Jn 17:20-24). To believe is to be in communion "with the Father and with his Son Jesus Christ" (1 John 1:3). In this primal experience of divine love, the Son is the unique self-expression and self-gift of the Father: "God's love was revealed among us in this way: God sent his only Son into the world so that we might live through him" (1 John 4:9). Christian existence finds its focus, then, in the unreserved personal self-communication of God to the world. This phenomenon discloses the excess of self-giving and self-expression possible to God alone. The Word, who is what God is (Jn 1:1),[12] is made flesh and so enters into the darkening drama of human history. In that history there is enacted an event of divine self-giving love, working to open the death-bound world to the fullness of life (Jn 10:10). As Raymond Brown remarks, "The resurrection was and remains, first of all, what God has done for *Jesus* . . . Only because God has done this for his Son are new possibilities opened for his many children who have come to believe what he has done".[13]

Spirit: The Effusive Aspect of the Event

The saturated phenomenon of the resurrection is a uniquely effusive event. It overflows through the outpouring of the Spirit. The Spirit is the divine medium, as it were, through which the Father acts in raising Jesus, and continues to act in the lives of those who believe in him: "If the Spirit of him who raised Jesus from the dead dwells in you, he who raised Christ from the dead will give life to your mortal bodies also through the Spirit that dwells in you" (Rom 7:11). In this further dimension of given-ness, neither the Father's loving originality nor the cross and resurrection of Jesus are events isolated in the past. God's loving is originally and continuously communicative. It reaches into all times, and touches every dimension of individual and corporate existence. The Spirit is poured out as the enduring communication of God's transforming gift, testifying to all believers throughout history of the victory of Christ over evil in all its forms. We might say that the Holy Spirit is the "resurrection effect" in person.

In the excess of this outpouring, the activity of the Spirit of God cannot be expressed in any one perspective. In Acts, for instance, on the day of Pentecost following the Ascension of the risen Jesus, the Spirit comes on the disciples with the energy of a mighty wind and tongues of fire, giving an ability to communicate beyond the restrictions of any language (Acts 2:1-4). Jesus' promise of a baptism in the Spirit (Acts 1:5) and power directing the disciples' witness to the world is fulfilled (Acts 1:8). The Pauline perspective is different: the Spirit is more like a divine field of energy and relationships, pouring forth God's love in our hearts (Rom 5:5), the living assurance of resurrection for all who believe (Rom 8:11). Forming the followers of Christ into a free, fearless relationship with the Father (Rom 8:14-17), the Spirit aids human weakness and expands Christian hopes "with sighs too deep for words" (Rom 8:26). Paul connects the gift of the Spirit to the constant renewal of hope, as when he prays, "May the God of hope fill you with all joy and peace in believing, so that you may abound in hope by the power of the Holy Spirit" (Rom 15:13). This holy Breath of Life is therefore both the inspiration and expiration at the heart of Christian experience throughout history.

From a Johannine perspective, after the completion of Jesus' historical mission, God gives into human history the permanent presence of the "Spirit of Truth" (Jn 14:17). Yet this "other Paraclete" is intimately connected with the presence of the Son who is the incarnate "way" to the Father. John the Baptist had testified to this Spirit who, descending from heaven and remaining on Jesus, was to be the medium with which he would baptise (Jn 1:32-33). Accordingly, in the experiential realm of God's self-communication, the Holy Spirit is a living stream emanating from the glorified Christ (Jn 7:37-39). The coming of the Spirit is the "advantage" that would follow the departure of Jesus from the earthly scene (Jn 16:7). The effusion of this Spirit is expressed in the last breath of the Crucified (Jn 19:30), and the first breath of the risen One (Jn 20:22). In this, the Spirit is the gift that Jesus promises, "The water that I will give will become in them a spring of water gushing up to eternal life" (Jn 4:14). Christ invites those thirsting for eternal life to come to him to quench their thirst, since it has been promised: "Out of his heart shall flow rivers of living water"(Jn 7:38-39. cf. 19:30, 34).

It is not as though the Spirit is ever severed from Christ, or is sent as a replacement or substitute for him. The Spirit acts to connect, or reconnect, the Christian sense of God back to the form of love incarnate in the mission of the Son (Jn 16:14; 1 John 4:2-3; 2 Jn 1:7). Christ is "the way"; and the Holy Spirit guides those who follow the way of Christ into an ever fuller realisation of the form of true life (Jn 14:26). This Spirit-Advocate is the primary God-given witness to Christian faith, to strengthen believers in the midst of a world in which the excess of love is experienced as a threat to an existence of self-enclosure. The historical community of witnesses, despite their weakness, will not lack *this* witness, the ever greater testimony of God (1 John 5:9) in regard to what God has revealed through the incarnation of his Word. "By the Spirit that he has given us" (1 John 3:24; 4:13), those who have "this testimony in their hearts" (1 John 5:10) are conscious of living from a new centre focused on the love that God is. They abide in God and God abides in them (1 John 4:13).

As the atmosphere or milieu of the resurrection, the Spirit is at once the agent, the overflowing gift, and even the form, of risen life. Jesus himself has received the gift beyond measure (Jn 3:34). He breathes this Spirit on his disciples (Jn 20:20; cf. Rom 8:11; 1 Pet 3:18; 1 Tim 3:16; 2 Cor 3:17). The life-giving action of the Spirit is the real, enduring "proof" of the resurrection, witnessing to the truth and love that has been enacted in the coming of the Son (Jn 14:16-17, 25-26; 15:26-27; 16:7-15). To this end, the Spirit is both given and giving. The Holy Spirit acts by leading (Jn 16:13; 14:25), instructing (Jn 14:26), bearing witness (Jn 15:26), calling to mind (Jn 14:26) and revealing the things that are to come (Jn 16:13). When faith lives from this witness, the whole truth always lies ahead, as the world is convicted of its failure to grasp what has been revealed.[14]

Nevertheless, while the coming of the Spirit transcends in its freedom all human calculation, it is not capricious; it is always related to the risen One—an excess suffusing the ritual objectification of the Christ-event in the sacraments, and its literary objectification in the scriptures.[15] While the Spirit-Gift is beyond measure (Jn 3:34), it is always proportioned to Christ, glorifying him, and making him known (Jn 16:12-16). Paul can claim, ". . . no one can say 'Jesus is Lord' except by the Holy Spirit" (1 Cor 12:3). For Paul, the gift of the Spirit is related to Christ, to build up his body and to lead it to its full stature (cf. Eph 4:7-13). Thus, the risen Jesus and his Spirit are correlative: the mission of Jesus reaches its term in breathing forth the Spirit of new life, while the Spirit leads back to an ever-fuller apprehension of Christ and conformity to him in his paschal existence.

It has been noted that the gift of the Spirit by itself would have been a perfect vehicle to express how the cause of Jesus lives on, without the complications occasioned by the awkward particularities of traditions concerning the empty tomb and the appearances of Jesus to the disciples.[16] But this is not how the phenomenon of the resurrection appears to Christian faith. For the Spirit is the resurrection effect *par excellence*. While all phases of Jesus' ministry and mission were under the guidance

of the Spirit, his resurrection leads to an effusive excess: the Spirit which
had possessed Jesus, he now pours out and breathes into his disciples.

Sacrament: The Church as Body of Christ

The resurrection is an overflowing event. Its effect is realised in an
historically identifiable embodiment of a community of faith. This body
of believers is constituted by the sacramental enactment of dying and
rising with Christ in baptism, and in the eucharistic celebration of communion in him. As Christians are conformed to Christ, they are inspired
to a love that "bears all things, believes all things, hopes all things and
endures all things" (1 Cor 13:4-7). As members of his body, believers
already enjoy the fruits of the Spirit as "love, joy, peace, patience, kindness, goodness, faithfulness and self-control" (Gal 5:22-23). Christian
witness to the primordial love of the Father, as it is incarnate in Christ,
looks to the practical realisation of such love in the mutual relationships
of the members of the community and in its outreach to the world.[17]
The resurrection thus takes effect in the Church as it continues the mission that Jesus himself had received from the Father (Jn 20:21). As the
expansive unity of believers participates in the all-inclusive unity of the
Father and the Son, it witnesses to the world the vitality of the love that
has been made known (Jn 17:23, 26). Each Christian community, therefore, and the community of communities which is the Church, exists in
the world which is the object of God's love (Jn 3:16). In this regard, the
Church is that part of the world which has come alive to the extent of
God's gift. The Church, as the "place of revelation",[18] is the world's
access to what has occurred in the resurrection of the Crucified.

The resurrection of the Crucified takes immediate effect in the Church's
outreach to the world (Jn 20:20; Lk 24:47ff.; Acts 1:8; Mt 28:18-20).
He who has been given "all authority in heaven and on earth" commands his disciples to make disciples of "all nations", and to teach them
to obey everything, "all", that he commands, with the assurance that he
is "always" with them (Mt 28:18-20). This mission admits no limits to
its extent. Paul's apostolic calling is directed to "all the Gentiles" (Rom
1:5). In John's Gospel, the disciples share in the energies of his Spirit (Jn
20:21-23) to be sent by Christ as he has been sent by the Father. The
mission of the Church is not the result of a merely verbal commissioning, but a sharing in the Spirit-empowered self-giving that Christ achieved
in his death and resurrection.[19]

This is to say that the resurrection effect saturates the whole reality
of the Church, its scriptures, sacraments, community, mission and historical institution. It permeates every aspect of its mission with the sense
that a new creation, no longer divided in the conflictual forms of strang-
ers and enemies, is in the making.[20] Thus, the traces of the resurrection

are found "in" the Church. For outside its corporate consciousness, there can be no awareness of God's gift. More radically, the phenomenon of the Church can be appreciated when it is located "in" the resurrection, as it forms, within history, a distinctive consciousness of itself.

Eschatological Anticipation

While the resurrection is an historic event, its full impact is yet to be registered, and its consummation is still to be achieved. It is replete with an eschatological excess. For Christ's resurrection points beyond itself as the anticipation of a universal transformation. Though the stream of eternal life has already begun to flow from its source in Christ, it has not reached its eschatological plenitude.

The gift of God is irrevocable; the resurrection has happened, and the Spirit poured out. But the groaning ambiguities and tensions of this present existence remain. In Paul's idiom, the outward groanings of creation, and the inward groanings of the Christian are supported by the deepest groanings of the Spirit, in expectation of the fullness of revelation: "In this hope we are saved . . . we wait for it with patience" (Rom 8:18-25). In its present form, hope can claim only the first fruits of the Spirit. The full harvest is yet to grow and be gathered. And the prayer of Christ is still to be answered: "Father, I desire that those also whom you have given me, may be with me where I am, to see my glory . . ." (Jn 17:24). The world as loved by God (Jn 3:16) is the world into which Jesus has come as its saviour (Jn 4:42; 1 John 2:2). Yet that world is yet to respond to the love that has been shown it: "so that the world may believe that you have sent me" (Jn 17:21). Even though believers are already "God's children", it remains that "what we will be has not yet been revealed" (1 John 3:2a). Fulfilling our present relationship to God is a promised future revelation: "What we do know is this: when he is revealed, we will be like him, for we will see him as he is" (1 John 3:2b).

The courage of faith in Jesus' victory over the world (Jn 16:33) manifests itself in a hope that this cosmic triumph will be fully displayed (1 John 5:4-5). Though to faith it is given to see the opened heaven (Jn 1:51), it is yet to see the world "opened" and lifting its gaze to the glory that has been revealed. Only when the word of Jesus is fully kept will the love of the Father be manifest—"And we will come to them and make our home with them" (Jn 14:23). The self-giving love of God, already realised in the resurrection of the Crucified and in the outpouring of the Spirit, looks to a final consummation. What has already been anticipated in Jesus will overflow in its excess into the resurrection of all in the fullness of time, to the point at which "God may be all in all" (1 Cor 15:28). The eschatological sense of what is to come is far from any form of self-congratulatory enthusiasm or passive satisfaction, as though Christians were merely rejoicing in a kind of team victory. The earliest disciples were disturbed by the responsibilities of bearing witness within a history which will attain its consummation in a way and at a time determined only by God (e.g., Acts 1:6-7).

This eschatological character of time inspires an ethics of solidarity and hope, along with the patience required to witness within the present age. In the various resurrection appearances, Jesus is disclosed in terms of meeting, eating, touching, walking, and so on, as has already been mentioned. This almost mundane type of description contains no whiff of a celestial sphere beyond the world, as might appear in more apocalyptic expressions. What takes place is related to the here and now of present experience and responsibility. Yet what occurred is of immeasurably positive significance for the future of human time. It affects history in its entirety. For the risen Christ is the alpha and omega of all creation (Rev 1:17). As time unfolds, it is leading to the goal inscribed into cosmic history through "the firstborn of all creation" (Col 1:15). The freedom of the believer, operating within the eschatological sense of human existence, collaborates with what God is bringing into being, to be achieved only in the fullness of time. The love of God in Christ neither lags behind the times nor runs ahead. The "now" of grace is irreversibly present in the resurrection; the "not yet" unfolds from what has already happened.

However this eschatological sense was expressed, it is animated by hope. As Brian Daley writes,

> From the vantage point of faith in the risen Lord, human time is wrapped in eternal love: the many hopes that rise—gropingly, picturesquely—in the heart of the believer are really only attempts to articulate in words the one abiding "mystery, which is Christ in you, your hope of glory" (Col 1:27). It is an expression of the mystery of Christ in which all Christian eschatology finds its unity and its meaning.[21]

The saturated phenomenon of the resurrection overflows, then, into at least six dimensions, named here in paschal, generative, filial, pneumatic, ecclesial and eschatological terms. Each suggest the overbrimming excess of "the breadth and length and height and depth" (Eph 3:18) of the divine gift, realised in God's raising Jesus from the dead.

The Light of the Resurrection

The resurrection effect is registered in Christian consciousness as a light and illumination, even if not in terms of the "vision" that is still to be given. We shall refer later to Paul's witness to the radiance of "the light of the knowledge of the glory of God in the face of Christ Jesus" (2 Cor 4:6). In the Gospel of John, Jesus presents himself as the light of the world (Jn 3:19; 8:12; 12:36, 46). This metaphor carries over into a creedal form in the phrase, "light from light", illustrative of the Son's relationship to the Father.[22] Jesus is the light radiating from the God who is light (1 John 1:5; Jas 1:17).[23] To the degree followers of Jesus are exposed to this source of light, they themselves become light to the world (Mt 5:14).[24] In the crucified and risen One, the light of the invisible God shines through. Christ is the icon, the visible manifestation of the invisible God (Col 1:15; 2 Cor 4:4). The light he radiates has its source from beyond the vision and visibility of this world. Nonetheless, his light is not a haze, ghosting the created world with a strange glow. Rather, it plays already over the whole of creation, locating all that is in a luminous horizon of waiting and hope for a universal transformation.

Yet this light is never separable from the radiance of love, the characteristic of the God who is revealed in Christ (1 John 4:8). What is brought to light is the excess of this love disclosed in its shocking vulnerability through the cross, and yet powerful in its effect by releasing the Crucified from the bonds of death. Though this is indeed light, it is a light directed to the way of hope and "patient endurance" through time and history (Rev 1:9; 2:2, 19; 3:10). In this regard, light is the resurrection effect, though not in a Gnostic sense of a privileged experience from which the less adept are excluded. Nor does it shine as the light of reason intent on logical deduction nor as a scientific methodology verifying its findings through repeatable experiments. It is more the light that is received in love, from and for the other. This "love-light" derives from Christ as he prays to the Father, "so that the love with which you have loved me may be in them, and I in them" (Jn 17:26). Extending this Johannine perception, the First Letter of John affirms, "God is light and in him there is no darkness at all...if we walk in the light as he himself is in the light, we have fellowship with one another" (1 John 1:5-7). In stressing the relational, other-directed character of this light, John goes on to say, "Whoever loves a brother or sister lives in the light . . . whoever hates another is in the darkness, walks in the darkness . . ." (1 John 2:10-11a). Despite its seemingly terminal vulnerability to the dark powers of hatred and violence, love has not been defeated, "because the darkness is passing away and the true light is already shining" (1 John 2:8). Christ is the light in which the saving intentions of the true God for the world have been revealed. In him, a divinely-wrought transformation has taken place in human history. The radiance of this light reaches out through the power of love to provide its own evidence.

In this light, the resurrection of the Crucified is perceived as a "once and for all" event (Rom 6:10)—"once" because of the singularity of this climactic event, and "for all" as pointing to its unbounded significance. Jesus is irreversibly established in a new order of life as the form and source and further anticipation of God's saving action. The reach of the divine action is limitless, overflowing into the meaning of history

and the destiny of the universe itself. The resurrection of Jesus anticipates the new aeon (Heb 9:26; 1 Pet 3:18). In contrast to the death-
bound old aeon, Jesus lives forevermore (Rev 1:17ff.). In him, all creation is disclosed in its original and final God-ward form (1 Cor 8: 6;
15:21ff.), and brought to a head (Eph 1:10).

The light of the resurrection thus reaches to furthermost limits. Jesus
is risen in his self-giving solidarity with all humanity. It is expressed in
phrases such as "for the many" (Mk 14:24); "for everyone" (Heb 2:9);
"for all" (Rom 8:32; 2 Cor 5:14ff.; 1 Tim 2:6); "for the people"(Jn
11:50; 18:14); "for us sinners" (Rom 5:8); "for me" (Gal 2:20); "for
you" (Lk 22:19ff.; 1 Cor 11:24); "for the Church" (Eph 5:25); "for the
sheep" (Jn 10:11-15). His rising from the tomb is understood so as to
include all creation, as we see in the Johannine prologue and the great
hymns of Ephesians and Colossians: everything stands in him who is the
firstborn of all creation (Col 1:16), the firstborn from the dead (Col
1:18): "All things came into being through him, and without him not
one thing came into being" (Jn 1:3).

The Light and Its Meaning: Patterns of Rhetoric

At the centre of Christian existence is the luminous and life-giving
presence of the risen Jesus in whom God is self-revealed. Though scriptural testimony, doctrinal judgments and theological elaborations follow from this initial perception, the original phenomenon is Christ present
in a love stronger than the powers of death and evil. The perception of
faith is itself an aspect of revelation. It is a gift of receptivity intrinsic to
the event of God's self-revelation, being neither the cause of revelation,
nor an extrinsic and subsequent interpretation of what God has brought
about. As von Balthasar writes, "The decision of faith is the presupposition, not only for the act of seeing the event of Jesus correctly, but also
for the act whereby the event *lets itself* be seen correctly".[25] The resurrection event includes both the salvific objectivity of the Father raising
up Jesus in the power of the Spirit, and the subjectivity in which this
divine activity is received by faith. Its evidence is accessible to "the eyes
of the heart" (Eph 1:18). The self-revealing God, therefore, acts on both
sides of the event: the objective happening and in its subjective recognition.

Arcs of Rhetoric

The explosive character of what took place brought forth a great
variety of expressions. Despite confusion and even the apparent contra-
dictions on details (Galilee or Jerusalem?), there can be no doubt that
what occurred engaged the whole existence of those who witnessed it. A
remarkably unified testimony resulted. God had acted. Jesus had been

raised. Though no one witnessed the event as such, the risen Jesus revealed himself to some in a special way. These privileged instances involving chosen witnesses were an essential part of the entire event, given to make known to the world the beginning of a new age. Precisely because it was a culminating salvific event, human collaboration was necessary—in a pattern reaching back from Mary's consent to the incarnation to Mary Magdalene's evangelisation of the disciples.

Given the action of God on both sides of the event, the objectivity of its occurrence and its subjective reception, the resurrection of the crucified Jesus is the phenomenon that "saturates" Christian consciousness. For faith, liturgy, Christian praxis and theological reflection unfold only from within this event which has made all the difference. Faith is not as a mode of consciousness looking into a mysterious event from outside it in an unchanged world. It is rather a consciousness formed by and within the resurrection event from which believers look out on a world transformed by it. Through this kind of immersion in the event, Christian identity is constituted. The community of faith is therefore defined by no national, cultural or religious identity, located "neither on this mountain nor in Jerusalem" (Jn 4:21). True worship of the God revealed in spirit and in truth is not constricted by the limits of any time or place or culture (Jn 4:23). The risen One is not confined or possessed by any community. It is he who contains the community of his followers, as the firstborn of the dead and of all creation, in whom all things hold together (Col 1:17-18). The centripetal convergence of all in Christ is the source of a centrifugal movement of mission, as the followers of the risen Christ are inspired to world-transforming action.

Far from being a projection of a group ideology, the resurrection is then a divinely objective event. It irrupts into the former world so as to leave any settled understanding of self, community or the universe itself in a provisional status. Faith, as the resurrection effect, looks beyond itself to what can never be adequately described. The shattering otherness—of Christ and what has happened in him—disorients human existence in its totality. It can never be bounded by any human limit nor assimilated to the presumed way the world is and has to be. It brings its own evidence and forms its own witnesses. Faith lives only by its receptivity to the risen One who has come from beyond the world of human capacities, categories and expectations. The excessive, all-transcending character of what took place provoked a whole variety of conflicting reactions, even for those on the way to the unreserved commitment of faith.

Yet there are clearly defined patterns of rhetoric needed to evoke, if never fully to capture, the light of the risen Christ. The phenomenon is productive of meaning. Here, we note in its development at least four "arcs of meaning".[26] First, there is the rhetoric of fulfilment. In Christ the scriptures are fulfilled and the fullness of the ages has come with the coming of the Son (e.g., Heb 1:1; Jn 1:16-17). He is the Yes to all God's promises and the Amen to all our prayers (2 Cor 1:20). Secondly, there is the language of participation: to enter into the realm of salvation is to participate in what he is, be it in a Johannine mutual indwelling and communion (Jn 17:20-21; 1 John 1:1-3), or in the Pauline idiom of being baptised into his death and resurrection (Rom 6:3-11). Thirdly, from the earliest to the later New Testament documents, a trinitarian or at least triadic form is apparent (1 Thess 1:2-5; 1 Cor 12:4-6; Mt 28:19; Jn 16:13-15): the Father has glorified his Son, and the Spirit of both the Father and the Son is the gift[27] flowing into all believers. Fourthly, there is the rhetoric of cosmic extension as Christ is revealed as the Word in which all things were made, and as the centre, the goal and the coherence of all creation (Jn 1:3, 10; Eph 1:10; Col 1:15-20). In the resurrection the cosmic expansiveness of God's design in Christ comes to light, with everything created in him, through him, for him, so that in him "all things hold together" (Col 1:15-18). Christ is in this regard the one divine Word. Any attempt to capture its meaning can freeze into a Gnostic rigidity. The varied expressions of faith must be patient with a nexus of analogies and fragmented perceptions, ever disposed to defer to what can be revealed only in the end. Still, the language of cosmic extension resonates even more in these later ages as humanity is experiencing its global and cosmic proportions, as we shall remark in the concluding chapter to this book.

Dimensions of Meaning

The arcs of New Testament rhetoric here carry a multi-dimensional meaning. [28] If Christ is truly risen, then there is work to be done, and a mission to be accomplished. The meaning of the resurrection must therefore be *effective*, as an impulse to action: thus, theologies of liberation—faith seeking to promote a more appropriate political and economic expression—do not allow oppressors to go unchallenged, or the oppressed to be left without hope, or either to live without hope of reconciliation and forgiveness.

The meaning of Christ, crucified and risen, is *communicative*; it forms an historical community, living from and mediating "the resurrection and the life" (Jn 11:25). Alive to this dimension of meaning, theology becomes faith seeking to promote unity and reconciliation through ecumenical and interfaith dialogue: the risen Lord is the truth transcending all historical and religious differences to call forth an ever new search for the reconciliation in him of all destructive differences.

Further, resurrection faith is *constitutive* in its meaning. It informs Christian consciousness to affect the believer's sense of selfhood and identity: "If Christ has not been raised, your faith is futile and you are still in your sins" (1 Cor 15:17). At this point, theology becomes a radically spiritual theology, as faith seeks to promote a more discerning self-appropriation in the heights and depths of human experience.

Most obviously, the meaning of the resurrection must allow for its *cognitive* expression. Here, faith seeks to promote a critical and coherent understanding of what has been revealed. Systematic theology is most active in this dimension of meaning, as it makes its distinctions between promise and fulfilment, now and not yet, truth and illusion, divine action and human response, seeing and believing, and all the rest. For instance, N. T. Wright and J. D. Crossan would seem to agree on just about everything, save in the area of the cognitive.[29]

Might one suggest that the salvific realism inherent in the cognitive dimension of faith's meaning will be most served by a disciplined return to the phenomenality of the resurrection in the manner in which we have begun to approach it? The adjective "salvific" usefully highlights the precise kind of realism involved. It is not contrary to the respective realisms of phenomenological, historical, metaphysical, scientific and anthropological methods. Each has its own limitations, particular concerns, traditions of interpretation and criteria of evidence. But salvific realism is focused on a unique event. It is, first of all, intent on being receptive to the phenomenality of the event which is the focal point of faith and a shock at the foundations of every theology. If the methods of other forms of phenomenological disclosure and patterns of knowing end by declaring the resurrection to be a non-reality, a non-event, the problem could be one of unexamined prejudice against the effects of historical phenomena. If this is the case, it is not helped by a theological method either un-attuned to what is at stake, or simply taking for granted what should be taken *as* granted, and respected in the singular conditions of its "given-ness". Theology must not be distracted into apologetic concerns before discerning the unique form of what has been given. Apologetics is at its most persuasive when Christian faith risks being rejected for the right reasons. On the other hand, the resurrection offers reasons that reason has yet to discover.

CHAPTER 5

Paul and the Resurrection Effect

Though the resurrection effect permeates all the New Testament writings, it is especially so in Paul's life and theology. For him the resurrection of the Crucified is an intensely personal issue. He puts himself forward as one who receives from the risen Jesus himself a special mission to the nations. The thrust of his testimony demands that it be taken on its own terms—which, in the event, includes his own personal witness as the last one of the privileged list to whom the Lord had shown himself. In ways that are more explicit compared to other New Testament authors—whose identities in any case are not easy to pin down (e.g., John, the Beloved Disciple, Matthew, Mark, Peter, and even Luke)— Paul is clearly identified as a person and author in the history of the early Church. His conversion was at first an occasion of scandal because of his previous involvement in the persecution of the faithful, as we see in the reaction of Ananias to his reported conversion (Acts 9:13-14). Moreover, he emerged as a somewhat troubling presence within the developing tradition even if he is ever at pains to pass it on (Gal 2:11-14).

Given the immense scholarship in this area, I propose in what follows to offer a brief comment on three issues only, since, after all, the words and witness of Paul are referred to in practically every page of this book:

1. *Paul's Transformative Experience*
2. *Conversion to the Risen One: Its Narrative Setting*
3. *From Experience to Meaning*

Paul's Transformative Experience

To heighten a sense of the phenomenality of the resurrection, we refer now to Eric Voegelin's treatment of Paul's experience of the risen Christ, as it is set out in his great unfinished *Order and History*.[1] He locates this experience within the context of a profound contemplation of the direction of human existence and the meaning of history itself.

For him, history is the realm of existence in which the directional movement of the cosmic order becomes luminous in human consciousness.[2] It
is imperative never to foreclose on the openness of "being", nor lose its
"in-between" character—the *metaxy* in Voegelin's terms. Metaxic consciousness finds expression in the key "symbolic" experiences keeping
history open to a transcendent, ever-indefinable order of being and life.
As affected by the resurrection, Paul experiences a "theophanic" event—
in contrast to a purely human or "egophanic" projection. Here, Voegelin
is concerned to reject any doctrinally rigid or superficial objectification
of what occurs in the depths of existence. That would result in congealing the open-endedness of the quest, and reducing it to subjective or
"egophanic" limits of the self-projective ego. In contrast, participation
in the transcendent order is a depth experience, never to be fully objectified in mundane and established categories. Yet, as a movement "in-
between", it is, of its nature, future-oriented and provisional. In the in-
between-ness of this enlargement of consciousness, categories such as
subject and object, even human and divine, prove too dogmatically rigid
and exclusive. What counts is the occurrence of the irreducible experience. It can be expressed only in the compact "symbolic" terms determined by the experience itself, mediating the inspiration that moves the
historical passage through time and history.[3] From a luminous centre,
Paul looks outward to the whole of reality transfigured by what has
taken place.[4] His vision evidences a sense of passing from decay to transformation. It occurs beyond any mundane conception or calculation:
"If for this life only we have hoped in Christ, we are of all people most
to be pitied" (1 Cor 15:19).

Paul's experience is profoundly vertiginous. It leaves the apostle pushed
to the limits of language and expression. Voegelin describes the giddy-
ing character of this experience in a key passage:

> In its experiential depth, a theophanic event is a turbulence in
> reality. The thinker who is engulfed by it must try to rise . . . from
> the depth to the surface of exegesis. When he comes up he wonders
> whether the tale he tells is indeed the story of the turbulence or
> whether he has not slanted his account to one or another aspect of
> the complex event; and he will wonder rightly, because the outcome
> depends on the interaction of the divine presence and the human
> response in the depth, as well as the cultural context on the surface
> that will bias his exegesis toward what appears at the time the most
> important part of the truth newly discovered.[5]

The impact of revelation occasions a "turbulence" in Paul's way of seeing the world, even if his vision remains always vulnerable to a pragmatic or ideological reduction. Though the experience occurs as an event
in the depths of reality, "engulfing" its addressee, its wording and com-

munication are inevitably conditioned by the surface needs of social and cultural concerns and structures. The temptation is so to shape the event that it will lead eventually to conceptual abstraction or pragmatic usefulness as to be assimilated by routine patterns of thought and expectation. On the other hand, if the irruptive and turbulent excess of the event is respected in its given-ness, if its witnesses and participants communicate its novelty, its effect continues, moving history forward by enlarging the sense of the transcendent order of existence.[6]

Attempts to define precisely what has taken place float on the surface of the experiential turbulence from which it has emerged, ever in danger of being lost in superficial concerns. The eventful "mutation"—a term borrowed from evolutionary science and increasingly favoured in recent writings[7]—can be missed. A theophanic experience can be reduced to "egophanic" projections of either a dogmatic or pragmatic type. When this happens, the self-referentially structured consciousness becomes closed in on itself and loses the "metaxy" of its depth-experience. The theophanic character of the Pauline vision of the risen Christ is no longer permitted to affect the constitutive meaning in history. The advance of insight is frustrated.[8] As a result, the egophanic revolt of modernity disallows the breakthrough that has taken place, and floods consciousness with new forms of ideology and Gnostic totalitarianism.[9]

Voegelin sees a symptom of this in the modern concentration on the "historicity of Christ," which reduces the "symbolic" character of the event to the world of abstraction and pragmatic control. This mind-set of historical analysis has been irremediably infected by centuries of separating symbols from experience. As a result, both the experience and its meaning are missed, and new mystical possibilities are not pursued.[10] Under the dead hand of analysis, abstraction and control, existence atrophies; and the vacuum of forgetfulness is filled by egophanic ideologies of power. The radically world-forming event is interpreted on the surface-level of rational analysis in terms of cause and effect. The revelatory "given" thus loses its originating uniqueness. As a result, the glory on the face of Christ becomes a mirror-image of self-projective ego.

There is no need to pretend that Voegelin's account of the revelatory impact of the risen Christ on Paul comprehends the full scope of Christian experience—in all its historical, liturgical, mystical, doctrinal, moral and theological dimensions. He is more inclined to consider the Christ-symbol than the historical person of Jesus—which is, in fact, not the focal concern of Paul's approach. Moreover, key Christian doctrines are interpreted as dogmatic distortions. Here, Voegelin falls short of an adequate appreciation of the historic objectivity of revelatory events in which the incarnation of the Word, the realism of faith and its differentiated sacramental and doctrinal expressions each have their part to play.

Nonetheless, Vogelin's analysis is immediately relevant to our investigation in five ways. These can be summarized as follows:

- The Pauline vision of the risen Christ constitutes a decisive event in the openness of history towards its consummation
- It communicates a quality of self-transcending consciousness, opening its horizons to the radically new
- It eludes all articulation, so that any social or cultural effort to put a meaning on it can easily end in forgetting the experienced event
- The turbulent fertility of Paul's visionary experience, though never objectifiable, comes to expression in different contexts
- The egological or self-enclosed character of modernity, because of both its ideology and pragmatism, works against an appreciation of the singular originality of the phenomenon

Each of these five points underscores the need for a refreshed phenomenological approach to what Paul witnesses in such a personal manner. Taken together, they serve to direct our attention to the unobjectifiable density of the event that so involved the Apostle, and now suggest the following brief reflection on his conversion to the risen Jesus.

Conversion to the Risen One: Its Narrative Setting[11]

Paul's own accounts of seeing the Lord can never be kept apart from the Gospel accounts of the resurrection and the eyewitness experiences of "seeing the Lord" sedimented in the whole tradition. Paul himself makes this point as he summarises the tradition in 1 Corinthians 15:3-11—to be treated more fully below. When it comes to Paul's own experience in this regard, Luke's account of what happened differs in some ways from what Paul himself describes. Luke's concern is missionary, and so he presents Paul's experience with that in mind. Luke is telling the story for his own readers, highlighting how the former persecutor was transformed into an apostle (Acts 9:3-9). In reporting this transformation, Luke highlights Paul's Jewish credentials and the reasons for his turning to the Gentiles, in the face of the often violent rejection from his own people (Acts 22:6-11, 15, 21). Paul's experience also figures in the account of the favourable impression Paul made on King Agrippa II and Berenice (Acts 26:12-19), to the point of exonerating him from anything blameworthy (v. 32). Luke's descriptions of the Pauline experience of Christ employ the conventional symbol of light: "a light from heaven flashed around him" (Acts 9:3), "a light shining from heaven" (Acts 26:13), intended, as Paul himself is quoted as saying, "to open their [the Gentiles'] eyes, that they may turn from darkness to light" (Acts 26:18), and "to proclaim light both to our people and to the Gentiles" (v. 23). Light-symbolism was an available and traditional mode of speaking of divine revelation. Though it resonates with Paul's appeal to the light of Christ in 2 Corinthians 4:4-6, an experience of illumination is not mentioned in Paul's first-hand account of the grace of God who had set him apart and "was pleased to reveal his Son to me" (Gal 1:15).[12]

But Paul's own direct testimony has other concerns (Gal 1:11-17). He is first of all at pains to suggest the originality of what he has personally received: "For I would have you know, brethren, that the gospel which was proclaimed by me is not of human origin; for I did not receive it from a human source, nor was I taught it, but it came through a revelation of Jesus Christ" (1 Gal 1:11-12). He is therefore stressing that his reception of the gospel had not been mediated to him by others, even if he stands with others in the way the risen Christ has disclosed himself to them (1 Cor 15:3-8). Still, a commanding "otherness" had broken into his life in a way that transcends any human agency. To this degree, his experience is reminiscent of the prophetic calls of Isaiah (Isa 49:1, 5; 44:2) and Jeremiah (Jer 1:5). His energetic commitment to Judaism and his equally energetic rejection of the followers of Christ were of public record (Gal 1:13-14). But, then, something happened to change all this, ". . . when God, who had set me apart before I was born, and called me through his grace, was pleased to reveal his Son to me, so that I might proclaim him among the Gentiles" (Gal 15-16).

While puzzles abound, we might single out five aspects of Paul's distinctive experience. They can be usefully related to the slightly fuller statement at the opening of his letter to the Romans:

1. It is *God* who has acted in his regard, not something or someone else, to bring about the change that has made him "a servant of Jesus Christ" (Rom 1:1). Though what God has done places him in the community of Christ's followers—and as the last in the line of privileged seers—Paul will insist on the originality of his experience of God's intervention on his behalf (cf. Gal 1:17-24).
2. The God who has so acted had sovereign power over the adverse conditions that affected Paul's origins and history. Before he was born, he had been "set apart for the gospel of God" (Rom 1:1).
3. God has acted through the gift of a special vocation, described in Romans as that of "grace and apostleship" (Rom 1: 5), mediated by the risen Christ to bring faith to the nations.
4. A new psychological attitude or religious sense on Paul's part is not the primary consideration, but the startlingly objective revelation of God's own Son. Paul is to proclaim the "gospel of God" which is further specified as "concerning his Son" (Rom 1:3). Jesus, like Paul, has his origins in Israel—"descended from David according to the flesh" (v. 3b), but is now made known to Paul as the risen Messiah and "our Lord" (Rom 1:4).
5. The irruption of this divinely-wrought revelation of the risen Jesus is not simply an individual grace for Paul, but given to equip him with

the power and content of the gospel in view of his mission to the nations, beyond restrictions of a previous horizon shaped by "the traditions of my ancestors" (Gal 1:14).

In discussing the responsibilities and privileges of Christian freedom, Paul intrudes the question, "Am I not free? Am I not an apostle? Have I not seen Jesus our Lord? Are you not my work in the Lord?" (1 Cor 9:1). From within this connection of freedom and vision, Paul offers himself as an example to others. His authority is based on his being an apostle, one who has seen the risen Lord and borne fruit in the mission received from him. Here we note the perfect tense of "seen", *heoraka*, connoting the present and continuing sense of a singular action occurring in the past. Clearly, this "seeing" is different from other visionary experiences in that it is associated with a particular self-disclosure of the risen Jesus. This singular realism, to be further discussed in relation to 1 Corinthians 15:8-11, suggests an objectivity that is more than a subjective vision or ordinary seeing. For the economy of these singular "seeings" had then come to an end, even though their occurrence can be widely verified by interrogating still living witnesses.[13] Though Paul is familiar with the various traditions of the logia, parables, miracles, and exemplary actions, condemnation and crucifixion in the narrative of the earthly life and fate of Jesus, he concentrates on what he takes to be the fundamental datum. As a teacher in Antioch, he would have been familiar with all the developing traditions as the details of Jesus' life were recollected and shaped into various forms for the instruction of Christian communities (Acts 13:1). But all this was not to be taken as the starting point. The original moment of truth was not a matter of knowing Jesus "in the flesh" (2 Cor 5:16), for that, by itself, would be a case of the idolic historicism that Voegelin criticizes. Separated from the resurrection, the recollection of Jesus' life and teaching would not raise Christian existence above an improved Jewish ethics or Greek wisdom; nor, for that matter, would it escape the preoccupations of an overheated apocalyptic vision. For Paul, everything must be centred, and continually re-centred, on the resurrection of the Crucified, in anticipation of a completely new creation (2 Cor 5:17).[14] He will not say that if Jesus had not proclaimed the reign of God, taught in parables, performed miracles, or suffered condemnation and death, then his followers are without hope of salvation. But what he does assert is this: "if Christ has not been raised, your faith is futile and you are still in your sins" (1 Cor 15:17). In the light of that event, all else made sense. Indeed, as we shall see below in reference to the Philippians hymn (Phil 2:6-11), the light deriving from the risen and exalted Christ enables Paul to read the humble service that so marked Jesus' earthly life back into its eternal, transtemporal origins.

To anchor Paul's experience of the risen One more firmly, let us gather together some of the strands of how his Judaic inheritance was affected by his encounter with Christ. The "turbulence" or "mutation" that occurred in Paul's experience affected the totality of his outlook and identity. It finds expression in the following declaration:

> From now on, therefore, we regard no one from a human point of view; even though we once knew Christ from a human point of view, we know him no longer in that way. So if anyone is in Christ, there is a new creation; everything old has passed away; see, everything has become new! (2 Cor 5:16-17).

Previous fixations of prejudice and antagonism to Christ (and to his followers) have been dramatically dissolved. A new horizon has opened up at the heart of what had seemed to Paul most authoritative. A new event had occurred to put everything on a new footing: "everything has become new!" The context of Paul's words indicates the theophanic nature of the event in bringing about in both Paul and his hearers a new transparency to God: "knowing the fear of the Lord . . . we ourselves are well known to God, and I hope we are well known to your consciences" (2 Cor 5:11). The "outward appearances" (v. 12) that had structured conflicting identities of Jew and Gentile are dismantled, to inspire a new self-transcending sense of life and reconciliation. In consequence, Christians "may no longer live for themselves, but for him who died and was raised for them" (2 Cor 5:15), for in Christ, "God was reconciling the world to himself" (2 Cor 5:19).

For Paul it was never a matter of rejecting the identification of Christ with Jesus. He is, however, intent on witnessing to the complete about-face that the revelation of the risen Lord had effected in him, compared to what he knew before *kata sarka*, "according to the flesh". The "human point of view" (RSV trans., 2 Cor 5:16) envisaged humanity as subject to the power of sin and burdened with the weight of the law. But now, in the light of the risen Christ, everything is seen differently, so differently in fact, that Paul is now free to admit his pre-conversion antagonism to Christ and the fury of his persecution of Christ's followers (Acts 9:1; Gal 1:13; Phil 3:5). What before had been for Paul a privilege and an advantage was now revealed as loss and, even more strongly, as "rubbish" (e.g., Phil 3:2-10).

Let us now look in more detail at what Paul saw himself converted from. From his own autobiographical remarks and the testimony of Luke in Acts, the following sketch emerges. He was a Jew with Palestinian ancestry (1 Cor 11:22); he had come to Jerusalem for schooling and rabbinical training (Acts 22:3; 26:4). As a Pharisee, he had been "far more zealous for the traditions of my ancestors", which included a refined articulation of the law (Gal 1:14; Acts 26:5). He had enjoyed the honour of studying under the celebrated Gamaliel (Acts 26:4). Within a few years of Jesus' death, he assisted as a young man at the stoning of Stephen (Acts 7:28). It seems that he was more than a mere student: he received a commission from the senior Jewish leaders to root out the Christians in Damascus (Acts 9:1; 26:9-11). He obviously shared their conviction that Jesus was the leader of an alarming new splinter-group. Jesus, despite his lack of formal training (Jn 7:15) and his more relaxed approach to the law, had tended to be taken as sympathetic to the Pharisaic party. But observant Pharisees had been scandalised by his association with sinners (Mk 2:16; Lk 7:36; 15:2), his interpretation regarding work on the Sabbath (Mk 2:24; 3:6; Lk 6:7; 14:1; Jn 9:13), and his neglect of rules of ritual purity (Mk 7:1). Some aspects of his treatment of the tradition were unsettlingly radical in regard to divorce (Mk 10:2) and the necessity of interior purity of heart. Most galling was that this Jesus pretended to a privileged position, not only in interpreting the law, but also in his relationship to God. The Pharisees could not escape the implication that Jesus was a messianic pretender. Their demand for some sign of the legitimacy of his activities (Mk 8:11) culminated in the questioning at his eventual trial, "Are you the Messiah, the Son of the Blessed One?" (Mk 14:61). After his death, they saw the potential danger in the claim on the part of his disciples that he had been raised, and how this could be sustained had his corpse been stolen from the tomb (Mt 28:13).

Paul clearly shared in this perception of Jesus and his followers. And it was this hitherto unassailable perception that was contradicted by his encounter with the risen Jesus. Not only was Jesus risen, not only had he appeared to Paul, his former antagonist, but he had also been divinely vindicated in the uniqueness of his relationship to the God of Israel in a way that left the law-structured religious world of the Pharisees radically relativised.

Paul's encounter with the risen Jesus is described in three places in Acts (Acts 9:1-9; 22:5-16; 26:9-18). Apart from recording the decisive effect on Paul himself, Luke's accounts are not uniform—with regard to Paul being blinded, the explanation he receives, or in the experience of his companions as regards what they heard or saw. Paul himself locates his experience as the last in the series of post-resurrectional appearances to chosen witnesses (1 Cor 9:1; 15:8). He shares with these others the in-breaking character of Christ's self-disclosure. It occurred at the initiative of the risen Jesus, with no expectation on the part of those who received it. In contrast, however, to the Gospel accounts, say, in Luke 24:13-43, any sense of growing recognition is lacking. The other witnesses were re-converted, or more fully and finally converted, to the One they had followed, and whose loss they had suffered, in grief and disappointment. Paul's "conversion" is more immediate, not only in terms of how Jesus intervened in his life, but also in the way that the fury of his former antagonism was forever reversed.

What occurred for Paul was a direct and immediate "revelation of

Jesus Christ" (Gal 1:12). It dramatically changed the horizon of Paul's previous convictions: Jesus was not a messianic pretender, but the Messiah, the Christ. He was not the troublesome leader of a splinter-group, but God's own Son. In him, a universal salvation was being offered, overflowing even to the Gentiles, beyond any restriction of the law.

While Paul turned away from his previous negative preconceptions about Jesus and his followers, his conversion did not leave him as an independent "free agent", with no further interest in the earthly life and ministry of Jesus, isolated from the tradition being handed on in the Christian community and with no responsibility for it. His experience of the risen Christ brought with it that profound sense of the self-giving love of Jesus as the historical appearance of the grace and mercy of God. Furthermore, what Paul individually had received never dissociated him from the emerging body of Christian tradition—as we have already emphasised. His experience was a variation of the melody pervading the larger symphony of Christian witness. For example, he cites the eucharistic formula (1 Cor 11:23-25), and primitive creed (1 Cor 15:3-5). He knows that Jesus is a Jew (Rom 9:4-5), of the line of David (Rom 1:3), that he had a mother (Gal 4:4), that he was betrayed (1 Cor 11:23) and was crucified (1 Cor 2:2), that he died and was buried (1 Cor 15:3-4) and raised from the dead (v. 5). Though he never feels the need to repeat everything that is in the tradition that he received, the historicity of Jesus is a basic datum. At no point may one preach "another Jesus than the one we have proclaimed" (2 Cor 11:4), so that "the life of Jesus may be visible in our mortal flesh" (2 Cor 4:10). He quotes the teaching of Jesus on divorce (1 Cor 7:10-11) and support for pastors (1 Cor 9:14). Some scholars have suggested that the agrarian metaphors he employs may well resonate with the parables, especially given the largely urban location of Paul's life.[15] Then, there are his multiple and extended contacts with various Christian communities and active involvement in their ministry (Acts 22:22), for example, in Damascus (Acts 9:19; Gal 1:17-18). His familiarity with the earliest communities included a visit to Peter—he uses the early Aramaic form of the name, *Kephas*—in Jerusalem (Acts 9:26; Gal 1:18). There, he presumably became aware of the tradition of Jesus naming Peter as the "rock" on which he will build his Church (Mt 16:13-20). After some years in Tarsus, he is summoned to Antioch for an active year, where "he met with the church and taught a great many people" (Acts 11:26). Hence, whatever the distinctive emphasis of his preaching, a background knowledge of the person, deeds and sayings of Jesus preserved in a number of early communities must always be presumed. The manner in which he tells of his personal encounter with Christ is firmly linked to the emerging traditions of the earliest Christian communities in and for which he worked.

We now pass on to two key texts relevant to his encounter with the risen Jesus which serve to elaborate the meaning of his experience.

From Experience to Meaning

1 Corinthians 15:1-28[16]

In his letter to the Corinthians, Paul explicates an earlier expression of his apostolic concern—written probably about 50 AD:

> But we do not want you to be uninformed, brothers and sisters, about those who have died, so that you may not grieve as others do who have no hope. For since we believe that Jesus died and rose again, even so, through Jesus, God will bring with him those who have died (1 Thess 4:13-18).

Christian hope penetrates into the world of hopeless grief. Death is not a grim barrier separating the living from those who have passed from this world before us.[17] The resurrection disrupts the power of death, and the meaning of time itself. As the risen Christ is the anticipation of the future, those who are with him are no longer lost in the past, but already populate the eschatological future in store for all. Despite the obscurity of the apocalyptic rhetoric, the message is clear: ". . . we who are alive . . . will by no means precede those who have died" (Gal 4:15), but will be "caught up" into a new order of existence with them, to meet Christ in his final appearance, "so that we will be with the Lord forever" (1 Thess 4:17).

Four years later, in his letter to the Corinthians, Paul refers first of all to the tradition he has both received and handed on (1 Cor 15:1-3)— "as of first importance" (v. 3) concerning the gospel he proclaimed. He appeals to this as something well known and widely received in its formulation, and bigger than any individual experience, even though he contributes his own singular and independent witness to its content:

> For I handed on to you as of first importance what I in turn had received: that Christ died for our sins in accordance with the scriptures, and that he was buried, and that he was raised on the third day in accordance with the scriptures, and that he appeared to Cephas, and then to the twelve. Then he appeared to five hundred brothers and sisters at one time, most of whom are still alive, though some have died. Then he appeared to James, then to all the apostles. Last of all, as one untimely born, he appeared also to me. For I am the least of the apostles, unfit to be called an apostle, because I persecuted the Church of God. But by the grace of God, I am what I am, and his grace toward me has not been in vain. On the contrary, I have worked harder than any of them—though it was not I, but the

grace of God that is with me. Whether then it was I or they, so we proclaim and so you have come to believe (1 Cor 15:3-11).

Here there are several critical points to note:

1. Christ's death for "our sins" is a confession that could be made only in the light of the resurrection. The cross certainly manifested the power of evil, but that it could be understood as victory over evil presupposes the resurrection of the Crucified. And in that victory over evil and the power of sin, the great prophecies of the past can be newly understood (Isa 40:1-11; Ezek 36:22-32; Ezek 37; Jer 31:31-34; Dan 9), as "according to the scriptures".
2. The repetition of the twofold "in accordance with the scriptures" in relation to the confession of the death and resurrection of Christ is no simple appeal to proof-texts. Christ himself is the living proof of what the inspired writings of Israel promised—as is more fully explained in Luke 24 when "beginning with Moses and all the prophets he interpreted the things about himself in all the scriptures" (Lk 24:27; cf. vv. 32, 44-45). The significance of the phrase "was buried" in the formula can be elaborated only as framed by the death and resurrection, as the Gospel narratives make clear.
3. The phrase, "was raised", is an example of the divine passive: God is the agent of the resurrection. The perfect form of the verb suggests an ongoing effect. It might be better rendered as "he has been raised", in preference to the more delimited and episodic connotation of the aorist form, "was raised", connoting a completed action in the past. Moreover, whatever the possible connotations of "on the third day"—say, in reference to Hosea 6:2—the reality of time following Jesus' death and burial is recognised, leading to the "day of the Lord", the first day of the week in the Christian tradition. These two points are not irrelevant to the discovery of the empty tomb.
4. Commentators make much of the precise connotations of the Greek form of the verb, *ôphthē*, here translated as "appeared". It could be just as well, if not better, translated as "was seen by"—thus accenting the objectivity of the disclosure.[18] Opinions differ as to the precise translation of *ôphthē*—usually taken as the aorist passive of verb *horao*. It is used nine times in relation to the risen Jesus (Lk 24:34; Acts 9:17; 13:31; 26:16), including four times in 1 Cor 15:5-8, all pointing to the idea that he "let himself be seen" in a special, free mode of self-disclosure. Here philosophical and even the theological presuppositions of scholars come into play. The context, however, is clearly one of an all-decisive realism, not of a subjectivist imagination or projection.
5. The list of those by whom the risen Christ "was seen", has a precision that underscores the reality in question. The mention of the early

form of the name of Peter as *Cephas* points to the original form of the tradition to which Paul is appealing—in contrast, say, to the designation *Simon*, as given in Luke 24:34. The "five hundred" suggests both the objectively public nature of the "seeing", and the possibility of its being checked by contemporary survivors. The mention of James, who was the leader of the church of Jerusalem up to the middle of the first century, provides a further fixed point of reference. "All the apostles" seems to suggest a group larger than the twelve; it is not unlikely, therefore, that the women who figure so largely in the later Gospel accounts are included here. After all, Paul employs the term "apostle" in a rather open-ended designation (cf. Rom 16:7), so as to include one who has seen the Lord and been involved in a life of witness to others (1 Cor 9:1).

6. There is the witness of Paul himself. As a former persecutor of the followers of Jesus, he was "one untimely born"—in contrast to the considerable gestation experienced by other apostles who had been disciples of Jesus in his ministry.

Paul proceeds to expound on the significance of the phenomenon of the appearances in a rapidly developing logic extending in many directions—the fate of the dead, the fact that Christ had been raised, the validity of faith, the character of God, the forgiveness of sins, and the provisional nature of this life. By arguing from within the existential "turbulence" of the resurrection experience, Paul is not appealing to an extrinsic proof in an apologetic manner intent on defending a truth revealed in some other way. He moves immediately into the existential significance of the Christ's resurrection for Christian life:

> Now if Christ is proclaimed as raised from the dead, how can some of you say that there is no resurrection of the dead? If there is no resurrection of the dead, then Christ has not been raised; and if Christ has not been raised, then our proclamation has been in vain, and your faith has been in vain. We are even found to be misrepresenting God, because we testify of God that he raised Christ—whom he did not raise if it is true that the dead are not raised. For if the dead are not raised, then Christ has not been raised. If Christ has not been raised, then your faith is futile and you are still in your sins. Then those also who have died in Christ have perished. If for this life only we have hoped in Christ, we are of all people most to be pitied (1 Cor 15:12-19).

A world-transforming event has occurred. Paul attests to it with an assurance founded on the transformation he himself has experienced, acutely aware of what is at stake, namely, the reality of Christ's resurrection, the authenticity of the gospel, the truth of faith, the character of

God, hope for the dead, the forgiveness of sins and the value of Christian life.

With this realisation, Paul meets head-on the doubts and objections regarding bodily resurrection from Jewish or pagan sources. He stresses the historic significance of Christ's resurrection as an event that has already taken place and radically affected the world. A new age has been inaugurated, and the reign of sin and death has in principle been terminated. If the resurrection of Jesus and its ongoing effect is denied, then the will of God, the creator and giver of life, has been frustrated. It would be tantamount to saying that God had not been revealed, that the dead will live no more, and that hope is useless.[19] In contrast to that bleak possibility, Paul presents a larger picture: the creator is leading creation to its fulfilment in Christ. For he is the God-intended truly human one, made in God's image: in him the destiny of all creation is anticipated (cf. Gen 1:26-28; 3:17-19; also Ps 8 and 110).

But in fact Christ has been raised from the dead, the first fruits of those who have died. For since death came through a human being, the resurrection of the dead has also come through a human being; for as all die in Adam, so all will be made alive in Christ (1 Cor 15:20-22).

For Paul, then, the resurrection is the vital originating factor. It is an event of expanding significance and influence—for Paul himself, for his hearers and for history itself. God's design takes its own time and is realised in its own conditions. There is a divinely established "order" or arrangement (cf. Ps 8:7), in which each divinely-timed phase has its place: "But each in his own order [*en to idio tagmati*]: Christ the first fruits, then at his coming those who belong to Christ" (1 Cor 15:23). The full extent of the divine design will be unfolded when what has happened already in Christ, the first fruits, will be extended to all who belong to him: "For since we believe that Jesus died and rose again, even so through Jesus, God will bring with him those who have died" (1 Thess 4:14). But under the rule of Christ, the end will take effect in a cosmic and even political manner: "Then comes the end, when he delivers the kingdom to God the Father after destroying every rule and every authority and power" (1 Cor 15:24), including "the last enemy"—death (v. 26). As the new Adam, having established dominion over all creation, the Son, in contrast to the old Adam, subjects himself in the end to God: "When all things are subjected to him, then the Son himself will also be subjected to him who put all things under him, that God may be everything to every one" (v. 28). Christ is not the idol of human projections or hopes, but the Son in and through whom God is acting. Though the resurrection of Jesus is an event of universal significance, it never separates its origins and ultimate purpose in God.

The aim of Paul's rapid-fire exposition is to expose his readers to the keen edge of their faith in the resurrection. Only there can hope find its justification in the midst of the world of aggressive certitudes and imperial power. Only at this keen edge of faith can present expressions of care for the dead mean anything: "If the dead are not raised at all, why are people baptised on their behalf?"(1 Cor 15: 29). Struggles inherent in witnessing to Christ need prophetic hope: "What do I gain if, humanly speaking, I fought with beasts at Ephesus? If the dead are not raised, 'Let us eat and drink, for tomorrow we die' " (v. 32; cf. Isa 22:12-14). Such hope can be compromised by the desperate presuppositions of the surrounding culture lacking the true knowledge of God. The community of faith, formed by the testimony of privileged witnesses and by the more encompassing witness of the tradition, supports a life of hope. Being apart from this corporate solidarity undermines the faith and hope of the community, as the popular epigram from Menander's play *Thais* suggests: "Do not be deceived: 'Bad company ruins good morals' " (v. 33-34).[20]

Though Paul's explanation of the precise character of the general resurrection proceeds by a *via negationis*, it takes the reader further into the "genesis" that the creator is enacting:

> But some one will ask, "How are the dead raised? With what kind of body do they come?" You foolish man! What you sow does not come to life unless it dies. And what you sow is not the body which is to be, but a bare kernel, perhaps of wheat or of some other grain. But God gives it a body as he has chosen, and to each kind of seed its own body. For not all flesh is alike, but there is one kind for men, another for animals, another for birds, and another for fish. There are celestial bodies and there are terrestrial bodies; but the glory of the celestial is one, and the glory of the terrestrial is another. There is one glory of the sun, and another glory of the moon, and another glory of the stars; for star differs from star in glory (1 Cor 15:35-41).

Clearly Paul is looking beyond the limits and miseries of biological life to the uniqueness of personal existence and the manner of its embodiment in Christ. Creation already includes a variety of different bodies: celestial and terrestrial, plant, animal and human. Each has its own "glory" or mode of appearance. Implied here is also the God-given character of humanity's dominion over all (Gen 1:28). But this can be fully realised only in the "last Adam". For the human body to be raised after death (v. 36) means being subjected, by the gift of God, to the final Adam, and so to bear his image (v. 38). Compared to the present state, there is both continuity and discontinuity involved (v. 37). The analogies that follow do not serve to clarify the composition of the resurrected body. They point, rather, to its gifted, final state in which its present mortality, lowliness, weakness and physicality are reversed:

So is it with the resurrection of the dead. What is sown is perishable, what is raised is imperishable. It is sown in dishonor, it is raised in glory. It is sown in weakness, it is raised in power. It is sown a physical body, it is raised a spiritual body. If there is a physical body, there is also a spiritual body (1 Cor 15:42-44).

Though reference has been made to celestial bodies, the resurrected state is not an astral existence, but a genuine bodiliness adapted to the milieu of the Spirit in which Christian consciousness lives and breathes (1 Cor 2:14-15; Gen 2:7).[21] The risen Christ is the form and source of the life-giving Spirit, to transform the still-mortal bodies of those united to him. Consequently, a final freedom from the limitations of the flesh inherent in its exposure to conflict with the world, and in the historical conditions of this present time, will be enjoyed (Rom 8:9-11; 2 Cor 3:17-18). This new embodied form of life will not lie at the mercy of the biological entropy characteristic of mundane time. No more will it be subject to the oppressive power of the rulers of this world. Present incapacities will make way for the energies of a new spiritual vitality, living and breathing in relational openness, and gifted with the freedom of the Spirit: "Thus it is written, 'The first man Adam became a living being'; the last Adam became a life-giving spirit. But it is not the spiritual which is first but the physical, and then the spiritual" (1 Cor 15:45-46).

The point is not that the human being is relocated or "spiritualised" in opposition to bodiliness, but of a bodiliness transformed in the milieu of the Spirit. If there is any suggestion of a local metaphor, it is that of being "in Christ", united to him, conformed to him, and participating in his mode of risen existence. Eschatological humanity conceived not as being "taken up to heaven when we die", but as being made the recipient of a final transformation. It is a mutation wrought by the transcendent power of "heaven", already effective in Christ, the image of what is to come:

The first man was from the earth, a man of dust; the second man is from heaven. As was the man of dust, so are those who are of the dust; and as is the man of heaven, so are those who are of heaven. Just as we have borne the image of the man of dust, we shall also bear the image of the man of heaven (1 Cor 15:47-49).

Though life is the gift of the creator, because of Adam's sin it has been disfigured. But, in the end, it is destined to be re-modelled in a heavenly, transformed mode. It will be reconstituted in that larger communion of life that is already partially realised. This celebratory sense of this ultimate form of life is reiterated in Paul's letter to the Philippians. In contrast to the flesh-bound unredeemed existence, "our citizenship is in heaven, and it is from there that we are expecting a Saviour, the Lord

Jesus Christ" (Phil 3:20). From the transcendent realm in which God's creation will be consummated, Christ comes as the agent of our transformation: "He will transform the body of our humiliation, that it may be conformed to the body of his glory, by the power that also enables him to make all things subject to himself" (Phil 3:21).

The discontinuity of the future with present existence is emphasised in explicit confrontation with the reality of death: "I tell you this, brethren: flesh and blood cannot inherit the Kingdom of God, nor does the perishable inherit the imperishable" (1 Cor 15:50). God's giving, far from being exhausted in the limitations of the present, looks to a great transformation of embodied existence: ". . . the dead will be raised imperishable, and we shall be changed" (v. 52). The limitations, degradation and entropy of our present bodily condition will be replaced by the deathlessness that is the gift of the risen One: "For this perishable nature must put on the imperishable, and this mortal nature must put on immortality" (v. 53). Christ's victory over the powers of death draws the "sting of death" (v. 55). Death has infected human history with sin working through oppressive power of the law (v. 56), thereby intensifying the alienation, incapacity and futility of existence. The Christian, then, gives thanks to God who has already conquered sin and death in Christ (v. 57). Our existence "in the Lord" (v. 58) is already drawn onward by hope and the energies of creation transformed.

The resurrection effect is registered, therefore, in a new sense of bodily life. A further witness, often associated with the Pauline tradition, speaks of enlightenment and a "tasting " of the heavenly gift and a receptivity to the powers of the age to come (Heb 6:4-6; cf. 1 Pet 2:3). As faith moves in "a new and living way" (Heb 10:20), its light, its taste, its energies are marked also with the invigorating "fragrance of life to life" (2 Cor 2:16). Faith's perception of God revealed in the risen Christ is anchored in the transforming activity of the Spirit already working in sacramental forms: "But when the goodness and loving kindness of God our saviour has appeared, he saved us, not because of any works of righteousness that we had done, but according to his mercy, through the water of rebirth and renewal of the Holy Spirit" (Tit 3:4-5).[22] Human existence is subsumed into the dynamic of a transformation that is already fulfilled in Christ: "Therefore we have been buried with him by baptism into death, so that just as Christ was raised from the dead to the glory of the Father, so we too might walk in newness of life" (Rom 6:4).

Paul's conclusion to his treatment of the resurrection and its effect does not allow for any kind of mystical passivity: now that faith stands at a point when it can look back to what God has done in Christ, to look forward to the fulfilment of God's good creation, there is work to be done: "Therefore, my beloved, be steadfast, immovable, always excelling in the work of the Lord, because you know that in the Lord your labor is not in vain" (1 Cor 15:58). If Christ is truly risen, neither faith nor its collaboration with God is in vain.

Paul's spirited exposition of the resurrection effect presupposes the background sense of creation in Genesis 1-3. His logic is animated by a primordial sense of the God-originated, God-imaged and the God-ward movement of creation itself. As Paul's argument plays around the focal reality of the resurrection of the crucified One, he shows how creation is completed and humanity becomes the true image of God. The immortality of the soul is not at stake, for that was a general belief. The critical issue is the full-bodied resurrection of Jesus, and its effect on human destiny. Christ, for the Apostle, is the anticipation, agent and exemplar of a promised universal resurrection, with its cosmic and historical effects. He allows that the nature of the risen body is radically unimaginable, except in terms of the analogical indications that he somewhat impatiently offers.

Paul is contending with difficulties and denials that arise in appropriating faith in the risen Jesus as he has presented it. He is not primarily concerned with the resurrection of Jesus himself, since that is inextricably embedded in the tradition he has received and handed on in his role as a chosen witness. More directly, his concern is the eschatological extension of what happened to Christ in his rising from the dead. If Jesus is truly risen, the resurrection effect is of real consequence in the intentionality of Christian faith. Neither the resurrection of Jesus nor its extension to others can be allowed to degenerate into some form of mythic construction on a reality that remains radically unchanged (cf. 2 Tim 2:17-18), without truly eschatological significance. Paul has both Jewish and pagan adversaries in mind as he asserts the eschatological turning point that is centred in Christ. He admits that the time and mode of a particular visual revelation to chosen witnesses has already come to an end. Still, an unapologetic appeal to the "seeing" of the privileged witnesses is an element in the realism of both the resurrection as an event and in the intentional response of faith to it. Consequently, Paul rehearses both the witness of the tradition that he has received, and his part, not only in receiving the tradition, but also as occupying it in a special manner as the last on the list of privileged witnesses. The profound "turbulence" (Voegelin) in which he has been caught up is presented as drawing others into it. Christians live in a new "in-between"—not between this life and a shadowy afterlife—but between this present form of existence in Christ and its complete fulfilment.

Philippians 2:5-11

Given that the resurrection saturated every aspect of Paul's life, mission and teaching, 1 Corinthians 15 is an example of Paul's creativity in extending the meaning of the resurrection to all believers and to the whole of creation. In what follows, we will suggest another dimension of resurrection effect, precisely as it is derives from a unique act of self-giving on the part of Christ, and the God who glorifies him in his self-abasement "for us and our salvation". Paul interprets the phenomenon of his encounter with the risen Lord as the outcome, not only of Jesus' surrender to the divine will even unto death on the cross, but also as originating in a transcendent order beyond time. In this it is revelatory of the character of God himself.[23] In this regard, Brendan Byrne, the eminent Pauline scholar, presents the following thesis:

> Not only does the interpretation of certain texts (notably Phil 2:6-8 and 2 Cor 8:9) require Christ's pre-existence but that, more importantly, the full force of Paul's soteriological thought is under-cut if the one whom he, along with the early Christian tradition, came to call Christ did not emerge from the eternity of God in such a way that his personal human history is preceded by this existence with God, and plays out an intimate relationship that is prior, in a unique way, to his human history.[24]

Byrne goes on to argue to "neglect the pre-temporal aspect of this relationship gravely erodes . . . the sense of the extremity of divine love and grace which lies at the heart of Paul's gospel".[25] Implicit in Paul's view of the origins of his experience is a sense of God who, in Jesus Christ, has reached out to the world in the costly vulnerability of love (see Rom 8:32, 39; cf. Paul's hymn to love in 1 Cor 13). There is no question of appealing to a mythic "pre-existing humanity" of Jesus, but of finding in Christ Jesus the enactment of a divine form of self-giving in the sphere of humanity. Christ is not an intention in the mind of God, but the embodiment of the mind of God in the flesh-and-blood costly vulner-ability of love. Presupposed in the self-giving love of Jesus is freedom and self-dispossession of a divine subject. This is not incompatible with the basic monotheism of the OT as scholars such as Hurtado[26] have shown, but represents this monotheism in a new key. Paul's experience of the crucified and risen Christ provided the impulse towards a concep-tion of God that his Jewish background could neither provide nor ex-plain. Despite the turbulence of the experience, the dismantling of pre-vious horizons, the discontinuity occasioned by this mutation in religious consciousness, "the carriers were at hand to encapsulate and express this mutation . . . early enough to find reflection in Paul".[27] Paul's state-ments dealing with God's "sending his own Son in the likeness of sinful flesh" (Rom 8:3-4), and presenting the God "who did not withhold his own Son, but who gave him up for all of us" (Rom 8:32) point to the transcendent origins of the gift that has been made (cf. Rom 15:3; Gal 4:4-5). But Byrne points to a further implication: Christ as a personal subject existing in the divine realm has himself exercised an act of choice in a manner that precedes his temporal existence.[28] Here we follow Byrne's careful exegesis of Philippians 2:6-8.

When Paul cites what appears to be an early Christian hymn, he presumes general acceptance on the part of his readers of what he is about to present and its existential relevance to them—because of their proneness to "selfish ambition and conceit" (Phil 2:3) and the tendency to "look to your own interests" (v. 4), at the expense of others. An authentic form of Christian consciousness is at stake: "let the same mind be in you that was in Christ Jesus" (v. 5). Receptivity to nothing less than that primordial divine act of generosity which has already terminated in the resurrection of Jesus is demanded and, with it, conformity to Christ's unreserved self-giving in which he has been glorified. It is rooted in the supra-temporal divine freedom which has reached into the heart of the human predicament. There may be an allusion to Adam in this text, but that is not the basic referent. Christ is not compared to Adam, but contrasted to him.[29] Adam's likeness to God as expressed in Genesis 1:26-27 is, therefore, not the key. Certainly, both Christ and Adam can be taken as being "like God"; but where Adam exploits and distorts the divine image, Christ, in humble love and obedience, reveals its true meaning.

"Though he was in the form of God, he did not regard equality with God as something to be exploited" (v. 6). The force of *harpagmos* suggests exploitation for selfish gain, the act of an all-dominating self-referential subject. On the contrary, as the verse continues, Christ, though enjoying a divine status, "emptied himself". This early hymn thereby suggests the character of God—a "key definition of divinity".[30] Not only is the "form" of God self-transcending, but self-transcending to an extreme degree. For Christ empties himself "taking the form of a slave" (v. 7a). The word *morphe* is used to point the contrast between the "form" of God and the "form" of a slave. It is best understood as "the specific form in which the identity and status of someone/something is expressed and can thus come to be known and recognized".[31] Given the resonances of identity and status connoted in such a "form", Christ is depicted as moving from a position of being Lord of all, to that of freely occupying a status in which he is exposed to the domination of the powers of this world ranged against God. He enters into the sphere of unredeemed human existence, a condition of enslavement. Paul elsewhere described this condition as that of humanity "enslaved to spirits of the world . . . to beings that by nature are not gods" (Gal 4:3, 8). For Jesus to enter into such a realm means exposure to the idolatrous and demonic forces of violence and pride. By his free act as a pre-existent, divine subject, Jesus deliberately assumed the state of "being born in human likeness, and being found in human form" (v. 7b). There is no implication of his retaining merely a docetic likeness to the human, but of his free self-immersion in what is furthest from the divine. By entering into the realm of human existence, Christ Jesus is "found in human form"—a divine passive suggesting that he stands before God in a representative capacity. He therefore enacts in the human world both God's outreach to humanity, and the form of obedience to God appropriate to human beings. As this representative human being before God, "he humbled himself and became obedient to the point of death—even death on a cross" (v. 8). This further act of freedom in the human sphere expresses the astonishing excess marking Christ's original decision. He does not opt to live by sharing in a self-contained human existence alienated from God, but in a mode of self-surrender to God through obedience even to the point of death—marked with the further limits of condemnation, rejection, abandonment and disgrace.

But now there is a shift of perspective. Where Jesus was the agent in the previous verses, God is now the main actor. The introductory "therefore" signals not simply a reversal of Jesus' humiliation unto death, but the culmination of God's original purpose behind the self-abasement of his Son. What comes to expression only at the end of the hymn is first in the divine intention, and, in fact, primary in Paul's own encounter with Jesus as Christ and Lord:

> Therefore, God has highly exalted him, and gave him a name that is above every name, so that at the name of Jesus every knee should bend, in heaven and on earth and under the earth, and every tongue should confess that Jesus Christ is Lord, to the glory of God the Father (Phil 2:6-11).

So completely does Christ express and enact God's outreach to the human and humanity's surrender to God that the Father from whom he comes, and whose form he expresses, "exalts" him as the bearer of the divine name and as deserving of universal adoration. Hurtado, in his study of this text,[32] provides further support for Byrne's interpretation, and helpfully locates the self-abasement of Jesus within the larger scheme of Jesus' glorification and the spiritual experience behind Paul's presentation of this early hymn.[33] Now the exalted and risen Christ is presented as the bearer of the very name of God, as identified with God—having come in the name, from the freedom, and in the form of God (cf. Isa 45:18-25). The universal submission of all to the creator now extends to the crucified and risen One.[34] Sharing the divine name, he is Lord over every dimension of creation, not only over the human world. It is the one God who shares his name with Jesus so that his glory will be revealed. Jesus is, thus, the manifestation of the name of God, exalted to further the glory of the primordial Other from *which, whom,* or *whence* he has come: "to the glory of God, the Father" (v. 11).

Byrne, therefore, can speak of "the phenomenon of Christ as an invasion of divine grace and generosity into the human sphere from outside".[35] The "invasion" concerned is not that of aggressive intent, but one of self-giving, costly love. It originates from the outside. It is embodied in the opaque and recalcitrant reality of human existence, and yet leading to a God-determined outcome in which this "invasion" reaches its term in the exaltation of Jesus. Within the horizon of faith, God has acted to acclaim the transcendent status of Jesus in relation to all creation. As Paul came to bend his knee and confess the Lordship of the crucified, risen and exalted Christ, he was caught up in the "turbulence" which would dismay his previous religious horizons, and make him a witness to the God-given "mutation" that had occurred in the world's history. Christ has been raised up and glorified as the revelation of God's self-giving love: hence, his appeal to the Philippian community, "let the same mind be in you that was in Christ Jesus" (Phil 2:5)— despite the endemic pull to the contrary (Phil 2:20-21). When he appeals to Corinthian generosity in the collection for the Christian community in Jerusalem, Paul employs the same logic: "For you know the generous act [*charis*] of our Lord Jesus Christ, that though he was rich, yet for your sakes he became poor, so that by his poverty you might become rich" (2 Cor 8:9; cf. Rom 15:3). The alienated and self-serving mode of death-bound existence that entered the human condition through the sin of Adam is now being reversed: ". . . much more surely have the grace of God and the free gift in grace of the one man, Jesus Christ, abounded for the many" (Rom 5:15). The *charisma* of Christ is "the concrete instantiation of or effect of (divine) grace (*charis*)",[36] as the self-giving love of Christ enacts the compassionate love of God himself. Through his death and resurrection, Jesus has become the revelation of God. To enter into the mind and consciousness of Jesus is to live in a milieu in which self-giving love is the form and energy of creation made new.

Byrne concludes his incisive study with a reference to the mentality of the post-Easter community:

> My point would be then that the sense of Christ as "God's own Son" (Rom 8:3, 32) and as pre-existent Son is truly central to the biblical revelation of God and cannot be downplayed without serious loss. The witness of Paul, in which the Christology of Phil 2:6-8 must be included rather than excluded, indicates the remarkably early presence of this conception in the post-Easter Christian community.[37]

We are left with a question: "What the impulse for this may have been remains a central question for Christology, as well as for the historical inquiry into the rise of Christianity".[38]

Conclusion

In different perspectives, we have been presenting an answer to exactly that question: the resurrection and its effect—above all, in the consciousness of Paul.[39] He speaks of the saturated phenomenon of the risen Christ. He does not offer any doctrinal exposition of what is termed "high Christology". Still the depth of his experience of Christ invites the early post-Easter community to work out the implications of what is expressed in this and in other hymnic forms.[40]

Paul's experience, to recall Voegelin's term, is "metaxic", but in two senses: First, he is at pains to keep vividly to the forefront of consciousness the experience of the risen Christ, even if this means for him relativising to some degree the importance of historical recollections of the life and teaching of Jesus to this end. Secondly, he occupies a place that is in a sense mid-way between his own privileged "seeing" and the experience of the community of faith he seeks to educate in its capacities to appropriate, in the economy of non-seeing faith, what he had seen. To this degree, he opens a door, never to be closed, onto the mystical experience of the later ages of the Church and the multiple discernments that characterise Christian life conformed to Christ through the indwelling Spirit.

Our next chapter will take up this theme more specifically.

CHAPTER 6

Resurrection:
The Visual Phenomenon

In the pastoral conduct of the Church, visual phenomena, especially "apparitions" of any kind, are usually regarded with some suspicion. They are subjected to a vigorous discernment, the basic criterion being the good of the Church as whole in its faith and mission. Nonetheless, the tradition of Christian faith holds within it a strongly visionary element. From its beginnings, the testimony of the privileged eyewitnesses to the risen One has a formative role. Though the time of such privileged "seeing" has passed—with Paul as the last instance of this kind of experience—it is possible to inquire into the extent these visionary origins have given a certain visual and contemplative aspect to Christian experience of the risen One as the light of life.

Yet the question stirs. Are we of these much later times and wider communities left only with ever-weakening and vaguer traces of what was originally so vividly and uniquely "given" to the experience of the earliest post-Easter community? With the passage of time and the history of conflicting interpretations, is there not an inevitable haemorrhaging of original significance? It would seem that the experience of later believers must inevitably fall short. We are deprived of the first hand experience of the earliest witnesses that was evidently, for them, so completely decisive. If this is so, the sense of objectivity must diminish with the passage of time, perhaps lost in the relativity and critical reflection of centuries of theological thought and secular experience. That feeling of a loss of objectivity may well give rise to versions of fundamentalism of either the fideistic or rationalistic variety. Far removed from the resurrection effect experienced by those early witnesses, faith is prey to the questions and doubts of a world far changed from the situation two thousand years ago. The temptation is to seek a substitute, either in the subjectivity of mysticism or spirituality, or in an ideological or even purely theological assurance. The present situation of the "not-seeing" is cut off from that "seeing" of the early witnesses. At one extreme, it is declared to be irrelevant. At the other, we might seek to recapture it in some other way by striving for a vision that is neither possible nor intended. Both paths peter out and pose other questions: how was the original "seeing" of the risen Christ meant to affect the history of "not seeing"? And, how does this "not seeing" still retain for the life of faith the salvific reality that the early disciples witnessed to?[1]

In this chapter we will argue that the gift of the "many and convincing proofs" (Acts 1:4) of the risen Jesus' self-disclosure must be set within the larger economy of the Spirit's witness. In such a setting, the experience of those early witnesses has a long-range effect in those who no longer see, but believe. The evidence of their testimony enters into the tradition of faith. What was given to them is for the sake of the ongoing life of the Church.

We will approach this question from four different but converging perspectives.

1. *A Continuing Dialectic* argues that there is no simple resolution of the terms "seeing" and "not seeing" outside of the phenomenon of the resurrection itself.
2. *The Appearances of the Risen Christ* considers the role of the original witnesses and their place in the New Testament and for later ages.
3. *The Economy of Seeing: An End and a Beginning* treats of the manner in which the end of one form of visionary seeing introduces a "seeing" of another kind in the life of faith.
4. *The Other Paraclete* considers how the "Spirit of truth" is the primary witness to the resurrection and the milieu of Christian experience.

We will then summarise and briefly conclude.

A Continuing Dialectic

Within the New Testament itself, there is a continuing dialectic of seeing and non-seeing that is left unresolved, at least in any theoretical sense. All agree that Christians live by faith, and not by sight. But this does not mean that faith is entirely sightless, or that Christian experience of Christ is a form of blindness. The kind of seeing that faith is opposed to is not always evident, so that the relationship between seeing and not-seeing gives rise to any number of questions.

Take, for instance, the question of seeing and not-seeing as it arises in the Gospel of John. It recalls the pre-resurrection confusion and foreboding of the disciples as they sensed things moving to a violent climax—the point at which Jesus would be removed from them. They are depicted, in their fear of what is impending, still limited to the conditions of the visibility of the earthly Jesus. He meets their forebodings by declaring, "A little while and you will see me no more; again a little while and you will see me" (Jn 16:16). The puzzlement of disciples over this implication of phases in their present "seeing" Jesus, and then losing sight of him, is dramatically recorded (vv. 17-19). In the gathering darkness, they interpret any promised "little time" of absence as the long time of death—when the dead stay dead, and human fate is wrapped in dread and obscurity. They have no eyes to look forward to the visibility of the glorified Jesus resulting from his going to the Father, and to his subsequent return as a source of life beyond the limits of death. In the history of faith, they are not the last to express the limitations of both their vision and their patience: "we do not know what he means" (Jn 16:18b).

The faithful in every age hear Jesus' emphatic assurance as resonating from the event of his resurrection. The dispirited sadness of the disciples is met with the vitality of "the resurrection and the life" (Jn 11:25), in his return to the deathless realm of the Father. At the depths of apparent defeat, and in the face of the world's celebration of victory, a great transformation—which has already occurred for the readers of the Gospel—is promised. The glorification of Jesus will mean a transformation of the consciousness of his disciples: "Amen, amen I say to you, you will weep and lament, but the world will rejoice; you will be sorrowful, but your sorrow will turn into joy" (Jn 16:20). This new consciousness derives from the joyous event of a new birth from above (cf. Jn 3:3, 6; 16:21). Isaiah had foretold that "the earth will give birth to those long dead" (Isa 26:19). In this God-determined hour, there will be a new birth, a new beginning for human existence in which the followers of Jesus are destined to participate. Their present sorrows are not symptoms of terminal distress, but of the travail connected with being born from above to abundant life (Jn 10:10). But here there is a surprising twist. The sorrow resulting from Jesus' departure and no longer seeing him leads to the joy, not of seeing him again, but of being seen *by* him from the vantage point of glory: "So you have sorrow now, but *I will see you again* and your hearts will rejoice and no one will take your joy from you" (Jn 16:22). The followers of Jesus will experience their lives unfolding in the sight of Jesus, to experience a joy that pierces the veil of death and defeat. They will not be found looking into an empty tomb or up to a closed heaven, nor as looking into the sightless eyes of a dead Jesus. Their faith will meet the gaze of "the one whom they have pierced" (Jn 19:37), in the joy of knowing that all their hopes and prayers have been answered (Jn 16:23-24). Despite the time in-between of struggle and conflict, the joy is not moved indefinitely into the future.

The life of faith lives under the gaze of Jesus from beyond and with the assurance of the Spirit from within. The void of invisibility left by the departure of Jesus is filled by witness of the "other Paraclete", the "Spirit of truth". The presence of Jesus in the flesh, his resurrection and subsequent self-disclosures, and the coming of the Spirit are not essentially unrelated or opposed moments. In different ways, these phases interpenetrate: the risen Jesus breathes forth his Spirit, and the Spirit leads back to and enlarges faith's perception of Jesus as the truth and the life, and as the light of the world. Within this two-dimensional economy of revelation, the non-seeing of faith, the visual experience of the chosen witnesses and the testimony of the Spirit are factors in the one living tradition in which all believers share, and to which all contribute.

The experience of Jesus' self-disclosure to chosen witnesses affects the later faith of the community. Though the life of faith is "unseeing" compared to the kind of seeing enjoyed by the original witnesses, there is still a multi-dimensional visual perception. The "eyes of faith" are illumined by the Spirit to find their focus through the community's sacramental signs and sacred scriptures. It recognises a spectrum of colour in the witness of saints and martyrs, mystics and theologians, artists and pastors. It would seem, then, that the original seeing of the chosen witnesses continues as a multi-layered element in the developing tradition of faith to give it both conviction and ever richer content. Deprived of the visual aspect of the risen Jesus' self-revelation, faith would lack an historic assurance of eventually seeing with full evidence what has been inscribed into its beginnings. Paul hits the nail on the head: "for now we see in a mirror, dimly, but then we will see face to face. Now I know only in part; then I will know fully, even as I have been fully known" (1 Cor 13:12). In short, faith is enriched and supported by the witness of the privileged recipients of Jesus' self-disclosures, just as their gifted testimony looks beyond itself to the larger community of faith in every age.

The movement from privileged seeing of the early disciples to the non-seeing of the later followers of the risen One is, therefore, not a one-way street. It is not as though the original seeing is followed by an unqualified not-seeing. For the resurrection event includes within it the visionary experience of the early witnesses in such a way as to serve the historical development of faith. For instance, the self-disclosures of the risen Jesus to Peter, Paul, James, and the five hundred are clearly not detachable from the communal commitment of faith. However we might express the connection, the blessedness of those who do not see but go on believing (Jn 20:29-30) would be deprived of some essential ingredient if the original vision were lacking. Von Balthasar cites Cajetan, the great Thomistic commentator, who highlights the necessity of some form of first-hand evidence of witnesses in what we might term the "ecology" of ecclesial faith: "otherwise the Church would not possess in herself any certainty about what ought to be believed—that is, if she did not have within herself any witnesses".[2]

The dialectic of seeing and not-seeing bears another feature, namely, the dialectic between seeing and hearing. Aquinas makes an intriguing observation in this context, to point to the primacy of hearing in regard to seeing:

> The apostles could testify to the resurrection of Christ also by seeing, because they saw Christ alive after his resurrection with a sightful faith [oculata fide], when before they had known him as dead. But just as we come to the beatific vision through the hearing of faith, in the same way human beings came to the vision of the rising Christ through what they had first heard from the angels through hearing.[3]

Aquinas is suggesting here that, in all revelatory experiences, a hearing precedes the seeing—even in the original experiences of seeing related to the risen Jesus. The disciples hear the angels as heavenly messengers, or the women, or others of their number, before they see;[4] and, in the more general case, the hearing of faith is required if it is to lead to the beatific vision and the kinds of knowing that anticipate it.

There is another aspect of experience that resonates with the Johannine theology of the Word who became *flesh*. It is communicated in terms of seeing and touching (1 John 1-3), so that on occasion such modes of sensing predominate over the more traditional experience of hearing the Word of God.[5] But images of visibility and tangibility do not of themselves evoke the excess of God's self-giving or the self-surrendering receptivity of faith. They can slip toward an idolic representation or projection.[6] No one form of "sensing" is sufficient; hence the importance of the more comprehensive experience of "knowing" so as to include the seeing, touching, and hearing in the inter-subjectivity of communion with Christ in the Spirit (Jn 16:30; 1 John 5:20).

On the other hand, there is a more comprehensive contemplative sense of seeing, an "ocular" or sightful faith, *oculata fides*. We speak, as mentioned above, of "the light of faith". It is related to the illuminating guidance of the Spirit as, for instance, in traditional accounts of the gifts of Spirit: wisdom, understanding, counsel, fortitude, knowledge, piety and fear of the Lord (note that four of the customary seven gifts deal with some special form of illumination as we will treat below). While Paul is quite clear about himself as the last in the privileged series of "seers" of the risen Christ, he can still speak of "the God who has shone in our hearts to give the light of the knowledge of the glory of God on the face of Christ" (2 Cor 4:6). It would seem, then, that the visionary experience of the early witnesses assures and enlarges the contemplative experience of the community of those who believe.

The Appearances of the Risen Christ

What then was the role of the chosen eyewitnesses in the resurrection event?[7] While the presence of the risen Lord is the central factor in the Gospel narratives and the tradition that gave rise to them, the authority given to these various witnesses is a complex question. For example, Paul in 1 Corinthians 15 names Peter, clearly identified as *Cephas*, as heading the list of accredited witnesses at a very early stage. The puzzle with Paul's list of witnesses is that the women are not specifically named, given that they, especially Mary Magdalene, figure so largely in the later Gospel accounts (Mt 28:1-10; Mk 16:1-8; Lk 24:1-11; Jn 20:1-18). As the Gospels developed, the role of the women becomes more dominant in the tradition, and the concentration of Peter lessens—but then to be re-emphasised in John 21. One must defer to exegetical experts to un-ravel this complexity.[8] But no comprehensively ordered historical ac-count is possible. Byrne has already reminded us of an essential prin-ciple of interpretation in this matter: "But the Gospels are not primarily biographies. From beginning to end they are replete with the deeper awareness of Jesus' identity, status and function that came to the dis-ciples along with faith in the resurrection. We never meet in the Gospels the purely 'pre-resurrection' Jesus".[9]

In the Gospel of Mark, the women are instructed to report to Peter: "But go tell his disciples and Peter that he is going ahead of you to Galilee" (Mk 16:7). The Galilee-connection is especially poignant, given that it was the scene of Peter's previous dubious leadership (cf. Mk 8:31; 9:31; 10:34; 14:28). Further, despite the primacy of Peter in Matthew and John, his role as witness to the resurrection is not singled out in any way—but rather upstaged by Mary Magdalene and the Beloved Dis-ciple. On the other hand, the Johannine community's eventual accep-tance of Peter's special role is vividly expressed at the end of the Gospel (Jn 21:1-25). It can be taken as the fulfilment of the promise made in Mark 16:7. Luke's account, however, proves rather complex and elusive concerning Jesus' appearance to Peter. Nonetheless, he had prayed for Peter specifically (Lk 22:31-32), even though this is followed by Peter's triple denial (Lk 22:54-62). Still, the Emmaus disciples have their expe-rience confirmed, for "the Lord has risen indeed and has appeared to Simon" (Lk 24:34). The element of the tradition that was expressed in John 21 is reclaimed by Luke, who inserts it into an earlier part of the narrative of the Galilean episode described in Lk 5:1-11. This throws some light on the primacy of Cephas in Paul's list (1 Cor 15:5-9).

As mentioned above, the tradition of women's witness waxed rather than waned in the early decades of Christian existence. Mary Magdalene is depicted as the prime witness (Jn 20:1-18; Mt 28:1-10; Mk 16:9-11). How this cast of "Marian" characters relies on the special role of Mary, the mother of Jesus, as described in both Luke (Lk 2:19, 51) and John (Jn 19:26-27) is a fascinating question, even if beyond our present scope—save to observe that in the event of this new birth the role of women resonates strongly with feminine symbolism (cf. Rev 12). Aquinas calls on a tradition that sees the witness of women as reversing the role of Eve tempting Adam, to become the bearers of the message of life. Their greater love for Christ, given the sorry performance of the male disciples, made them the first to see the risen Jesus.[10] As we shall see below, there are important epistemological considerations of a more "feminist" experience of knowing, as Sarah Coakley has noted.[11] A flatly objective, rationalist, "masculine" mode of cognition is challenged at this point to appreciate a more participative, subjectively-engaged and affectively charged, interpersonal mode of knowing or "seeing", and its relevance to the matters we are considering.[12]

But to make a general remark: the Petrine (or "masculine") and Marian (or "feminine") modes of witness are different aspects of the resurrection effect in the history of faith. The Petrine dimension comes out in the institutional form of the Church in history, and its experience of conflict, repentance and conversion. The Marian dimension suggests more the experience of new birth and transformation: it is expressed in the sponsal and maternal receptivity of the Church, and is evocatively affirmed, for instance, in the Catholic dogma of Mary's Assumption into heaven.

As to the "appearances" of the risen Jesus, they cannot be adequately described as apparitions or visions of a purely subjectivist character. They bear the stamp of an encounter in which the subjectivity of the witnesses is laid bare, and their perceptions transformed.[13] There is a further intriguing point. The appearances of the risen Lord do not bear directly on the fate of the disciples who were the recipients of such disclosures. For instance, they are not assured that they too will rise. It is true that the event of the appearances will overflow with such an implication, as the Pauline logic in 1 Corinthians 15 attests. Certainly, Jesus appeared to these disciples in "a different form" (Mk 16:12; Lk 24:4; Jn 20:15; 21:4). Yet there is an objective austerity about these accounts which bear no resemblance to the startling transfiguration as recounted in the Gospels (Mt 17:1-9; Mk 9:2-10; Lk 9:28-36—and probably Jn 12:27-30). Though at the tomb, the angels "shine", as an indication of the hidden glory of the risen One, this occurs only when Jesus is not there! Even though his appearances lead the disciples to an eventual joyous conviction and a sense of missionary responsibility, the "many proofs" (Acts 1:3) do not suggest otherwise striking phenomena. Indeed, the appearances are so discrete in this respect that the disciples are still faced with some rather large questions: "Lord, is it at this time that you will restore the kingdom to Israel?" (Acts 1:16). The full evidence of what has occurred is reserved for the future.

The discrete objectivity of the resurrection narratives in the Gospels contrasts with the more elaborate hymnic depictions of Christ as found, say, in the Captivity Epistles and in the Book of Revelation.[14] Yet any such elaboration would be meaningless unless set within the eschatological horizon opening out from the resurrection itself. For the risen One is never an object to be grasped within the projections and figures of the passing world. The angelic figures, associated with the discovery of the empty tomb, are designed to evoke the cosmic significance and hidden glory of the resurrection event in its uniqueness. These angelic witnesses ask, "Why do you look for the living among the dead? He is not here, but has risen" (Lk 24:5). Similarly, at the end of the economy of privileged seeing, they ask, "Why do you stand looking up to heaven?" (Acts 1:11). Jesus comes, goes, and will return again, in a timing and condition that elude all human perspectives.

There is another striking feature. These self-disclosures of "the resurrection and the life" (Jn 11:25) are not only directed to chosen witnesses, but are also Jesus' self-interpretation in the light of the whole revelatory experience of Israel in the past and of the Church in the future. Hans Frei remarks on the various accounts of the appearances of the risen Lord, "What the accounts are saying, in effect, is that the being and identity of Jesus in the resurrection are such that his non-resurrection is inconceivable".[15] Jesus disclosed himself as the living interpreter of the whole trajectory of his life, communicating how the witness of scriptures converge in him (Lk 24:26; Jn 2:22; 12:16). The early traditional phrase, "in accordance with the scriptures", thus takes on its deepest meaning. Yet Jesus' coming looks beyond itself—to his sending the Spirit and to the mission of the disciples to whom he appeared.

While reflection on the resurrection appearances understandably highlights the "seeing" on the part of the various disciples, what is often passed over in the character of such experiences is the experience of "being seen through" by him who sees into the heart. We have already mentioned above the Johannine aspect of Jesus "seeing" the disciples after "the little while" of his passion and crucifixion (Jn 16:22). The Book of Revelation takes this aspect of Christian experience further. The visibility of faith is that of being seen through by the One who sees with "eyes like a flame of fire" (Rev 1:14; 2:18). Jesus repeatedly declares, "I know your works"—or "your affliction and your poverty", or "where you live" (Rev 2:2, 9, 12, 19; 3:1, 8, 15). This experience is common to all the Gospels (e.g., Lk 9:47; 11:17), and is implicit in the resurrection appearances. Before the disciples see Jesus, he sees them. And from this experience of being seen through and faced with him, they are empowered as witnesses.[16] Von Balthasar cites Bornkamm to good effect:

The people with whom he speaks, and with whom he has anything to do, are there in undisguised reality. They all bring something with them into their encounter with him; the righteous bring their righteousness, the scribes the weight of their learning and arguments, the tax collectors and sinners their guilt, those who seek help their sickness, the demoniacs the fetters of their possession, and the poor the burden of their poverty. All this is not wiped out and a matter of indifference: but in this encounter, it no longer counts. For in this encounter, each one is required to leave what he was before. In all the narratives about Jesus, the moment occurs when people have to stand forth as the people they really are.[17]

Not only does all this variety of human beings stand before Christ in what they already "really are", but also in what they are called to be. The resurrection is, therefore, a constitutive event for Christian identity. The transparency of the disciples to the gaze of Jesus is a moment of conversion—especially at the point where faith had been lacking, had waned or even died. Without this personal sense of being "seen through", the witness of others will never be enough, as the disciples found in the resistance of Thomas to their testimony (Jn 20:24-29). The women met with similar resistance in their reports to the apostles (Lk 24:11). The Gospel narratives, formed as they are in the light of Easter, recall a humbling fact. Before the resurrection, the earliest disciples had missed the point, and had been consistently slow to understand (Lk 9:45; Jn 2:22; 12:16; 13:7; 16:4). Although in one sense they had heard the Word, they still needed to be "faced" by Christ in his risen vitality. Even if the economy of privileged witnesses "seeing" the risen Christ comes to an end, he is ever present in the Spirit as the one who sees into the hearts of all. Paul is eloquent on the passage from blindness to the new form of "seeing" that occurs in "the light of the gospel of the glory of Christ, who is the image of God" (2 Cor 4:4). The creator of light has "shone in our hearts, to give the light of the knowledge of the glory of God in the face of Christ" (2 Cor 4:6).[18]

The "seeing", as well as the sense of "being seen through", are clearly aspects of a many-sided experience. Although the most direct form of expression is "seeing",[19] a larger sensory field of experience is implied. For example, there is the disciples' experience of hearing Jesus speaking (Mt 28:9, 18-20; Lk 24; Ac 1:4-8), walking with them (Lk 24:13-28), preceding them to Galilee (Mt 28:16), and of ascending out of sight (Lk 24:50; Acts 1:9). There are instances of meals, in which he both eats and gives food (Lk 24; Jn 21:13; Acts 1:4; 10:41), as well as many other signs (Jn 20:30), including gestures of blessing (Lk 24:50), his breathing upon the disciples and their touching him (Mt 28:9; Lk 24:39; Jn 20:17, 27). In the case of Thomas and Paul, faith in any ordinary sense was not presupposed. Yet they too became part of the limited circle of those whose experience was expressed in visual terms: "God raised him up on the third day and allowed him to appear, not to all the people, but to us who were chosen by God as witnesses, and who ate and drank with him after he rose from the dead" (Acts 10:39-40).[20]

Appreciated in this light, the appearances can be understood as educative within the more ultimate domain of the gift of the Spirit. Jesus comes only to bid farewell, but in such a way as to lead to his deeper mode of presence within history itself (Mt 28:20; Jn 14:18ff.). Through this continuing presence, history is exposed to the life-giving love that has been revealed, and to the witness of the communal faith of the Church. It transforms both the presumed objectivity of the world, and the enclosed subjectivity of those to whom it is given.[21]

The Economy of Seeing: An End and a Beginning

The experience of privileged eyewitnesses is, then, deeply formative of the tradition of faith in which "seeing" (Jn 14:19; 1 John 1:1-3), "non-seeing" (Jn 20:29) and only obscure seeing (1 Cor 13:12) are irreducible aspects. Yet that initial seeing on the part of the eyewitnesses is a determining element in later seeing and non-seeing of the Church. Paul's "last of all" seeing bridges the gap between the original visionary experience and the contemplative vision of faith in later ages.

All this suggests that both the visibility and invisibility inherent in the New Testament expression of faith are not so much contraries, but converging perspectives. They point beyond themselves to a resolution on another plane. Both perspectives open to the self-giving presence of the risen Jesus in the life of faith. He gives himself to his followers through the witness of the Spirit (Jn 14:25; 16:13-15), through the witness of others (Jn 17:23; 20:21), through the word of scripture,[22] and through the sacraments of water and blood (Jn 19:34; 1 John 5:8). Phases of seeing, non-seeing and seeing again interweave within the experience of the "little whiles" that mark the history of faith (cf. Jn 16:16-23).[23]

On the one hand, when the crucified and risen One departs and a divine "cloud took him out of their sight" (Acts 1:9), the previous time of a particular "seeing" is over. Jesus is no longer visible to human eyes, either in the mode of his earthly life, or in the privileged economy of seeing that followed on his resurrection. His Ascension metaphorically depicts the accomplishment of his earthly mission through his return to the Father. On the other hand, he is now to be found in another field of perception formed by the witness of the Spirit and the recollection of the whole Christ-event it inspires. The perception of faith brings its own kind of vision and wisdom. It enables faith to contemplate Christ, not in his human form within the created world, but as the one in whom all creation finds its coherence, destiny and fulfilment (Col 1:15-20; Eph 4:10). Christ is risen, but not so as to be a visible object within the world. It is more a matter of the world and its history being taken up in the risen Christ in an eschatological anticipation of what is to come. Paul's words to the Colossians awaken Christian experience to its full proportions:

> So if you have been raised with Christ, seek the things that are above, where Christ is seated at the right hand of God. Set your minds on the things that are above, not on things that are on the earth, for you have died, and your life is hidden with Christ in God. When Christ who is your life is revealed, then you also will be revealed with him in glory (Col 3:1-4).

There is, then, a "seeking" for what is not yet possessed, and the "hidden" quality of what is not yet revealed. This "not yet" suggests a tension between what is "above" and the mundane reality "of earth". Christian consciousness ("your minds") is elevated to what is above, and orientated to what is yet to be revealed. This uplifting and future-directed experience affects the values that faith lives by, and reaches into the deepest sense of identity—"the new self, which is being renewed in knowledge according to the image of its creator" (Col 3:10), to be clothed with "compassion, kindness, humility, meekness and patience" (Col 3:12), in a "love that binds everything together" (Col 3:14). What is implied is a distinctive form of wisdom born of being indwelt by the "word of Christ" (Col 3:16).

Yet faith's vision of Christ must accept that the economy of privileged "seeing" is over. It has led into another kind of experience. In this phase, a privileged kind of seeing is not the leading experience. That is now best expressed as "hearing", and being possessed by the Spirit of what has been given in the baptismal washing and eucharistic eating and drinking. Nonetheless, there is still a visual dimension. Knowledge, wisdom and insight find their object in sacramental signs and in the words of scripture, through the mystical dimension of Christian consciousness, and in the (discomforting) visibility of our neighbour (1 John 4:20). As hearing and tasting of the Word of God predominate in the sensory field of faith, there is too a "breathing" of the "Breath of Life", and an inhalation of its fragrance.[24] In fact, Aquinas ascribes the most intimate form of experience to taste:

> One experiences a thing by means of sense, but the experience of a thing present differs from the experience of something absent. One experiences a distant reality by sight, smell, and hearing. Whereas one experiences a present reality by touch and taste. Still, while touch attains this present reality in an extrinsic way, taste attains what is present in an interior way. Now God is neither distant from us nor outside us . . . and so the experience of the divine goodness is called tasting.[25]

The sensory field of Easter faith is never adequately expressed in the five senses of our physical organism. Still, they provide a rich fund of analogical expressions in order to evoke the experience of contact and assurance embedded in a love-guided knowledge that reaches beyond the capacities of sight: "Although you have not seen him, you love him; and even though you do not see him now, you believe in him and rejoice with an indescribable and glorious joy, for you are receiving the outcome of your faith, the salvation of your souls" (1 Pet 1:8-9).

The Other Paraclete

All this would all be very precarious if the memory of Jesus and his words were to be subject to the erosion of history. Hence the importance of the Paraclete. "The Paraclete, the Holy Spirit, whom the Father will send in my name, will teach you everything, and remind you of everything I have said to you" (Jn 14:25). The resurrection effect would wane and fade without its principal witness and agent (Rom 8:9; 2 Cor 3:18). We have already remarked that the gift of the Spirit has been interpreted by some as an expression of the resurrection itself: the cause of Jesus lives on in the minds of his disciples, without having to rely on the dubious historicity of either his empty tomb or his appearances to chosen witnesses. The phenomenon of the resurrection does not permit such a separation. The productive novelty of the event is not found merely in a change of heart in the disciples of Jesus, but in a change that has occurred in Jesus himself. He is no longer dead and buried, but generated to new life in the power of the Spirit, given back to the disciples as the exemplar and source of a transformed existence. Through the Spirit the Father has eternally engendered the Son, and now generates him into the fullness of sonship in time and creation. It is this Spirit of his risen sonship that Christ breathes into his followers, to establish them in intimacy with the Father and as a pledge of their resurrection to the fullness of life. Thus, the Spirit is the milieu or eschatological atmosphere, as it were, in which Christians are united to Christ and to an ever deeper knowledge of him.

The New Testament witnesses to an experience of a transformed consciousness, as the Spirit of the risen One saturates all dimensions of Christian experience: ". . . no one comprehends what is truly God's except the Spirit of God. Now we have received not the spirit of the world, but the Spirit that is from God, so that we may understand the gifts that are bestowed on us by God" (1 Cor 2:9-10). A new field of communication results: "And we speak of these things in words not taught by human wisdom but taught by the Spirit, interpreting spiritual things to those who are spiritual" (1 Cor 2:9-13). Faced with these and similar texts (e.g., 1 John 2:27), theology is always somewhat at a loss. Something intrinsically elusive to any kind of rational mastery is at stake.

There is a gifted excess, in the gift itself, in the mode of its giving, and in the way it is received. The difficulty lies in adequately naming the way in which the Spirit of Christ affects the intentionality of faith. A certain affective and cognitive "feel", "instinct" or "sympathy" is implied in the effusive character of the gift.[26] Von Balthasar interprets this experience in relation to the activity of "spiritual senses", as found with different emphases in the writings of Origen, Augustine, Bonaventure, and Ignatius of Loyola.[27] Augustine gives arresting expression to this spiritual sensuousness in a passage from his *Confessions*:

> But what am I loving when I love you? Not beauty of body nor transient grace, not this fair light which is now so friendly to my eyes, not melodious song in all its lovely harmonies, not the sweet fragrance of flowers or ointments or spices, not manna or honey, not limbs that draw me to carnal embrace: none of these do I love when I love my God. And yet I do love a kind of light, a kind of voice, a certain fragrance, a food and an embrace, when I love my God: a light, voice, fragrance, food and embrace for my inmost self, where something limited to no place shines into my mind, where something not snatched away by passing time sings for me, where something no breath blows away yields to me its scent, where there is savor undiminished by famished eating, and where I am clasped in a union from which no satiety can tear me away. This is what I love when I love my God.[28]

Von Balthasar goes on to elaborate the manifold senses of faith by mining especially the works of Barth, Guardini, Siewerth, and Claudel. The knowledge of faith is most profoundly a *con-naissance*, "being born with" the one who is the firstborn from the dead into the fullness of life. Receptivity to this gift brings its own new perceptions. Here, in line with his aesthetic method, von Balthasar makes a general remark that harmonises deeply with the phenomenonological approach we have been commending:

> The human person sees truly when prepared to receive . . . what spontaneously offers itself: here the person seeing is first of all a becoming aware, a hearing, which then, step by step—penetrates the sphere of understanding.[29]

A receptive attentiveness leads to the play of sense, imagination, insight and judgment as progressive interiorisation of the phenomenon. This is a special feature of Johannine pedagogy, with its many stages, "leading the outside to the inside, from the inchoative to the perfect".[30]

In this context, a remark on the traditional "seven gifts of the Holy Spirit" is relevant. The theology of the gifts is usually tucked away in specialised soundings within the history of Christian mysticism. Take

Aquinas' theology on this topic. His treatment of the gifts of the Spirit suggests the special receptivity of Christian consciousness to the gift of God, and serves to work a healthy deconstruction of the conceptual idols erected by a one-dimensional rational mode of thinking.[31] This is an aspect of Aquinas' thought that von Balthasar especially praises.[32] Thomas' theology is explicitly related to the experience of the gift of grace as it saturates every aspect of the cognitive and conative life of faith. But this general consideration of the life of grace can be profitably refocused on the gift behind the gifts, namely the risen Christ himself, the incarnate form and revelation of such grace.

For Aquinas, the gifts of the Spirit are given to enable the graced subject to receive and act in a manner that is "beyond the human measure".[33] While the Christian phenomenon is given into the hardy world of objective and rational theological discourse, there is always a vertically given excess extending or even disrupting the horizons of reason alone. Intelligence must be receptive, waiting, as it were, on the gift from above, in order to know and to act in a way that respects the irruptive and transformative character of what has been given. This is not unlike the disposition of those who had followed Jesus to his death, and the transformation they experienced following his resurrection. Though Aquinas' treatment is more generalised at this point, it does suggest a God-given ability to yield to the initiative of God's self-giving.[34]

Presumed in the Thomist account is the recognition of a certain strain or dislocation inherent in responding to our God-given destiny. While there is a native aptitude for the pursuit of the good and the truth proportionate to our mode of present existence in the world, a "connatural" proportion to our "super-natural" destiny is lacking. We might add that this is more so when it comes to the irruptive manifestation of Christ risen from the dead. A necessary complement, therefore, to this "new creation" is found in the gifts of the Spirit attuning the mind and heart of the believer to the milieu in which faith must now live. Only through these gifts can the gift of life in the risen One be received and integrated into human existence by means of "an instinct and movement of the Holy Spirit".[35] If believers are not given a more lively, supple and receptive attunement to the Spirit's interior action, Thomas seems to fear that our sense of God will be annexed to—or seduced by—a limited rational mode of knowing and acting. In the terms we have been employing, this would mean that the "idolic" character of rationality has a tendency to edge out the receptivity and surrender required by the "iconic" character of revelation. More positively, the self-revealing God equips faith with a special instinct, enabling it to reach beyond a routine, rational pattern of activity.[36]

Thomas considers the sevenfold gifts of the Spirit following the traditional enumeration: wisdom, understanding, counsel, fortitude, knowledge, piety and fear of the Lord. Focused specifically on the resurrection event, these gifts suggest an instinct for new life in Christ, life to the full, a new creation. The psychological transformation in those who have received "the Word of life" (1 John 1:1) means a new identity, a new birth, manifested in a new level of spiritual activity and experience. This entails a special "taste" for the things of God through the gift *par excellence*, "wisdom"—*sapientia* (from *sapere*, "to taste").[37] It is at once a tasting and an attunement to the character of the self-giving mystery of love, a "feel for" the totality of the divine economy.[38] Christian consciousness operates in an intimate sense of filial relationship (*pietas*) with the God who has acted in glorifying his Son and in uniting us to him. The gift of *timor Domini* ("fear of the Lord") brings with it a radical poverty of spirit along with a reverent sensitivity to the way God has acted in raising the crucified Jesus.[39] On a more cognitive level, the Spirit-given gift of "understanding" (*intellectus*) would suggest a clear-eyed perception of the uniqueness of the resurrection event, protecting it from the images and projections that would work to distort its transcendent originality compared to other kinds of events or apprehensions.[40] The gift of *scientia* ("knowledge") likewise bears on the uniqueness of such an event, to save its universal significance from being lost in an empty and aimless contingency.[41] In the domain of moral action, the gift of *consilum* ("counsel") is the special Spirit-guided instinct for freedom responding to God's act in Christ: in the light of the resurrection, all ethical action is concretely affected with a new capacity for discernment. The hierarchy of values structuring any cultural world must have room for a love stronger than death, beyond the world of even ethical calculation.[42] Finally, "fortitude" is an experience of the Spirit manifest in resoluteness in living in the light of the risen Victim, despite the violence of a world intent on crucifying what stands in the way of its self-serving projects.[43] Far from destroying or compromising human liberty, the instinct of the Spirit of the gifts enlarges and completes it: "Spiritual persons are not only instructed by the Holy Spirit on what they should do, but also their hearts are moved by the Spirit".[44] Human liberty is at its height when it is receptive to the surprises of God.

In short, as the event of the resurrection disrupts the horizons of reason, the Spirit of Christ is manifested in a range of special gifts to inspire in the believer a receptivity to what is given from beyond the horizons of the reason-structured world. The gifts of the Spirit are thus one aspect of the resurrection effect as it affects faith when it "sees" and acts in the light of what has occurred.

From different perspectives, the "seeing" of faith possesses a holographic sense of the self-revelation of the risen One. It is not distracted into a collage of visual images drawn from mundane experience, for the focus is fixed in the living reality of the risen Christ himself.[45] The resurrection affects Christian experience in all its modes of seeing, hearing and touching of "what was from the beginning" (cf. 1 John 1:1-4). It results in something like the tact which Coleridge understood to be the special gift of the poet:

> He may not have it in logical coherence, in his Brain & Tongue; but he must have it by *Tact*: for all sounds and forms of Nature he must have the *ear* of a wild Arab listening in the silent Desert—the *eye* of a North American Indian tracing the footsteps of an Enemy upon the Leaves that strew the Forest; the *Touch* of a Blind Man feeling the face of a darling Child.[46]

We have been considering various perspectives of how the seeing and non-seeing of faith in Christ are related. All that has been said so far can be taken as a variant of the Johannine answer to these questions. Note, in the first place, the words of the risen Jesus to Thomas, who had just uttered his individual confession, "My Lord and my God!" (Jn 20:27). Jesus goes on to say, "Have you believed because you have seen me? Blessed are those who have not seen and yet have come to believe" (Jn 20:29). The "blessedness" concerned is related to the larger context of the "advantage" connected with his departure from the historical scene. It is found in the Advocate whom Jesus will send (Jn 16:7). The Holy Spirit "whom the Father will send in my name, will teach you everything and remind you of everything I have said to you" (Jn 14:26). The Paraclete will come as the crowning glory of Jesus' mission, to guide the disciples into an ever-fuller perception of the incarnate Word. This other "Advocate" will fill the void of invisibility that Jesus' absence will create. But this further gift is not just a remedy for his absence, nor merely a consolation for the grieving disciples. For Jesus will send the Paraclete as the promised fulfilment of his revelatory mission to them—and to the world to which they will be sent. Such will be the advantage that awaits them, not as a consolation, nor as a substitute, but as the fulfilment to which everything is moving, and despite the momentous conflicts and rejection that the disciples will suffer.

The conflicts occasioned by the Christian phenomenon given into the self-limited phenomena of mundane experience are indicators of the "saturating" evidences of the gift that has been given. This "other Paraclete", the "Spirit of truth", is the field of turbulence, breathing where it will (Jn 3:8), beneath the seemingly untroubled surface on which all forms of self-containment float. The Spirit of Jesus is a disturbing presence at the heart of idolic self-enclosure that resists seeing the event that has made "heaven opened" (Jn 1:51). The world refuses to be drawn beyond itself to the transcendent realm of the Father, and to follow "the way" of Jesus. For Jesus has "come as light into the world, so that everyone who believes in me should not remain in darkness" (Jn 12:46). A terminal conflict is envisaged: "all who do evil hate the light, and do not come to the light, so that their deeds might not be exposed" (Jn 3:20-21).[47]

Like Jesus himself, the other Paraclete will confront pretended judges and teachers with the truth about themselves (Jn 3:19; 5:22, 27, 30, 44-45; 8:16; 9:39). The radical cause of the world's self-enclosure will be made clear. The doers of evil will be shown to be doing their ". . . father's desires", the "murderer from the beginning" who is alien to the truth, a liar and the source of lies (Jn 8:44). The unholy generativity at work in the world will be identified as a web of violence and idolatrous untruth, in allergic reaction to the life-giving truth of the love offered it (Jn 3:16).

There is a second crucial consideration: "concerning righteousness". The Paraclete reveals the idolatrous self-righteousness of the world. Jesus has been condemned for blasphemy in breaking the Sabbath and calling God his Father (Jn 5:18). Consequently, he has been declared to be demonically possessed (Jn 8:48), and a sinner (Jn 9:24b). In their refusal to receive "the gift of God" (Jn 4:10), the "righteous" ones of this world have clung to a pretended justification in claiming to be the children of Abraham rather than receive the Son of the Father (Jn 8:39-59). In their refusal of the full gift of the truth as it has come in Jesus (Jn 1:17), their identity is limited to that of being the disciples of Moses (Jn 6:30-31; 9:28-29). They reckoned themselves to be obedient to the law,[48] rather than allowing the word of the One whose voice they have never heard, whose form they have never seen, abide in them (Jn 5:37-38). In the tiny world of their self-glorification, they would shut their own people out of the synagogues of Israel rather than welcome the glory that comes from God (Jn 12:43). The Father's house of many dwellings is closed to them.

Thirdly, there is the matter of "judgment". The world will bring about the death of Jesus through a quasi-judicial execution. But the coming of the Paraclete will not allow this verdict to remain. The cross will not be seen as a vindication of worldly justice, but, in its fullest paschal light, it will be revealed as the lifting up of Christ, the Son of Man, for the world's salvation (Jn 3:14; 8:28; 12:32-33). In that hour of glory, the true God will be revealed (Jn 11:4; 12:23; 13:31-33). In the world of darkness, the execution of Jesus appears as the triumph of the forces intent on removing him and on scattering his disciples. Yet the full luminous reality will result in gathering into one the scattered children of God (Jn 11:50, 52; 12:11, 19), as the Crucified draws all to himself (Jn 12:32). Far from being the infliction of divine punishment, or the triumph of the forces of evil, his death is disclosed as his return to the Father (Jn 13:1): the crucified One is now risen (Jn 20:17). Through the paschal event of Jesus being "lifted up", the heavens open to dimensions of peace and joy that the closed world cannot imagine.

As a result, the activity of the Spirit means the radical reversal of the history of the self-serving, murderous judgments of human glory. The age of sacred violence is over; for its "god", the ruler of this world, is already judged (Jn 16:11; cf. 14:30). Grim though this exposure may be, the action of the Paraclete will ensure that history continues to be the theatre in which the glory of God and the truth of Christ will be experienced. Exposed to the counter-action of the Paraclete, the world will nonetheless continue to find itself as the object of God's love (Jn 3:16).[49]

More positively, "When the Spirit of truth comes, he will guide you into all truth; for he will not speak on his own, but will speak whatever he hears, and he will declare to you the things that are to come" (Jn 16:13). The Spirit's activities, described as guiding, speaking, hearing and declaring, are explicitly related to Jesus: "He will glorify me, because he will take what is mine and declare it to you" (Jn 16:14). The christocentric character of the Spirit is reinforced in the First Letter of John: "we know that he [Jesus] abides in us, by the Spirit that he has given us" (1 John 3:24), so that "every spirit that confesses that Jesus Christ has come in the flesh is from God" (1 John 4:2). Moreover, the witness of the Spirit of truth is associated with the sacramental significance of "the water and the blood" (1 John 5:8). This is to say that the presently "unbearable" (Jn 16:12) fullness of revelation still comes to believers in every age. The witness of the Spirit gives an incarnational, sacramental and scriptural density to the salvific reality of the gift— even if it requires ongoing discernment in the world of rejection and conflict.[50]

As a result, the ongoing history of faith means neither a slow haemorrhaging of the original truth, nor a tranquil self-possession of its radiance. It is peace, certainly, but a peace that is ill-advised to lean on any mundane support. It is a joy, too, but not as arising from any approbation or acclaim on the part of the world. Indeed, though faith will have its own history as it advances to a fuller knowledge of the things that are to come, with a deeper penetration of the truth incarnate in the crucified and risen Christ, that history is not one of untroubled progress. It is inextricably interwoven into an exposure to a world all but convulsed by the Spirit's witness to the one it had condemned and executed.

It is necessary to separate the coming of Christ from the prior perceptions, desires or cultural systems that the Spirit comes to contest. The world may need Christ, but be shocked by the manner of his appearing. And yet there is an obvious sense in which it cannot allow itself to wait for him, nor to see in him the answer to its hopes. Even the disciples, insofar as they had imbibed the culture of their world, were inevitably surprised and shocked by the resurrection of the Crucified. He summons his followers into a radical form of self-dispossession. This will mean being drawn out of a world-conformed self to find an identity in the disturbingly other (Jn 12:24-25). With a distinctively revelatory emphasis, Jesus declares, "Amen, amen, I say to you, unless a grain of wheat falls into the earth and dies, it remains alone; but if it dies, it bears much fruit" (Jn 12:24). To behold the glory of the cross is to enter another realm. The barren isolation of a world refusing to be transformed will be reversed. The grain of wheat, sown in the mysterious ground of the Father's will, is a long way from the palm branches of worldly glory. To cling to a life cut off from the true form of life in the crucified and risen One is self-made solitude. But to stake all on the glory revealed on the cross will mean finding that the promise of eternal life with God will be kept.

The true disciple follows Jesus on his way to the Father. This means following him both in the depths of "falling" down into the earth, and into the heights of his being "lifted up" (Jn 12:26). Such followers will be honoured by the Father (12:26). The paternal life-giving mystery is thus presented as the ground into which the grain falls. In that ground, it sprouts with the energies and fruitfulness of abundant life. By rejecting the superficial glory of this world, believers, as they follow the way of the Son, receive the glory that only the Father can give (cf. Jn 9:22; 12:43; 16:2).

Conclusion

This chapter sought to address the visual character of the phenomenon of Christ's resurrection. We have to conclude that the resurrection effect results in such a saturation of human vision that any terms employed to express it are pretty much defeated. Still, this is a defeat that is not altogether dishonourable: it simply highlights both the transcendent and transformative character of God's self-revelation in the resurrection of the Crucified. We have indicated something of dialectical interplay that occurs in the experience of faith in the risen One. No synthesis is possible when trying to appreciate the seemingly conflicting aspects inherent in this experience: the "seeing" of the chosen witnesses as a result of the self-disclosures of Christ, and non-seeing and seeing—in other forms—of believers generally. We have kept the emphasis on the self-revelation of Christ and the gift of the Spirit of truth. We set this in the context of the interactions between seeing and being seen through, between seeing, hearing and sensing in other modes, between the light, receptivity and the darkness of faith. Complexities abound; but the focus remains: the resurrection effect reaches into every aspect of the believers' experience, and makes each one, according to the gift he or she has received, a witness to what has been given from beyond this world. The words of the poet are apposite:

> . . . I looked
> at him, not with the eye
> only, but with the whole
> of my being, overflowing with
> him as a chalice would
> with the sea . . .[51]

CHAPTER 7

Subjectivity, Objectivity and the Resurrection

In this shorter chapter of our exploration of the resurrection effect, we pause over the polarity of subjective and objective.[1] A line cannot be simply drawn between the objectivity of the resurrection appearances and the subjectivity of the disciples[2] involved. To put the matter most directly, in the event of the resurrection something and someone was disclosed to the disciples, not nothing and not no one. The passive form of the Greek verb, *ôphthē*, "was seen", suggests that there is something for the seer to see, something given and disclosed.[3] On the other hand, nothing is seen without a seer. But there is the further point: the risen Jesus is seen in such a way as to elect and empower special witnesses in the economy of his divinely-given mission. Though what was seen was not seen by everyone, anyone, in principle, could once have interrogated the witnesses on what they had seen (cf. 1 Cor 15:3-9).

Let us look a little more closely at the endemic problem of distinguishing and uniting these polarities in relation to the resurrection. For our present purposes, I approach the matter under the following headings:

1. *The Polarities of Subject and Object*
2. *The Complexity of Experience*
3. *Five Assumptions Questioned*
4. *The Saturation of the Phenomenon*
5. *Conclusion: The Play of Polarities*

The Polarities of Subject and Object

If we are to respect all the facets of what took place, it is impossible to avoid shuttling between the objective and subjective polarities of what the chosen disciples witnessed to. Yet there is no question of a symmetrical correlation in accord with some predetermined form, as might be attempted by appealing to the fragmented totalities of a reductive subjectivism, on the one hand, or an objectivism that ignores receptivity to the matters in question, on the other. There is no facile symmetry: the objectivity of the divinely enacted event is not relatable to a kind of expectant subjectivity on the part of those to whom it is disclosed. Despite Jesus' efforts to instruct his followers as to the true nature of the Reign of God, they evidently took a long time in getting the point (Acts 1:6). In the end, it is only the horizon of the reign of God that remained for them, bearing its eventual fruit in the resurrection of Jesus himself. Their subjectivity anticipated nothing like what happened, and yet the resurrection event called into existence a new intentional consciousness. And once this transformed subjectivity is constituted through what must have been an extremely surprising and disorientating experience, it could proceed to explore the objective dimensions of the reality concerned, in line with the Lonerganian axiom, "genuine objectivity is the fruit of authentic subjectivity".[4] When the resurrection is the basic datum, or better, *donum*, there is a new experience to name and understand, a new meaning to elaborate and explore, a new truth to affirm, new values to live, and a new reality to communicate. The phenomenon of the resurrection brims over into every dimension of meaning: cognitively, it is the God-wrought event in the light of which all else is interpreted—the cross, the Kingdom of God, and the universe of God's creation. Constitutively, it informs Christian consciousness with a new sense of identity, be it described as participating in the divine life, as being indwelt by the Spirit, or being a member of the body of Christ. Communicatively, it brings the community of the Church into existence, celebrating and living from what has occurred. Effectively, it inspires the authenticity of Christian living. It inspires a morality unconstrained by the violent and vengeful proclivities of all cultures and societies to witness to all nations of the unbounded salvific will of God. Naming, exploring and applying the meaning of the resurrection is the ongoing business of theology in all its forms—biblical, fundamental, systematic, moral and pastoral.

The Complexity of Experience

Let us now attend to some of the complexities involved in the use of the subjective-objective polarity. When approaching the focal experience of Christian faith in the risen Christ, discussions tend to fall immediately into considerations of subjectivity on the part of the early witnesses (and those who would rely on their testimony), and the objectivity of the event—the action of God in raising the crucified Jesus. The polarity in this regard is already determined, permitting no crossing from one to the other. The terms of debate are, as a result, already laid out. For instance, the appearances of the risen Jesus are so objective that anyone there would witness them. Or, not infrequently in the modern discussion, the resurrection is simply a symbol for the dramatic change that occurred in the disciples. It is regarded as psychologically explicable in any number of psychological ways, and so indifferent to anything that actually happened to Jesus himself. The resurrection is merely a psychological event. When the tortured body of Jesus is left dead and buried in the tomb, his resurrection must be all in the mind of his disciples.

A kind of mental myth is constructed. It may prove useful for polemical purposes, but it remains strangely inapplicable to any familiar experience. We might question, for example, whether the beauty of a Mozart symphony is an objective or subjective experience. Is beauty only in the eye of the beholder or in the ear of the listener? Is it possible, for instance, that the kind of objectivity which the classic musical tradition associates with the genius of Mozart can be appreciated only by those who come to a discerning appreciation of music and its possibilities, whose ears and hands are trained through a long tradition of musical discernment? Furthermore, is not the recognition of the Mozart symphony in its normative classical status the reason why so many generations have put so much of their time into trying to appreciate it? If that is the case, the objective work of art is a catalyst for an ever renewed subjectivity.

Something similar might be said about Shakespeare's *Hamlet* or *King Lear*. Exposing a group of children, say, to either kind of classical masterpiece without adequate preparation would risk the unfortunate and culturally destructive outcome of having the symphony dismissed as mere noise, or the play regarded as an unintelligible jumble of exotic verbiage, with the interest reduced, say, to the ghost scenes or the bloody duel at the conclusion. Wise educators will point to the need of leading the young from a point of ignorance or neutrality or incapacity through exercises designed to broaden their horizons, to develop a sensitivity that would allow them to participate in the classic events of the cultural tradition; and even to lead them, at least in some cases, to some form of appropriate performance. The postmodern critique of classical forms may well object that there are other forms of music and drama that deserve attention. But here, too, preparation is needed; otherwise, the youthful generosity behind an invitation to accompany grandparents to a rock concert might lead to confusion! Any appreciation of art would seem to rely on a tradition of prior witnesses—good critics, for instance. Because of a refined discernment, the fruit of long years of personal and aesthetic development, these critics become authorities on the artistic work in question. In that capacity, they may invite new generations to participate in the subjectivity of their taste and appreciation. In regard to the tradition of Christian faith and its focal mystery, the task of catechesis, mystagogy and theology is not unlike the role of the critic in the world of art.

On the objective side, there is that elusive wager expressed in the phrase, "the test of time". History is always moving on. Yet, there would be a sense of impending cultural self-mutilation if in any era the music of

Mozart were dismissed as cacophony, or if the plays of Shakespeare were regarded as the unintelligible posturing of premodern human beings. The indefinable impact of works of art themselves and a tradition of appreciative witnesses keep alive for others the possibility of discovering something to be disclosed and experienced in its transformative effect. Again, we find an analogy for the resurrection effect in the life of the Church. The ministries of Word and sacrament, the witness of believers through the ages, all face the "test of time" in an even more radical sense—as time and all the unpredictable dramas of history test faith; while faith, in its wisdom and hope, contests any sense of time as a succession of meaningless moments on the way to nowhere.

The object-subject polarity discernible in the world of art is akin to the experience of love itself. In anyone's dedication to a beloved other, what is objective and what is subjective in such an experience? The more Jack embarks on the life-determining commitment of love for Jill, the more Jill is recognised in the objectivity of her personal uniqueness. Eyebrows might arch from a long experience of the vanity of romantic attachments and infatuations, and the peculiar tragedies inherent in this domain of life. Yet there is a truth here: the only way to know the other is through love, just as the attractiveness of the beloved other can bring about such a transformation in the life of the lover so as to "mean the world" to him or her. Without this recognition, human relationships would be corroded and collapse into a manipulative cynicism: the other would be only a function of the closed, immutable, all-consuming ego. Against the prejudice of those who have been hurt and disappointed in love, there is the witness of those who have found that love, realised only in self-giving and commitment, is the most illuminating and enduring reality in the course of life. Here, again we find the resurrection effect, in the imperative of faith to be ever disturbed in its subjectivity by the love of God and neighbour.

These remarks on the complexity of experience and of language dealing with subject and object, both in general and in regard to the resurrection of Jesus, have one purpose: to undermine any assumptions that the subjective and objective are mutually exclusive. To put it another way, these two poles of experience are not incompatible. The greater the subjective engagement does not mean the less there is of the objective reality that calls it forth. Nor does it mean that the greater and more overwhelming the objectivity of the reality—person or event—that the less there is of a subjective response to it. Paradoxically, these two polarities of experience are, in fact, not poles apart. It is a denial of experience to assume that there is no crossing from the one to the other, or any possibility of relating the two. An objectivity that owes nothing to subjectivity, or a subjectivity necessarily undermining the objectivity of what is given in its arresting otherness, be it an event, a person or a work of art, are both caricatures. The stricken look on the face of a bag-lady on the corner may call me to a conversion in my social conscience. And that change in my social conscience inspires in me a more compassionate recognition of the poor whom I have hitherto ignored. Moreover, the witness of the notably compassionate people who hunger and thirst for justice on behalf of the poor and forgotten powerfully affects our routine indifference by calling forth greater efforts to make the world more hospitable to those whom society has marginalised. The polarity of subject and object, if grounded in personal experience and open to the testimony of others, is not a dichotomy: subject and object, though they may be distinguished, cannot be separated.

Five Assumptions Questioned

Since the language of subjectivity and objectivity is pertinent to the Christian experience of the risen Jesus—on the part of the privileged witnesses, and the community formed by a tradition of faith which accepts such testimony—let us look at this polarity more fully. Five assumptions must be questioned:

First, we need reject the assumption that *we already know in a particular context what the subject and object mean*. What these polarities might mean is determined by the field of experience, the dimensions of its meaning and the values that motivate it. That field of significance, be it in art, love for the other, moral responsibility or religious faith, provides the particular contexts in which a discriminating employment of the subjective-objective polarity comes into play, each relying on a formative tradition animated by its respective witnesses. Here a more deft phenomenological approach is required. An all-significant event must be allowed to present itself on its own terms. It is does not come "prepackaged", wrapped in notions of what the subject is capable of, or of what is objectively possible in the ontological domain. While the world of routine communication employs symbolic or verbal signs to refer to the phenomenon of the resurrection—and so name Christ as the risen One, and Peter, Paul or Mary Magdalene as those who "saw"—it is not as though the event or the privileged experience of those so named are automatically conjured up as presently available realities. Our signifying activity cannot endlessly repeat and represent past historical events or persons. What is most obvious is that this past complex event has left a trace or effect in our history which retires into its own uniqueness even as it is invoked. It occurs as a summons to wager oneself on the truth of what has been revealed, to be judged by it, to enter into its field of communication, to receive its witnesses, even without being able to "signify" or ever represent it fully. History as a consequence is an endless hermeneutic of the excess that defies objectification.

The peculiar nature of this hermeneutic for Christian faith is instanced in a number of ways. A certain number of Christian symbols are cel-

ebrated as "sacraments"—*efficax gratiae*, "as communicating the original gift". The sacred texts of Christian faith are recognised in a canon of
scripture, to be accepted as the inspired Word of God. Its original witnesses form the apostolic tradition, and its present and past saints, martyrs, mystics, doctors and artists enrich the tradition of faith and expand its subjectivity. All these suggest an excess of significance to
challenge the community of faith in every stage of its historical development.

Second, there is the assumption which pretends that *the polarities of
subject and object are mutually exclusive and set one against the other.*
To repeat Lonergan's axiom: genuine objectivity is the fruit of authentic
subjectivity. The more I seek to be fully attentive to what is given, the
more vigorously I try to understand what has been disclosed, the more I
weigh the evidence in order to arrive at a judgment regarding the objective truth of what has been revealed, the more I try to respond to the
implications of what is so given, the more genuine the objective grasp of
the reality in question. There is the other side to this: the more communicative and transformative the event or reality, the more it has the capacity to involve those it affects, and to draw them into its special field
of evidence. This is of clear importance when discussing the resurrection, the appearances of Jesus and the witnesses involved. Though, in
this case, we are dealing with a uniquely transcendent event, it does not
abolish subjective and objective polarities, or place them in a situation
of some kind of psychological or ontological rivalry. The subjectivity of
faith must still attend to what it experienced and go on to ask what,
who and why, when confronted with what is luminously and radiantly
given beyond all subjective capacities or expectations.

This is not to deny that that there is a self-enclosed subjectivity that
pretends to restrict reality to the ambit of its own fears, needs, imagination or ideology. Nor, for that matter, do we intend to deny that there is,
so to speak, an imperious objectivity in actions or events that crush,
disable or belittle those affected by them. But the phenomenon of the
resurrection is not so, either in its effects or in the witnesses it calls
forth. Hence, it is better not to play off subjectivity and objectivity, as
though the more of one, the less of the other, but to locate both polarities in the field of communication and participation proper to this unique
divinely-wrought event. All this suggests an exchange in which the objectivity of the event enhances the subjectivity of those who witness it
and of those who will profit from such testimony. Conversely, the transformed subjectivity of those who have experienced the self-disclosure of
the risen One, and who now know themselves caught up in his risen life,
makes them key witnesses to the world-transcending objectivity of what
has taken place.

Third, we reject as unwarranted the assumption that *the subject-object distinction can be univocally applied in all circumstances.* There is

what we might call the objectivity of experience, in terms of what is immediately given. This empirical component is only one feature of the objectivity of full knowledge. In a critically-established form of objectivity, the given experience is (eventually) located in a meaningful context, its truth is assessed, and an appropriate moral response may follow. That, in turn, affects the character of the witness it engenders.

There is a further kind of objectivity which affects both the fundamentally empirical and the fully formed critical forms of objectivity. We might call it the objectivity of interpersonal communication. It is not neatly subsumed under objectivity of either an empirical or critical kind. There are three special aspects to be noted in an interpersonal encounter: First, what is immediately given has the character of personal self-giving, or "givingness", if you will. Secondly, rather than calling forth a primarily critical or purely intellectual evaluation of the other so experienced, the imperative is more like a summons or call emanating from, and for, this other who is so given. Thirdly, rather than terminating solely in a particular objective judgment or moral decision, it inspires an unreserved commitment, realised in self-surrender, fidelity and belief. Reverting to the first-person mode of expression, it can be stated thus: my experience of being loved by another, or of loving the other, leads me to an ongoing, open-ended way of experience in which the other is allowed to mean the world to me. The person-to-person relationship is the appropriate site in which the meaning and value of the other comes to light.

Yet how much an interpersonal context is the basic determinant of empirical and critical objectivity would be a matter of endless discussion. For example, the love of a parent is the formative experience shaping the child's basic experience and interpretation of the world. The love of spouse, children, friends and colleagues inserts one in a particular tradition of feeling for the world. It intensifies certain ranges of meaning and emphasises some values over others. An inspired teacher is likewise profoundly formative of one's taste and discrimination, at least in certain areas of life and learning. The face of the poor and the suffering may call me out of myself into a lifetime of compassionate commitment.

This is to say that there is one level of self-transcendence implied in being attentive to the data, to the given, on the empirical level. There is the further self-transcendence instanced in exploring, questioning, locating what is experienced in the world of meaning. There is the decisive self-transcendence of the judgment which moves beyond impressions or ideas to the reasonably affirmed fact or probability. In all this, I go beyond myself, not simply to interpret the world, but to shape it, in a responsibility deriving from the objectivity of my knowledge. Decision is based on judgment; and judgment is based on facts. As this experience is assimilated into personal consciousness, as its meaning enlarges one's capacity to understand the whole of reality, as its truth extends to the whole world, as its values include the whole human race and the universe itself, witnesses emerge who will form and enrich the tradition in which the experience, understanding, judgment and responsibility of later generations will occur.

All this is put on a new footing in an interpersonal context. If the experience is in fact that of the self-giving of the other or the self-disclosure of the other, a more radical form of self-transcendence emerges in the encounter and commitment that follow. A new and transformed self comes into being in the light of the self-communicating other; deep calls unto deep; existence is now radical co-existence, as being by, from and for the other. The most objective world-determining fact is, in this way, profoundly inter-subjective.

Applications of the subject-object polarity must, therefore, share an analogous character. The more singular the object or event, the more transformative and communicative is its import, and the more distinctive its witnesses. And the more "excessive" this singularity, the more flexibly the language of subject and object must be employed. A chair in one's room, a tumour in one's body, a fellow driver on the road, a loved friend or spouse or child, God, the risen Jesus, or his presence in the Eucharist, represent a range of different "objects". Each of these entails its own kind of relationship to the subject who affirms them or is affected by them. I might look out on the world from the undisturbed comfort of sitting in a favourite chair. I may be rather more apprehensive over an impending medical report in the case of the tumour. I would find routine vigilance appropriate in regard to other drivers on the road. I might relate in an elementally enjoyable way to friends and family. Or, I might feel awe in the face of infinite mystery, and feel drawn to wager all on the truth of faith, and to celebrate its liturgy with reverence. For its part, the event of the resurrection is a phenomenon which, to use Marion's metaphor, "saturates" a whole field of communication between God and Christ, between Christ and the chosen witnesses, and between Christ, the apostolic witnesses and the whole Church. In that field of brimming communication, different determinations of objectivity and subjectivity are inevitable in the light of the overwhelming objectivity of the divine action, and the initiative of the divine self-giving involved. Once there is evidence of an initiative and a self-giving on the part of the other subject, let alone on the part of the divine Other, all clearly determined categories of subject and object are "saturated" in a field of inter-subjectivity, and not so easily pinned down. The objectivity of an historical or physical fact, the objectivity of gift and the love from which it comes, the objectivity of witnesses transformed in the event, are all part of a larger movement of communication and transformative action.

Fourth, we question the assumption, that there can be *an objectivity that can do without subjects, and a subjectivity that is entirely unbeholden*

to some objective content. Put simply, there can be no objective statement unless it is registered in the mind and heart of a subject. To pretend otherwise would be to banish objectivity from the realm of experience and to lift it out of classic formative traditions as they are found in
all forms of learning, science, faith and art. Reality may indeed be infi-
nitely more than the human mind can grasp or the heart imagine, and
certainly far exceed any human need or usefulness. To allow for that
possibility of "excess" is already an indication of how both mind and
heart experience intimations of something more. This is to say that revelation inspires faith. It cannot be so objective as to bypass those who
receive it. The Word of revelation presumes a human hearing and even
"seeing"—as we suggested in the previous chapter. It reverberates in the
human mind, heart and imagination. It is not the source of irrelevant
information, even when it might appear to be so, say, in the doctrine of
the Trinity. For all "revealed mysteries" derive from data registered in
the human mind and heart. The divine object is never unrelated to the
human subject.

On the other hand, subjects are without a world unless there are
varieties of objects—even if these were to be considered as pure ideal
forms. More to the point, the more developed one's subjective capacities, the greater and wider the range of objects is disclosed: the keener
the sight, the further one sees. There is a further consequence: the more
world-transforming the object, the more it impinges on subjectivity and
affects our forms of experience and knowing, and our capacity to witness to what has occurred. A driver placidly passing me on the road
provokes a different reaction from one who suddenly swerves and crashes
into my car. A God conceived as a remote world-principle of some kind
would make less demands on me than the God who has raised the crucified Jesus from the dead.

Fifth, we need not assume that *we cannot be objective about subjectivity, nor subjective about objectivity*. To the contrary, we can be objective about subjectivity, and refer to the state of the subject, to his or her
reactions in fear, awe, doubt, puzzlement, joy, courage—as is the case
with the disciples who "saw the Lord". Similarly, there can be no particular problem in admitting subjective responses to what is revealed in
the resurrection event. If the Lord is risen, the alleluia expressed in feel-
ings of joy, thanksgiving and awe, is not inappropriate.

The Saturation of the Phenomenon[5]

The reason for dwelling on these five misleading assumptions is to
clear the ground for two remarks: First, the value of a different approach to the phenomena of Christian experience is clarified. Rather
than straightjacket reactions to the resurrection in terms of subjective-
objective considerations, it is useful to appeal to the phenomenon of the

resurrection as it is given, in its saturated significance. Only then can we allow consideration of what is objective and what is subjective to come into play in a way that respects the singular event in question and the witnesses it calls forth. The resurrection of the crucified One must be permitted to occupy Christian consciousness on its own terms. For that phenomenon *par excellence* "saturates" both the objective and subjective poles of Christian experience with its own excess, and situates them in its own field of God-originated communication and testimony. The "idol" of both subjective projection and objective neutrality is brought into contact with the "icon" of God's self-communication in Christ. This, in turn, overflows and dissolves the rigidities of the predetermined categorisation of what is subjective and what objective.

Furthermore, it is of special importance to acknowledge the divine subjects involved in the Resurrection, the Son as the one who is raised, and the Father who raises him by the power of the Spirit: it is a God-wrought objective event. The phenomenality of the Resurrection cannot be appreciated outside the inter-subjective field of communication in which it occurs. For this field embraces the inter-subjectivity of the Father, the Son and the Holy Spirit. It overflows into relationships between Jesus and the disciples. It inspires the apostolic witnesses and the wider community of believers, both past and present, and energises their witness to the world.

Implied in these varieties of inter-subjective relationship and encounter, there is the objective character of the event itself. God has raised Jesus, not someone else; God has done this, not that; and under these conditions, and so on. To that degree, there is what we might term an "inter-objectivity" implied in the resurrection. The Trinity is not only invoked, but affirmed in the actions proper to the Father, Son and Spirit. The witnesses to the resurrection are named and recognised as historical persons, as Paul lists them (1 Cor 15:3-8). Their objective witness is handed on in the tradition of the Church throughout history. That wider, later history of the Church is related to the early communities and their witnesses, to the contemporary world, and, indeed, to all nations. In each of these cases, the personal reference to "they" or "we" is compatible with the impersonal form of "it", in reference to the Church, the world and to all creation.

Conclusion: The Play of Polarities

To summarise: in the phenomenon of the resurrection, though distinctions related to subject and object are inevitable and offer desirable clarification, such terms are caught up in a kind of spiral of reciprocal redefinition. In such a moving viewpoint, genuine objectivity remains the fruit of authentic subjectivity. But the objectivity of God's act in raising Jesus summons the subjectivity of those it touches into an ever fuller self-transcendence and surrender. The language of subject and object must be sufficiently buoyant and flexible to serve "the saturated phenomenon" of the resurrection. By being alert to this excess or saturation, we are prevented from drying out the language of faith at its focal point so that it becomes a brittle form of apologetics or desiccated rationalistic reduction.

These considerations of subject and object are intended to serve what we might call "salvific realism". The adjective "salvific" is used to highlight the precise kind of realism involved. It is not contrary to the respective realisms of historical, metaphysical, scientific and anthropological methods. Each has its own limitations, particular concerns, traditions of interpretation, and criteria of evidence. Salvific realism is focused on a unique event. It is, first of all, intent on being receptive to the phenomenality of the event which is the focal point of faith, and thereby a shock at the foundations of every theology. If the methods of other forms of phenomenological disclosure or patterns of knowing end by declaring the resurrection to be a non-reality and a non-event, the problem could be one of unexamined prejudice against recognising the resurrection effect in history. This is not helped by a theological method either un-attuned to what is at stake, or which simply takes for granted what should be taken *as* granted and respected in the singular conditions of its "given-ness". It is of maximum theological importance not to be distracted into apologetics before discerning the unique form of what has taken place. Apologetics is at its most persuasive when Christian faith risks being rejected for the right reasons.

CHAPTER 8

The Salvific Realism of the Resurrection

After a detour into a discussion of the polarities of subject and object, we are now in a position to consider such polarities within the saturated phenomenon of the resurrection. We first consider the objective facets, and then move on to a number of subjective aspects.

Salvific Objectivity

Here, we dwell on some seven interrelated aspects of the objectivity of the resurrection:

1. *Salvific Realism*: however we might speak of objectivity, it is governed entirely by the divine saving will
2. *The Divine Initiative*: the resurrection and its associated phenomena all derive from the freedom of the divine gift
3. *Presence and Absence*: the "otherness" of the risen Christ allows for the play of presence and absence in his communication with the disciples
4. *The Humanity of the Risen Jesus*: while the humanity of Jesus is transformed, his humanity is not volatilised: he is the Jesus the disciples knew
5. *Forgiveness*: his return to the disciples is the revelation of a mercy and forgiveness for their previous failures
6. *The Empty Tomb*: ambiguous in itself, it serves as a provocative historical marker for resurrection faith
7. *Overture to World History*: the resurrection as an opening to the larger world and to an incalculable future

Salvific Realism

The adjective "salvific" underscores the significance of the resurrection, not as an act of capricious divine display, but a unique event determining the meaning of salvation and the manner of thinking about it. In this regard, the objectivity in question flows entirely from the divine act—the act of the divine subject who raises Jesus from the dead. Its objectivity, in other words, is precisely designed to serve the divine purposes "for us and our salvation". It is not something a group of human beings imagined or expected. Indeed, it was not even what they specifically desired. On the other hand, the occurrence of this unique event did not contradict a more general, inarticulate sense of longing for lasting life and for the vindication of those who lived for God. It was a particular answer to the immemorial prayer for justice, that God would not desert the victims who appeared to have suffered in vain, defenceless against the powers of evil and violence.

However historically verifiable the various New Testament reports associated with the resurrection, they are not, nor were they ever intended to be, dispassionately scientific records. Nonetheless, there is evidence of the "salvific realism" that we are here stressing. While the self-disclosures of the risen Jesus to the disciples ended by provoking their unreserved self-surrender and their conviction as witnesses, there is a mood of critical discernment in the various New Testament accounts of what took place. What is presented clearly differs from other reports of visions (Acts 16:9; 18:9; 23:11; 27:23), dreams (Mt 1:20; 2:12ff., 19-22), and ecstasies (Acts 10:9ff.; 2 Cor 12:2-4; Rev 1:10ff.). Luke is at pains to stress that the privileged early witnesses had to get beyond the terrifying impression of meeting a ghost, to be led by Jesus beyond fright and doubt to recognise him anew, even if he had appeared in a new form (cf. Lk 24:36-40). When Paul gives a list of witnesses ending with himself, he is clearly not talking about the varieties of gifts and spiritual experiences exuberantly present in the ongoing life of the Corinthian community (e.g., 1 Cor 12:4-11). What he does affirm is an originary series of self-disclosive events whose manifestation had come to an end: "Last of all, as to one untimely born, he appeared also to me" (1 Cor 15:8). In all this, none of the early witnesses ever pretends to describe the resurrection, save in these terms: the crucified Jesus, who had been known in the course of his earthly life and through the impact of his mission, is now glorified, and given back to them. In his return from beyond the domain of death, he comes "to mean the world" to them in a new way.

It is clear, too, that these witnesses show no inclination to prove the resurrection merely from the fact that the tomb was found by the women to be empty. Christ's rising from the dead is not reducible to the various accounts of miraculous resuscitations (Lk 8:49-56; Jn 11:1-53; Acts 9:36-42), even if these serve as a certain adumbration of the life-giving eschatological power of the risen Lord. Furthermore, it has been frequently noted that the theology and philosophy of the day provided no hope or expectation that such a resurrection could happen.[1] The prevalent Greek worldview found any concept of a new physical embodiment after death repugnant (see Acts 17: 18, 32). The Sadducees did not believe in the resurrection of the dead in any sense.[2] The Pharisees, only a small percentage of the population, believed in a resurrection of the just on the last day. Instances of this belief are found in the account of the martyrdom of the seven brothers in 2 Maccabees 7:1-41 and in hopes expressed in Wisdom 3:1-9 and Daniel 12:1-3. While the hopes of Israel looked forward to a resurrection of the just on the last day, no one was expecting the resurrection of this executed criminal on this particular Easter day. Something thought of as happening only at the end of time had been disconcertingly anticipated in what had occurred in Jesus of Nazareth. A shared eschatological hope focused on the end of time now came up against a new barrier—the "too-good-to-be-true" quality of what had actually taken place: Jesus had risen and appeared to his disciples (Lk 24:41). There were simply no clear terms and categories by which to express adequately what happened. The transformation of the crucified Jesus and his new, living presence to the disciples were something "out of this world" and the scope of its experience. But the evidence these disciples offer points to the inarticulate groping of the early community of faith to express some massive and transforming reality. The crucified One lives; and he has revealed himself in ways unconstrained by time and space and the expectations of this world. Though the appearances of Jesus are limited to a few, they are given for the sake of all. The Second Letter of Peter knew about "cleverly devised myths". Compared to such, the "power and coming of our Lord Jesus Christ" was something quite different (2 Pet 1:16).

The contrast to the disciples' experience of the transfiguration (Mt 17:1-8; Mk 9:2-8; Lk 9:28-36; 2 Pet 1:16-18) is also informative. For example, in the transfiguration, the witnesses recognised that it was Jesus all along; they responded by wanting to make the three "dwellings" to house or commemorate Jesus' communication with Moses and Elijah; they see the bright cloud, and hear the voice of God; and finally, Jesus orders them to "tell no one about the vision until the Son of Man has been raised from the dead" (Mt 17:9). However the experience of Peter, James and John is to be interpreted, it is clearly quite different from their witness to the risen Jesus. In these appearances, God does not speak, but Jesus—who is not clearly recognised at first; and, of course, there is no question of keeping it secret. The resurrected Christ, the saturated phenomenon *par excellence*, overwhelms all categories,[3] while the transfiguration suggests that the disciples' experience was of a more "idolic" character. They had responded to a theophany by wanting to locate it—and keep it—in the world of their previous experience (Mk 9:2). But in the event of the resurrection, it is Jesus who acts and shows himself in a manner that disrupts any previous experience, and renders it incapable of holding him. The risen Christ is "the image [*eikon*] of the invisible God" (Col. 1:15). The Father is revealed in his act of raising the Son. His resurrection manifests the incalculable activity of the Spirit, given now as both witness to Christ and the bond of unity with him.

The resurrection event, therefore, overflows any idolic limit, either that of a projection of past expectations or of present comprehension. What has taken place does not occur as a mundane fact—however surprising—but as the event overflowing with world-transforming energy and inexhaustible significance. As a result, it dismantles previous horizons and categories, and introduces the radically new in which the past is interpreted and the possibilities of the future are re-defined.

The Divine Initiative

God has acted. In traditional theological language, we can speak of "grace"—the sheer gift and giving of God (Jn 4:10-11). The resurrection is an act of divine grace: the crucified Jesus receives what only God can give, to become the form and source of such a gift for all. In a phenomenological idiom, faith is receptive to the "givenness" of an event that transcends any mundane category of appearance or possibility. It is not a matter of taking for granted a strand of doctrinal data or scriptural propositions to constitute a theological principle for systematic elaboration. Rather, theology is first of all receptivity to the experience of an event bearing an excess of significance—in terms of its source, its content, the witnesses to it, the receptivity it generates, and its ultimate purpose. This overbrimming prodigality derives from its character as a divine form of self-giving and disclosure. It not only surprises the death-bound world in which it occurs, but also reconfigures it: death and the powers that work through it are confronted by the revelation of the source and form of eternal life.[4]

This is to say that the resurrection is an originating event. Christian life and the tradition of faith have their beginning in the initiative of God's raising up the crucified One.[5] If this unique event had not happened, the Gospels would not have been written. Saul of Tarsus would never have become Paul, the apostle. The Church would not have come into existence, and theology would lack its primary impetus. There would have been no *triduum paschale*. Without this "third day", the "first day" would never have been known as *Good* Friday; nor the second day as *Holy* Saturday. Jesus would have been one more good man, swallowed up in defeat and death. But because of what is now named as the "the resurrection", the Friday of the death of Jesus is seen as the disclosure of that all-merciful love which he had always embodied, and now reaching into the world at its darkest point.[6] Likewise, the long liturgical day of that Saturday becomes "holy", as hope waits on that love to penetrate the lowest depths of human defeat, guilt and isolation.

Paul famously underscores the crucial character of the resurrection of Jesus, as we have already seen.[7] To deny it would be to misrepresent

God. It would negate the interrelated identities of the Father and the Son, and undermine the transformative impact of their Spirit. Because of what this God has done, there is hope of resurrection for the dead, mercy for the sinful, and assurance of the validity of the gospel (1 Cor 15:12-19). The event of Christ's rising saturates the consciousness of faith. It overflows into all dimensions of history and reaches into the dread limits of mortal life itself where death is experienced as sundering all communion between the living and the dead. The impact of Christ's rising locates the past and the future in a universe subject to God's transforming action.[8] God has acted in Christ, the first fruits of a cosmic transformation.

The New Testament offers both a list of witnesses (1 Cor 15:3-11), and a variety of accounts of how they came to see and recognise the Lord.[9] In contrast to a simple record of any event whatever, these accounts contain two excessive extremes. An inner-worldly factual event, a *fait accompli*, is experienced, if registered at all, in an impersonal kind of objectivity. It takes place within the horizon limited to one's routine existence in a pre-existing world. The self is not engaged, unless to dismiss an alleged occurrence peripheral to its interests. In contrast, the resurrection is an originary, saturating event. It introduces a new horizon, of a world made new by God's transformative action. It communicates a unique sense of both God as the giver, and of believers as the divinely gifted, in an eschatologically oriented universe of divine creation. It is given as something unforeseen, irreducible to explanations in terms of cause and effect. To that degree, it is "anarchic", for it owes nothing to any worldly principle or influence or capacities. It ruptures the flat fabric of previous existence by provoking a new understanding of self and world and the direction of time itself. The whole self is engaged, as it is drawn into the new adventure of life in its fullest and most ultimate form. Far from being the self-projection of the religious ego, this new self is called into existence by the self-communication of the divinely Other.

The resurrection is, then, the all-deciding event for Jesus himself, and a momentous awakening in the consciousness of those to whom he appeared in his risen form. In both instances, a divine initiative beyond any mundane expectation or possibility has occurred. For the resurrection is not so much the "next chapter" of a preceding story of Jesus' failed mission and tragic death—an improbable addendum to a narrative of defeat. In the radiance of what had occurred, the life-giving character of who God is and of how God acts is finally revealed for what it was all along. In this sense, it discloses what had been going on in every phase of Jesus' life, words, deeds and mission. In its expanding radiance, all creation appears in its true light, brought to its fulfilment in the triumphant cry of Jesus on the cross: "It is finished" (Jn 19:30). The creativity of God's self-giving love is revealed as the source originating all that had taken place. The powers or "rulers" of this world (e.g., Jn 14:30; 16:11) that have worked against it, and sought to displace it with other versions of reality, are unmasked as idols of deceit and delusion. God is not the "god" of the self-assertive forces that work to dismember creation violently, but the true God of an all-inclusive love for the world that is yet to discover its true history. The novelty of the true God breaks the old, closed circuit of violence and evil. God has worked within the world of violence and death, but not to be enclosed within it, nor caught up in its spiral of vicious circles. In this regard, the resurrection of the Crucified is the great disruption. Life is revealed, no longer determined by violence and bounded by death, but as participation in the vitality of the God of love. Following on this revelatory event, a new chapter does in fact unfold: with Christ risen from death, his followers are gathered into a new covenant; and the whole of creation awakens to the creative mystery of love at work.

What occurred in the resurrection event is divinely gratuitous. God's giving serves no human economy of merit or laws of exchange.[10] The resurrection is not contained in any law of reciprocity, nor any symmetry of subject and object. It derives from a divine freedom that owes nothing to human calculation, in a manner suggested by the words of Jesus in the Gospel of Mark, "for mortals it is impossible, but not for God; for God all things are possible" (Mk 10:27). This gift-quality irrupts into any previously established expectations. The shameful death of Jesus has ended the possibility of his relating anew to his disciples in the context of his earthly life. Coming from beyond any calculations of reward or punishment, the raising of the crucified Jesus breaks into the world with an incalculable initiative and originality. A disconcerting "other-ness" collapses all former frames of reference. It is so disruptive, in fact, that the disciples do not experience an immediate and joyous fulfilment, for "they were startled and terrified, and thought they were seeing a ghost. He said to them, 'Why are you frightened, and why do doubts arise in your hearts?' " (Lk 24:38; cf. Mt 28:10; Jn 20:19-26; 21:7).

The self-disclosures of the risen One (Acts 1:3) also bear the mark of gratuity. The various kinds of encounter between the risen Jesus and the disciples, with their respective emphases, suggest either a gradual unfolding of what has taken place (Lk 24:32), or a sudden irruption (Paul), or the intimacy of a personal address, as in the case of Mary Magdalene (Jn 20:16). In all cases, previous limited horizons had to be left behind (Lk 24:19). Christ's self-disclosures called forth a whole range of emotions from awe and fright to astonishment and joy, and different types of sensory experience of the bodily reality of the risen Jesus. The recipient of these disclosures is still left free. The Matthean phrase, "but some doubted" (Mt 28:17), however jagged an insertion in the narrative it might be, underscores this point.

The surprise of the disciples highlights the unexpected objective character of the divine initiative. The resurrection relies on an irruptively divine action "from beyond", originating in a realm of world-transcending otherness and freedom.[11] Jesus' appearances and departures are governed only by his freedom, within the economy of the "little whiles" that John presents (Jn 16:16-22). He comes and goes and gives himself, always as a sign of contradiction to the world that had condemned him. He appears to the disciples precisely at the time when they are suffering the disgrace of his shameful death and their own failure. Despite this, their expressions of dismay, doubt, later confusion, and eventual joy, are marked by a sense of overwhelming factuality (1 Cor 15:12ff.; 2 Tim 2:17ff.). Whatever their inarticulate gropings, the first witnesses were "dead sure" about the new thing that had happened and to whom it had happened.

This element of surprise in this event undermines all efforts to confine the resurrection to some pre-established religious horizon. The true God is the God of *this* essential surprise. It brims over as an excess hidden in the world of faith—in its signs, witnesses, varieties of gifts and vocations. As a non-representable "trace", it holds faith on edge, preventing it from falling back into religious routine or congealing into an ideological system. The original wonder of God's raising the Crucified unsettles the closed system of the world with a new contingency: for God, all things are possible (Mt 19:26; Mk 10:27; 14:36; Lk 8:27).

Presence and Absence

The salvific objectivity of Christ's rising and self-disclosure involves a disconcerting otherness. The risen Jesus is not present as a datum of experience in a world in which his visible presence could be enjoyed and his further violent removal feared. He is not available as a phenomenon offered for either inspection, address, manipulation or exclusive possession. There is no holding on to him, as it were, within the limits of the empirical world (Jn 20:17), just as his identity can no more be nailed down with his body on the cross, with its taunting inscription, "King of the Jews" (Jn 19:19). The impulse to confine or possess the otherness of the risen Jesus within previous limits is evident when some of the earliest disciples were appalled at hearing the risen Jesus had disclosed himself to Saul of Tarsus (Acts 9:13-16). As the risen One, his coming and going and giving are incalculable. His episodic appearances lead to a mode of disappearance from sight as he ascends into heaven. But this departure does not diminish his relationship to his followers, but opens it to its full cosmic and eschatological dimensions. Selective and incalculable as the appearances of the risen One were, they are given to promise his new mode of being present to the community of faith throughout history (Mt 28:20).

The Humanity of the Risen Jesus

However "other", disconcerting, surprising and irruptive his self-disclosure, Jesus still appears as a human being.[12] His humanity has not been volatilised by some other-worldly contact with the divine. He is not a ghost haunting the world that had rejected him; nor is he a spectre formed by the projections of a guilty conscience as is the case with Herod in regard to the Baptist (Mk 6:14-16). He is risen as the one who had been crucified under Pontius Pilate, but as now transformed, and embodying a new beginning for the death-dealing world that had gotten rid of him.

The evangelists stress that disciples eventually identified the risen One as the Jesus of Nazareth whom they had known—even to the extent of being able to recognise the wounds by which he died. While his otherness is not collapsed into the familiar, Jesus comes as one whom the disciples had previously known. He bears the stigmata of his death and evokes the memory of his past meals with them (Lk 24:39-41).[13] He is simultaneously dead to this world and alive in a new order of existence. It is not as though he is resuscitated to this life. His lethal wounds have not been divinely healed. What is communicated in his rising from the tomb is that the death that the world dealt him is not the defining factor, but God's glorification of this victim to self-giving love. He is the Lamb who was slain (Rev 5:6), the incarnation of the sacrificial self-giving that alone can undo the destructive power of evil and challenge the forces that work through the threat of death. His resurrection is, therefore, not simply the reversal of death, but, on a completely other level, the manifestation of life beyond death and its power. The reason for the continuance of the stigmata is suggested by Thomas Aquinas as he cites the venerable Bede, "He keeps the wounds, not because they cannot be healed, but that he may carry around the triumph of his victory forever".[14] The resurrection of the crucified One is the showing forth of divine glory and victory.[15] In the full-bodied reality of the crucified and risen One, the dark symbols of a death-dealing world are trans-valued. Mortality is not only transcended, but also death is radically transformed. It loses its immemorial sting. Jesus is risen, not only through an agency beyond this world of death, but also as revealing himself as a reality within it. In this regard, hope is not based on nice ideas, but on a living and life-giving fact: the risen Christ himself. In him, the deathward gravity of our experience is reversed: "The light shines in the darkness, and the darkness did not overcome it" (Jn 1:5).

The economy of the unique series of resurrection appearances will be finished when, ascended into heaven, Jesus is removed from any categorical levels of human relationships—either as the beloved master who had called his disciples (in the case of the Twelve), or as the one whose followers were persecuted (in the case of Paul). From then on, he will relate to followers in a manner unknown to the mundane world of experience—that is, through the gift of the Holy Spirit. He "ascends" from the death-limited world of human relationships. But the Spirit "descends" to fill that empty space to make of it a field of new forms of relationship to him and to the Father.

Forgiveness

A further aspect of the gratuitous appearances of the risen Christ to his disciples is forgiveness. He does not return as a judge to expose the betrayal and obtuseness of the disciples. He is not a judge fabricated by their "idolic" projections of guilt, but rather the icon back-lit by limitless mercy and forgiveness. The disciples' guilt and failure were not therefore the determining factor in their relationships to him and to the God he reveals. Rather, he comes as the embodiment of a gift and a love without condition. There is a judgment involved, but it is the judgment of grace on the human condition—of a love unconditioned by any human sin or weakness, opening into a new kind of relationship to Christ and the Father, as is dramatically portrayed in the case of Peter (Jn 21:15-19). Faced with the risen Lord, the early witnesses are not addressed either as subject to a judgment demanding punishment, nor as sinners called to repentance. Whatever their past failures, the risen Jesus finds them in a love and forgiveness that cause them to witness to others of what they themselves have received. Significantly, in John's Gospel, Jesus greets his disciples with the blessing of peace, and sends them as the Father has sent him (Jn 20:19-23). He then breathes the Holy Spirit on them, and commissions them as agents of reconciliation. They can forgive—and "retain", that is, confront and unmask the evil in the still-conflicted world to which they have been sent.[16] Paul can tell the Corinthians, that if Christ is not risen, they are still in their sins (1Cor 15:17). But since he has been raised, the all-determining factor of their identity, both now and in the future, is the love that has overcome the power of evil in all its forms. The "perfect love" that has appeared casts out all fear (1 John 4:18).

The Empty Tomb

The biblical data regarding the resurrection of Jesus and his appearances to various witnesses include a more ambiguous indicator, namely, the fact of the empty tomb. Its discovery is connected to a temporal reference to "the third day". There is also a personal connection as well, since "some women of our company" discovered it (Lk 24:23). How the confession of the resurrection is related to this tradition of the empty tomb remains a complex question. On the one hand, it never suggests, either for the disciples or for those who would profit from their testi-

mony, that the reality of the resurrection was founded on the mere emptiness of the tomb. A vanished corpse is not the same as the risen Lord.
Nor does an unoccupied grave mean a transformed creation. Nevertheless, a decaying corpse is not a very convincing sign of Christ's victory
over death, let alone of the beginning of a new creation.

The discovery of the empty tomb initially gave rise only to perplexity
and fear (cf. Mk 16:8; Lk 24:5, 11). The women, confronted with the
absence of the dead body of Jesus in the tomb, were exposed to a new
form of questioning, "Why do you seek the living among the dead?"
(Lk 24:5a). The sudden appearance of "the two men in dazzling clothes"
addressed the—at first perplexed, and then terrified—women with this
question. The declaration follows: "He is not here, but has risen" (Lk
24:5b). These factors indicate that the resurrection is a divinely-wrought
event—all along the God-intended culmination of Jesus' mission: "Remember how he told you . . . that the Son of Man must be handed over
. . . crucified . . . and on the third day, rise again?" (Lk 24:6-7).

What had taken place was not explicable in terms of the emptiness
and silence of the tomb. Its only explanation was to be found elsewhere,
in the transformative action of a love stronger than death. That would
bring its own kind of silence. But it would be the silence of mute wonder
and joy in response to an event for which the world had no words. But
before that, the women's first report to the apostles of what they had
seen and heard had seemed "as an idle tale" (Lk 24:11), even though it
led to Peter running to the tomb, seeing the grave-clothes, and coming
home "amazed" (Lk 24:12).

When that initial kind of silence, suspicion and amazement learned
to speak of what had taken place, it was not about the mere emptiness
of the tomb. It was in the words of joyful witness to "these things" in
which the power and mercy of God are manifest (Lk 24:45-49). The
resurrection does not mean, therefore, that Jesus returns to his disciples
as a striking figure within the conditions of the world in which he had
been crucified. He is no triumphant religious celebrity imposing himself
on gullible disciples and telling a tale of escaping death in a world in
which death still reigned. His resurrection is no narrow escape from his
adversaries or from mortality itself. The world of previous relationships
has died with him. But what happened to him opens his existence to
another realm of relationships, unbounded by death, transforming human freedom to levels of joy, hope and courage that nothing apart from
his resurrection can explain. Though an all-deciding event, it still demanded waiting for Jesus to send the Spirit his Father had promised (Lk
24:49a): "stay here in the city until you have been clothed with power
from on high" (v. 49b).

Such is the context in which the empty tomb became a sign of promise. There is no implication that the early witnesses to the resurrection
either haunted a grave or lingered among the dead. Rather, they were

empowered to be witnesses within history to that fullness of life which in Christ had already been anticipated. The empty tomb, therefore, has its place in the salvific realism of the Gospel narrative. It is an indicator of the incalculable excess of the resurrection event. The otherwise blank fact of the empty tomb is lifted out of its original ambiguity. Its inclusion in the Gospel accounts prevents faith from fabricating idols of an idealist or mystical ilk.

If theology dismisses or bypasses the significance of the empty tomb, there are inevitable negative consequences. The phenomenon of the resurrection would be left at the mercy of the kind of subjectivity that would prefer to be undisturbed by such an event. Christ's rising from the dead would tend quickly to become a nice thought in a world in which nothing had really changed, and in which the resurrection could not *really* happen. Eschatology would veer very quickly into an ideology. It would entice hope to trust in an exalted ideal, to the detriment of founding itself on a transforming divine event. Moreover, it would mean dismissing the special role of women in communicating the gospel of new life.[17] After all, unless it were utterly sure of what it was reporting, the gospel would hardly base its case on the testimony of women in a culture that scarcely accepted their credibility.[18] For that matter, neither friend nor foe pretended that the tomb contained the remains of Jesus. One Gospel writer at least is quite aware of the allegation that the corpse had been stolen (Mt 28:1-15). This was a quite predictable reaction on the part of those for whom, for whatever reason, Jesus had to stay dead and buried.

In this way, the empty tomb serves as an historical marker for a transcendent mystery. Right there, set within the history of human defeat and failure, it recalls Christian faith to be defiantly full-bodied in its realism. The emptiness of the tomb shows the power of the Spirit as a transcendent energy of world-shattering proportions. While the empty tomb can never substitute for Jesus' living presence, it inspires a keener awareness of the divinely transforming event that has occurred. It is not an idol of human projection and defensive apologetics. On the other hand, it does leave its trace in time and space and matter, thereby suggesting that there are far more surprises in store than scientifically predictable events can allow. It sows a seed of wonder and questioning in the ground of the material cosmos. A whole worldview is called into question. N. T. Wright underscores the political and cultural consequences:

No wonder the Herods, the Caesars and the Sadducees of this world, ancient and modern, were and are eager to rule out all possibility of actual resurrection. They are, after all, staking a counter-claim on the real world. It is the real world that the tyrants and bullies (including intellectual and cultural tyrants and bullies) try to rule by force, only to discover that in order to do so they have to quash all rumours of resurrection, rumours that would imply that their greatest weapons, death and destruction, are not after all omnipotent.[19]

David Bentley Hart makes a similar observation. Confronted with the empty tomb of the crucified Jesus, the powers that did away with him are made inescapably aware that they are not the forces that shape history:

> In a sense, the resurrection is an aporia in the language of the powers, a sudden interruption of the story they tell, and the beginning of an entirely new beginning of the story of the world: this is perhaps nowhere more powerfully expressed than at the end of Mark . . . when the empty tomb reduced the women come to anoint Christ's body to speechlessness, to an amazed inability to say what they have seen and heard.[20]

What is at stake is a whole worldview. For the powers of the world that rule this side of death, the tombs of those who challenged them are signs of their power to impose an unquestionable rule. Perhaps these tombs will be eventually permitted to be venerated as symbolic sites of what might have been, the places where dreams of better things and the bodies of these unworldly dreamers are confined. In the meantime, those who pretended to disturb the established world-order lie dead and buried—crushed, brought to nothing, shorn of all power to subvert the way things are. With that solid assurance, all the boundaries that had been essential for the maintenance of a violent world-order are fixed in place, once these disturbers of the peace are buried, and their tombs remain secure: "The tomb, after all, is the symbol *par excellence* of metaphysical totality and of the mythos of cosmic violence".[21]

If the powers that govern the world through the threat of death dance on the graves of those who pretended to challenge them, the emptiness of this tomb is an indicator of the fullness of life that a death-bound world could not allow. The world is not an enclosed totality. The empty tomb points beyond every limit, whether accepted or imposed. There is no definitive salvation in any system of thought or conduct which leaves the forces of oppression basically unchallenged.[22]

The empty tomb focuses faith at the clear edge of a new world in the making. What is coming to be, what has begun with Jesus rising from this tomb, goes beyond all desperate efforts to reduce the "real world" to the idolic certitudes of violence, pride and greed: "He has put down the mighty from their thrones and exalted the lowly" (Lk 1:52). Yet this event, given within history in the emptiness of this tomb and in the transformations it effects, causes a deep turbulence in which all established orders are destabilised: "The resurrection is a transgression of the categories of truth governing the world . . . Christ is a word that cannot be silenced; he can always lay his hand upon another and say, 'I am he that liveth, and was dead; and, behold, I am alive forevermore' (Rev 1:18)".[23] In contrast, the past world is wrapt in a classic fateful melancholy. The inscription on the ancient tombstone read, *et in Arcadia ego* ("I too was once in Arcady"). Virgil expressed it with immemorial poignancy: *sunt lacrimae rerum et mentem mortalia tangunt* ("tears are at the heart of reality and every mortal thing affects our thinking"). A kind of all-pervading sadness is never far from the coercive power of violence. It is a dismal concession to the loss of all ultimate hope. Yet both the defeats of melancholy and the pretensions of violence stand under the divine judgment of life to the full.[24]

The raising of the crucified Jesus from this tomb remains a scandal to all the despairing attitudes and desperate systems that would reject the power of God to transform the world. The emptiness of the tomb now "marks a boundary beyond which God has passed in Christ without allowing the beauty of his gift to be consumed by the indeterminate".[25] Every effort of thought to give meaning to death "has been surpassed by an infinite gesture, by the disorienting rhetoric of the empty tomb, by the radiance of the resurrection, and by the palpable wounds of the crucified".[26]

If his tomb is not empty, the creative force of the crucified and risen Jesus is easily accommodated to ideologies of whatever kind. Easter becomes a meaningless holiday and a marketing opportunity for chocolate eggs. Unless that sepulchral space is left empty, the resurrection of Christ is either lost in a mystical vagueness or replaced by a self-referential theological form of rationalism. However stupefying this emptiness is, it must be critically guarded. Nature abhors a vacuum; and the monuments to power and triumph begin to tilt dangerously when there is an empty space at their foundations. But in this indicator of a new creation, those united to the risen Christ share in his resurrection: "If the Spirit of him who raised Jesus from the dead dwells in you, he who raised Jesus from the dead will give life to your mortal bodies also through his Spirit that dwells in you" (Rom 8:11).

He died, and so shall we. He has been raised; and so shall we be. But, though his tomb is empty, ours will not be. His resurrection is materially complete; ours must wait, at least for its full eschatological realisation. Why is his case special? Even if his mortal remains were still in the tomb, theology could still think of him as newly embodied in a new form of existence, beyond the mortal limits of earthly life. What is the point then of holding to this singular material transformation of the dead body of Jesus so that his tomb is empty? Indeed, by focusing specifically on his empty tomb, might not faith be distracted from the cosmic and universal scope of a promised resurrection? But here, as with all aspects of Christian revelation, we must first of all be open to the phenomenality of the *economia*, the pattern of God's freely given salvation. Philosophy might be bewildered and religious projections scandalised, but the question is, has God acted or not? And if it is allowed that God could act, why did God act in this manner?

Theology must "seek understanding", but first of all it must be receptive to what is given to be understood. Here it is brought back to the concrete manner in which the Father has chosen to display the extent of his saving love in and for the whole of creation. The Word became not theory, not myth, but flesh—with all the contingencies and particularities that this implies. The raising of the dead-and-buried flesh of Jesus from the tomb is designed to serve the manner in which a love untrammelled by earthly conditions has acted.[27] Something of cosmic significance is being revealed when Jesus is transformed in the totality of what he was when laid in the tomb. The matter that made up his crucified body is transformed. His tortured corpse has been changed into his full-bodied risen existence. It cannot but have appeared as the least promising material for the glory of God to be revealed. His corpse is the remains of a man who had been executed in defeat, humiliation and apparent abandonment by the God in whose name he had claimed to act. What, then, is its significance?

Aquinas remarks that Jesus' risen body is not an imagined reality (*corpus phantasticum*), but the God-wrought embodiment of the saving Word.[28] His death is not the result of the entropic forces of nature which lead to decay. It figures in the way God has acted "to show forth the divine power" (*ad ostensionem virtutis divinae*).[29] In this showing-forth, the resurrection and the empty tomb belong together in the concrete particularity of the divine economy or pattern of action. Jesus' proclamation of the Kingdom of God led him to defeat, condemnation and execution. He was left dead and buried. His vindication by the God he has so intimately invoked as "Father" did not mean that he came down from the cross, nor that he walked out of the tomb to rejoin his distraught followers in life as usual. He came to them in a new realm of existence. For that reason, there is a certain appropriateness—or *convenientia*, as the Scholastics would say—in the transformation of his crucified body. It occurs to display, in an anticipatory manner, the Spirit of God at work. God's power is in no way constrained by the defeats, condemnations, violence and burials that mark the human history embodied in this man. Jesus rose to face his disciples who had looked on him transfixed on the cross (Jn 19:37; cf. Zech 12:10). The Lamb who was slain retains the marks of the cross even in his risen body. In his total physicality, he is given to faith in a form that anticipated a new creation: "I was dead, but now I live forever and ever" (Rev 1:18). He had been done to death as the representative and agent of God's reign.

His blood had been poured out for the new covenant. He has previously been present to the disciples who had had every reason to fear that death—for him and even for themselves—would result from his head-on confrontation with the violent powers of politics and religion with only God to defend him. Their fears were justified, as they mourned the execution that eventually occurred. His dead body was the gruesome expression of his failed mission, his prayer unanswered and his Father's defeat. For God to raise him from the tomb of disgrace and defeat would manifest the scope of a divine victory over the powers of death and violence that had, so they thought, terminally rid themselves of him. His tomb would become a provocatively empty space in the fabric of the world that had done away with him.

There is, then, a unique realism in this economy of salvation. God has acted in history, not by communicating a new idea, but by doing a provocatively and properly divine thing. Through Jesus' transformed physicality, the divine intention for the whole of creation is anticipated and manifested in this exemplary instance. As a result, the world is no longer a total system of entropy and decay, nor a theatre in which the scripts of self-justifying violence are enacted. Even though death is still our common fate, its dominion has been disturbed. The risen Christ is the first and last letter, the "alpha and the omega" (Rev 22:12), of an alphabet by which the great poem of the Word comes to expression. A love stronger than death has been revealed.

Overture to World History

The appearances of the risen Jesus, with their association with the empty tomb, are a history-forming phenomenon. As with all significant events, there is an inherent "structural delay": as the lethal limits of the pre-resurrectional world are thrown into disarray, a new realm of divine possibilities opens up. Jesus turns the gaze of the apostles away from the familiar regions of Jerusalem and Galilee, out to "the ends of the earth" (Acts 3:8). He discloses himself as moving forward to the Galilee of the Gentiles, not as gathering his disciples around him in the Holy City (Mk 16:7). His disciples are sent to witness "to all nations, beginning from Jerusalem" (Lk 24:37; cf. Mt 28:18-20). The risen Jesus thus discloses himself as the leading edge of the direction in which the Church must move, forward and outward. The resurrection of Jesus cannot be separated from his mission to the world in which his followers are to share (Jn 20:21). Though Jesus had appeared to them, his communication looked beyond the especially privileged few to the wider world of faith. Though they had "seen the Lord", blessed are those others who, without seeing, will simply believe (Jn 20:29; 1 Pet 1:8). His self-disclosure to chosen witnesses does not, therefore, enclose them in a privileged encounter with him in the familiar circumstances of the past. The primary purpose of these appearances is not to assure the disciples of their own future resurrection, but to empower them as witnesses of a boundless economy of salvation.[30] What they had seen and heard and touched (1 John 1:1-3) is given so as to overflow to all nations and throughout all time.[31] As a result, the resurrection is not given to stop history, but starts it on a new providential course. By raising Jesus from the dead, God has made time for the whole of human history—now affected by the all-deciding "mutation" that had occurred within it. Through the irruption of an incalculable grace into the world, the resurrection does not halt, but rather intensifies, the drama of human freedom. While the resurrection anticipates a creation transformed, it brings no premature fulfilment. The "opening of heaven" (Jn 1:51) that occurs in Christ suggests the horizon in which the unfolding of the whole of history will take place. The resurrection and the appearances of the risen One remain adapted to the life of faith. It will not be spared the burden of the mundane, ambiguous course of things, nor exposure to intense conflict.[32] For the self-enclosed world of the past is locked in a terminal struggle with the excess of the self-giving love that has revealed itself. It is as though a divine tact or discretion, ever respectful of human liberty, allows for both continuity and discontinuity. The continuity consists in free human beings acting in a biologically-structured and morally conflicted world in which human freedom must be realised. The discontinuity lies in the divinely instigated reversal that has struck at the heart of the powers of evil. It comes with a disruptive "otherness", impelling believers to live in the world "otherwise". For the resurrection of the Crucified punctures the desperate certitudes of a world for which such an event cannot, and must not, happen. Yet, because it has happened, a new liberty stirs. Freedom finds a new depth and breadth as it participates in the mission Jesus himself received from the Father (Jn 20:22). Faith must expand and express itself in a universe radically freed from the "power of darkness" (Col 1:13) by the gift of God.

Implied in each of these facets of the resurrection is the fact of an immense transformation having occurred in the minds and hearts of the earliest believers and witnesses. We now turn, then, to consider various aspects of such a transformation or "salvific subjectivity".

Salvific Subjectivity

The divine initiative in raising Jesus from the dead is registered in the consciousness of the disciples.[33] More particularly, the appearances of the risen Lord suppose a certain experience in those who witnessed them. We have already remarked on their passing from desolation and failure to a sense of joyous vindication and new beginning. The moment of recognition leads to the acceptance of responsibility, a point from which they never look back. They express their dedication to Christ in the language of worship and unqualified commitment (Jn 20:16ff.; Mt 28:9, 17).[34] Here, there are five related topics to be considered:

1. *A New Beginning*
2. *The Disciples' New Understanding*
3. *Called to Witness*
4. *A Universal Horizon*
5. *A Reactive World*

A New Beginning

The followers of Jesus who had been scattered following on the horror of the cross become a community of witnesses committed to proclaiming salvation in the name of Jesus to all nations (Lk 24:47ff.; Jn 20:21ff.). His execution and burial had the effect of scooping out of the religious mind and imagination every vestige of either worldly hope or simple optimism.[35] God was proved to be powerless by the criteria of devout or political expectations. Whatever the God of Jesus intended, it was not to be revealed as a mundane power meting out worldly justice. The experience of defeat and emptiness readied the early group of disciples to be witnesses to something utterly new. Love had acted on its own terms to constitute its witnesses and to inspire their mission. In this new field of consciousness, the reality of God, of the world and of the human self is newly defined.[36] The resurrection, as the "saturated phenomenon" *par excellence*, called into question all previous interpretative categories. It was an event, not as an objective *fait accompli* within the settled boundaries of an established world, but as destabilising any previous world, and overflowing in its transformative effect into the consciousness of faith.

The experience of this singular event was supremely meaningful. If it were experienced as meaningless, it would have passed unnoticed. It could not have been known or spoken of. But it was a densely meaningful event. In its light, the disciples were invited to reread "the law of Moses, the prophets and psalms" in which the hopes of Israel had been expressed (Lk 24:44). A new understanding of "all the scriptures" and of the sufferings of Jesus (Lk 24:25-26; cf. Jn 2:22; 12:16; 14:26) is provoked. As the culmination of all the saving works of God in the past, the Father had acted in an ultimately decisive manner (Gal 1:1; Acts 2:23, 32).

What had been experienced raised questions that demanded answers. One way or another, the apostolic group had to ask: What is the ultimate truth that has been revealed to us—about God, the world and ourselves within it? Similarly, given this displacement of consciousness, these early witnesses could not avoid questions as to who they now were—as loved, forgiven, and what they are called to be and do. Out of a new sense of corporate existence, questions would arise about what constitutes unity in Christ and communion in his Spirit. Further, drawn as they are to acknowledge the universal significance of what has taken place, these original disciples are impelled to question what was being asked of them in witnessing to their own age and the ages to come.[37]

This new beginning meant for the first generations of believers a passage from the sense of an overwhelming experience to an articulation of its meaning: there is a final truth to proclaim, a new identity to appropriate, a new community to recognise, and a world-transforming mission to promote. Because of the saturated meaningfulness of the resurrection event, it registered in the consciousness of the followers of Jesus in various ways. Here we touch on just some of them.

The Disciples' New Understanding

There is evidence of an expansion of the consciousness of the disciples. They come to understand what they had previously not understood. Moreover, they are quite aware of their change of mind and what had caused it. What had been hidden to them had now been made clear. In their corporate experience and expression of faith that resulted from the resurrection, they were free to record, not only that the apostles had previously missed the point of what Jesus was about—despite his efforts to instruct them—but also that they had deemed it scandalous, and rejected it. But then, the illumination: they could now understand his mission, his God, and the diseased nature of the world that had violently expelled him as subversive of the good order of religion and politics. This simple point suggests a striking cognitive gain on the part of the disciples, and the sense of themselves as constituted as privileged witnesses to what had occurred.

The expanded subjectivity of the disciples allowed them to appreciate more deeply the subjectivity of Jesus himself. In contrast to the continuity between Jesus' pre-resurrection self-understanding in terms of his identity and mission and his post-resurrectional consciousness, they confessed to the dramatic change that occurred in their own awareness of Jesus compared to their previous understanding of who he was and what he stood for. It was not only a matter of their now grasping what had been previously beyond them, but also that they were now enabled to appropriate what he had understood all along (i.e., what had motivated him, what he had refused to betray at any cost in his unique mission from the Father). His distinctive, uninhibited understanding has been described as "the intelligence of the victim".[38] The early witnesses and believers were now given the capacity to enter, in their respective ways, into "the mind of Christ" (e.g., Phil 2:5).[39] They began to share his understanding of God and to see themselves as extending his mission: "As the Father has sent me, so I send you" (Jn 20:21).

Before the resurrection, who Jesus was and what he was about had been a scandal. He represented an impasse that even his disciples could not negotiate. He was the stone rejected by the builders. What he stood for was too angular or misshapen for anyone intent on constructing a world resistant to the Reign of God that he proclaimed. His earliest followers came to admit that they had been unable to grasp some essential point. The blindness and narrowness of their expectations made his view of things seem impractical and dangerous. They did not then realise their complicity in the idolatrous violent world that he was radically contesting.

But after the resurrection, they awakened to God as the non-violent mystery of self-giving love. This awakening brought home to them how they had been part of the world of envy and exclusion. Yet, in their stumbling against the rock of scandal that he was to them, they were, in fact, being slowly prepared to accept what would be finally made clear. In rising from the tomb, the Crucified was not the stumbling block that had tripped them up, the stone to be rejected by the world's builders, but the chief cornerstone of a divinely designed edifice of a new humanity. They began to see things otherwise—their own resistance and confusion, and the filial identity of Jesus in his unreserved dedication to the saving will of the Father.

In short, these early Christians came to understand God, Christ and themselves in a new way. There occurred a remarkable, post-resurrectional increment in their understanding. They now enjoyed a dazzling insight into the divine economy—and their place within it.

Called to Witness

The early disciples are now confronted with the task of communicating their understanding of Jesus, crucified and risen. They had to assume new responsibilities involved in a world-transforming mission. Their awakening to the full scope of God's action as it was revealed in the cross and the resurrection is worked out in that matrix of experience out of which the New Testament writings emerged, with all the variety of their contexts and accents. These foundational writings are not like research papers prepared for a theology conference. Their purpose is to communicate a participation in "the mind of Christ Jesus" (e.g., Phil 2:5), as it was already shared in the consciousness of the early communities of faith. The kind of consciousness involved is not translatable as either a secret gnosis, or, for that matter, as a philosophical or theological system. Its character is conveyed as the state of being "in Christ", as in a new existential realm of grace—in the Pauline sense (2 Cor 5:17). It is expressed also in terms of the reciprocal indwelling typical of the

Johannine vocabulary, in a communion of life (e.g., Jn 17:21).

Being "in Christ", participating in his consciousness, does not detach his followers from history. It locates them in a specific past. Luke, for example, presents the risen Jesus interpreting himself for his disciples within the testimony of the scriptures of Israel as the fulfilment of "the law of Moses, the prophets and the psalms" (Lk 24:44-45; cf. Lk 24:27). Their minds were opened by his "exegesis" of the scriptures of Israel: he is the key to the larger story of election, hope and prayer. The "Old Testament" remains thereby ever integral to the Christian scriptures: the "New Testament" contains some three hundred and sixty references to the scriptures of Israel, a third of which are from the Psalms.[40] The traditional phrase, "according to the scriptures" (e.g., 1 Cor 15:3, 5) was not reducible to a collection of proof texts, but a formula aimed at recognising the salvific design of God operating throughout all history, manifest in all types of biblical witness.[41] On the other hand, there is a proleptic dimension, as is evidenced in the insistent eschatological orientation of the New Testament writings. In terms of Christian identity "what we will be has not yet been revealed . . . when he is revealed, we will be like him, for we will see him as he is" (1 John 3:2). God will act to terminate history and bring it the fulfilment of "God all in all" (cf. 1 Cor: 15:28). Yet there is progress in knowledge, under the guidance of the Spirit, "of the things that are to come" (Jn 16:13). The manner in which the resurrection saturates time itself, in the "now but not yet" of the experience of faith, works continuously to repristinate the "newness" of the New Testament. Its excess is evidenced, as already noted, in a strongly and widely articulated *theologia negativa*—a knowledge by way of negation—regarding the unimaginable consummation of what has begun.

A Universal Horizon

The novelty and expansion of the disciples' insight extends into the meaning of all creation centred "in Christ". In a manner inexplicable save in terms of the "saturated phenomenon" of the resurrection, the New Testament registers a many-sided conviction of the significance of Christ for all created realities (Jn 1:3, 8:58, 17:5; Heb 1:2; 1 Cor 8:6; Col 1:15-20; Eph 1:3-14). More surprisingly, there is a recognition that this was part of the original understanding of Jesus himself. He was the bearer of an understanding of an original creation, created in love, inclusive of all, and the goal of his mission of salvation. Indeed, his identity is tied into the aboriginality of creation, "before the foundation of the world" (Jn 17:5, 24). Inevitably, such a consideration pushes questions of the psychology of Christ to a new limit. For instance, did the early followers of Jesus later come to understand something about him that he had not understood beforehand himself?

In this limitless expansion of perspective, the resurrection appearances give rise to the imperatives of a new universality. The gift of the Spirit at Pentecost (Acts 2:1-36) reverses the disintegration of Babel (Gen 11:1-9). Philip enlightens the Ethiopian eunuch as to the true meaning of the Isaian prophecy (Acts 8:26-40). Peter eventually discerns the rightness of going to the house of Cornelius (Acts 11:1-19). Paul finds in the cross the dissolution of all divisions: "For he is our peace: in his flesh he has made both groups into one and has broken down the dividing wall . . . that might create in himself one new humanity in place of two . . ." (Eph 2:15).

It is a universality to be both formed and further discovered. It is formed in the inner imperatives of Christian community, "Little children, let us love, not in word or speech, but in truth and action" (1 John 3:18), and in its conduct toward the threatening other: "love your enemies, do good to those who hate you, bless those who curse you, pray for those who abuse you" (Lk 6:27-28). But it is also to be disconcertingly discovered, as in the parable of the Good Samaritan (Lk 10:25), and eschatologically anticipated in love for the suffering neighbour in whom Christ is present (Mt 25:31-46). Wherever "the mind of Christ", the life of self-giving love, is manifest, there the universal saving will of God is at work.

Jesus is risen as "the way" (Jn 14:6a) to the Father's house of many rooms. Yet this gracious space is no imaginary extraterrestrial location, but the final dimension of creation.[42] It includes the spiritual and material universe. By making all this his own, Christ has introduced every dimension of existence into the divine realm. In assuming humanity as the Word made flesh, in rising from the dead to a new realm of life, he takes with him our humanity, its world and the whole universe, into a final sphere of existence: "He is the image of the invisible God, the firstborn of all creation; for in him all things in heaven and on earth . . . have been created through him and for him. He is before all things and in him all things hold together" (Col 1:15-17).

A Reactive World

The resurrection provides the impetus to go out into the world as the object of God's love, and to recognise the mission of Jesus as the "saviour of the world" (Jn 3:16; 4:42).[43] On the other hand, the disciples, as they moved out into that world, were ill-advised to consider themselves in a tranquilised post-resurrectional state (cf. Jn 15:18-16:4). There were conflicts in store; and the burden of transgressing long-established boundaries had to be borne. Simon bar Jonah, even after being declared *Cephas*, Peter, "the Rock", in order to strengthen the new community of living stones (Mt 16:17-18), found this disconcertingly to be the case (Mt 16:21-23; Acts 10). Paul admits that we carry "this treasure in clay jars" in recognition that "this extraordinary power belongs to God and does not come from us" (2 Cor 4:7). The peace that Christ gives is not as the world gives or permits (Jn 14:27; 16:33). There would be a conflict, resulting in fierce opposition. Those serving the gods of this world would react violently to the revelation of the true God. For the God who glorifies the crucified Jesus is the God who undermines the idolatrous systems of violence and its vicious circles of hatred. The disciples register the realism of their position, and recognise that it will mean persecution, death, and a necessary participating in the sufferings of Jesus. Still, their candid acknowledgment of the virulence of the world's reaction does not diminish the universality of their Christ-given mission. For they must be agents of reconciliation and witnesses to a mercy greater than the evils that confront them, by praying for enemies, repaying evil with good, against the time when the fullness of salvation is consummated at the end of the ages. The transformed subjectivity of the disciples in no way represses the conflicts in store. In this context, Girard's comment is incisive:

> The delayed recognition of Jesus has nothing to do with a lesser visibility of his resurrected body due to the lesser reality of the shadowy afterlife to which he would now belong. The opposite is true. This resurrection is too real for a perception dimmed by the false transfigurations of mimetic idolatry.[44]

Each of these five aspects suggests something of the manner in which the God-wrought transformation that occurred in Christ overflows into the consciousness of his followers. In that consciousness the meaning of the resurrection is formed and takes theological shape. The following chapter gives a number of indications of how this occurs, and of how the resurrection has its theological effect.

CHAPTER 9

Extensions of the Resurrection Effect

As the resurrection saturates the consciousness of faith, it blooms into manifold meaning. Theology seeks to understand and to word what faith has received and what the life of faith entails. The resurrection effect resonates through the whole of theology. It carries over into every systematic theme and permeates the system in its entirety. In cognitive terms, through the resurrection of the crucified Son, the true God is revealed as unconditional love (1 John 4:8, 16)—as "light" (1 John 1:5), "true God and eternal life" (1 John 5:20). God comes as a gift, in a self-giving that overflows all previous conditions and ontological determinations.[1] In its constitutive meaning, the resurrection effect radically affects the consciousness of Christian identity. It refreshes and informs Christian subjectivity, expanding its awareness in a new field of relationships—intimacy with the Father, union with the Son, the indwelling of the Spirit, and participation in a creation which has already produced its "first fruits" (1 Cor 15:23). Then, the communicative dimension: the resurrection of Jesus, as the crucified victim, is an impetus to embrace the hitherto disowned "other", and to enter into solidarity with his fellow-victims sacrificed to the endemic violence that has excluded, or simply used, the defenceless for its unredeemed purposes. In this manner, the resurrection has an effective or world-changing impact, as it inspires and sustains liberation in the form of cruciform non-violent love, to contest the violence and inhumanity of every culture and every life-situation. To illustrate this larger theological effect, we consider here just three topics: the Trinity, moral theology and interfaith dialogue.

The Resurrection and the Trinity

Here we argue that a phenomenological consideration of the resurrection is a necessary preliminary to a theology of the Trinity, as say, it is represented in the classic Thomist exposition.[2] Aquinas' analogical method has an irreplaceable explicative power in a systematic comprehension of trinitarian doctrine.[3] But this classic exposition makes no explicit mention of the resurrection, even though it is the revelatory point of the trinitarian self-disclosure.[4] The resurrection does not pertain simply to a data-gathering phase preliminary to systematic exposition. Rather, it is a *donum*, a gift, to be received, affecting all systematic thinking with its inexhaustible significance. In this regard, the phenomenality of the resurrection event is not readily reducible to "visible" and "invisible" missions that conclude the traditional order of the Thomist procedure. For the "visibility" of this phenomenon is not that of mere historical empirical data; nor is its "invisibility" to be understood on that level, as though opposed to what is otherwise visible. The resurrection event leaves neither term clearly defined nor set against the other.[5]

Before any employment of systematic categories, the resurrection is the phenomenological locus of telling the story of God-with-us in a new way.[6] It amounts to discerning a quasi-autobiographical manifestation of God. In the light of the resurrection, the play of divine inter-subjectivity in the prayer of Jesus (Jn 17:1-26; Mt 11:25-27), the declarations of the Father (Mt 17:5; Mk 9:7; Lk 9:35; Jn 12:28), and the witness of the Spirit (Acts 13:2; Rom 8:26-27; Rev 22:17) might find expression as follows.

The Father who *so* loves the world, gives all to the Son. In the Gospel of John, for instance, the Father's giving is unstinted. There is a primordial superabundance of communication (Jn 3:35; 13:3; 17:7). The Father's giving to the Son includes his name (Jn 17:11), glory (Jn 17:22, 24), authority over all flesh (Jn 17:2), having life "in himself" (Jn 5:26), his activity and works (Jn 5:36), words (Jn 17:8), authority and judgment (Jn 5:2, 27), everything he asks (Jn 11:22), in such a way as to include believers in the present and the future (Jn 6:37, 39; 10:29; 17:2, 6, 9, 12, 24; 18:9). The Father thereby refuses, as it were, to have any appearance in that world other than through the self-giving of the Son. By raising him from the dead, the Father glorifies his Son as the embodiment and utterance of the excessive character of self-giving love which has gone to the extreme of the cross.

The Son, for his part, by receiving all from the Father, refuses any identity in the world save that of being the revelation of the Father and the agent of his will. Even as this entails a collision with the idolatrous and demonic forces that structure the world that rejected him, the whole mission of the Son is to glorify the Father, as the one, true God and creator of the world, even in its state of alienation. The mission of Jesus is completed in breathing forth the Spirit. The sending of this "other Paraclete" is the "advantage" that follows upon Jesus' departure and return to the Father.

Both the Father and the Son, once the divinely willed economy of the earthly history of Jesus is completed in his death and resurrection, yield all to their Holy Spirit who is sent by the Father to "take what is mine [i.e., of Jesus] and declare it to you [the disciples]" (Jn 16:14). This Spirit refuses any role or identity save that of leading to Christ and establishing the community of believers in an intimacy with the Father. The Spirit comes to "convict" the world of its perversity in rejecting the self-giving and forgiving love offered it (Jn 16:7-11). The character of this Spirit is discerned in relation to Jesus (1 John 4:2-3), and in its intercessory "groaning" within the groanings of creation and Christian life, thus expanding hope to its fullest proportions (Rom 8:22-27; Rev 22:17). For hope looks to the reconciliation of all things in Christ, the final emergence of creation transformed (Eph 5:16; Col 4:5).[7]

These brief indications suggest that the resurrection has, therefore, a trinitarian density. The resurrection of the Son cannot be located outside his self-giving for the glory of the Father; Nor can it ignore the originating dynamic of the Father's giving manifested in the glorification of his Son as the way of salvation. Nor can the gift of God ever be appreciated unless through the primary witness of the Spirit awakening Christian consciousness to an ever new awareness of life lived to the full (Jn 10:10).

The occurrence of the resurrection introduces a radical shift in the horizon of existence. It is the culminating "event" of divine self-involvement in history. Its culminating and saturating character cannot be reduced to an episodic divine interruption of the world's course. Rather, it discloses the divinely originated and finalised movement of history as a whole, affecting every aspect of faith's present experience. By raising Jesus from the dead, God is revealed, and hope awakens within a history that anticipates a divine fulfilment. It gives rise to a new narrative comprehension of life in its fullest dimensions: "this life was revealed, and we have seen it and testify to it, and declare to you the eternal life that was with the Father and was revealed to us" (1 John 1:2). However paradoxically, such revelation has an illuminating effect: "the darkness is passing away and the true light is already shining" (1 John 2:8). The light of revelation is the radiance of a love exceeding all mundane limits: "In this is love, not that we loved God but that he loved us and sent his Son to be the atoning sacrifice for our sins" (1 John 4:8-10). The resurrection becomes the telling point from which God's redemptive self-involvement in the history of creation can be told. In the strongest sense of the term, this narrative is God's own story, of how a primordial, engendering love reveals itself by raising the crucified Jesus. Admittedly, it can be banished to the margins of myth, an instance of what is "too good to be true" (cf. Lk 24:41) for a world that would be deeply troubled if it were true. But if it is received as true, then God is not an idea or a symbol or an outdated myth. The one, true God is the source of a self-revelation—the *I* who speaks and the *You* who is addressed: "This is my beloved Son. Listen to him" (Mk 9:7). At such a point, faith comes to "overhear" an intra-divine communication, "Father . . . all yours are mine, and mine are yours, and I am glorified in them . . ." (Jn 17:10; see also Lk 10:21-22). This expression in the "first person" autobiographical mode lifts the biblical narrative of the resurrection from an idolic projection to an iconic event of revelation. God is no longer locatable in the sphere of human projections, for "no one has ever seen God" (Jn 1:18). The knowledge of what and who God is comes from beyond, the three-dimensioned light and life radiating from the crucified and risen Lord. He is the revelation of the Father and the source of the Spirit.

The trinitarian event of the resurrection cannot be circumscribed. Its origins derive from the "anarchic" character of God whom no one has ever seen (Jn 1: 18). It is wrought by the Spirit who is unconditioned by all finite limits and all earthly powers. It cannot be predicted through any earthly calculation or causality. Its centre and circumference is determined by the risen Christ in whom all things cohere and find their purpose. All points of reference are lost in an overwhelming transcendent indefinability. Although the trinitarian event upends all human projections, it catches up into itself all who participate in it through the self-surrender of faith, hope and love. It thus discloses a new world of relationships and a new way of being in the world. For the world itself is reconfigured: the given world, dominated by earthly powers that crucified Jesus, is now a new world in which God has acted to raise him up: "so if anyone is in Christ, there is a new creation: everything old has passed away; see, everything has become new" (2 Cor 5:17).

This trinitarian form marks the earliest forms of the New Testament triadic rhetoric (e.g., 1 Thess 1:1-5 dating from A.D. 58). It thus presumes something already evident to the community of faith, even though this form has not yet been crystallised into the trinitarian doctrines of the fourth century. A post-resurrection triadic rhetoric pervades Paul's discussion of the law (Gal 3:11-14) and Christian freedom (Gal 4:4-6), just as it animates his expressions of thanksgiving (2 Thess 2:13; Col 1:3-8). Moreover, it is embedded in expressions of prayer and praise (Rom 15:30; Phil 3:3-6; Eph 3:14-16). Likewise, the unity and the variegated giftedness of the Christian community are presented in an explicit reference to the divine three (1 Cor 12:4-8).

What is simply assumed in the patterns of the early rhetoric of faith comes to a more determined expression in a number of liturgical formulations, as in 2 Corinthians 13:14. Significantly, at the conclusion of Matthew's Gospel, the risen Lord commissions the disciples to go forth and baptise the nations "in the name of the Father and of the Son and of the Holy Spirit" (Mt 28:19). But these inchoately trinitarian dimensions of early liturgical prayer-forms can be further specified. Some are more figurative while others appear more schematic. They interweave in various manners (cf. Acts 1:4-8; 2:23, 28; 9:17; 10:38; 11:15-17), as mind and imagination are reconfigured in the light of the resurrection event.

In the more figurative, symbol-laden instances, a post-resurrectional consciousness reaches back into the earthly history of Jesus to construct images disclosive of the salvation embodied in the risen Christ. This is especially so in the Synoptics. The Lukan Infancy Narrative gives something like a holographic impression of the power of the Holy Spirit to bring Jesus to birth in the fullness of his divine Sonship (Lk 1:32-35). In the various depictions of the baptism of Jesus, the Spirit descends in the form of a dove, the heavens are opened, the divine voice proclaims Jesus as the beloved Son (cf. Mt 3:16-18; Mk 1:9-11; Lk 3:21-23; and also Jn 1:32-34). The Transfiguration passages prefigure what is to come in their references to the cloud of glory (the *Shekkinah* of the Spirit), and the Father's voice from heaven proclaiming Jesus as the beloved Son (Mt 17:1-8; Mk 9:2-8; Lk 9:28-36). Likewise, Luke depicts Jesus rejoicing in the Spirit, expressing the intimacy of his communion with the Father, and his role in inviting all who renounce idolic pretensions into the experience of grace (Lk 10:21-22). These retroactive figurations of the resurrection find their completion in the narrative of the Ascension (Lk 24:50-53; Acts 1:6-12). The risen Lord ascends to the divine realm, from which he will send the Spirit, as "the promise of my Father" (Lk 24:49).

Somewhat in contrast to these figurative representations of the trinitarian form of the resurrection event are those of a more schematic type. Here, the accent is less on the symbolic figuration and more on the conceptual presentation of the fullness of salvation in Christ. For example, major sections of the Pauline writings (Rom 8; Gal 3; 1 Cor 12; and Eph 1) show in their construction a clear outline of the trinitarian dimensions of the mystery of Christ: believers celebrate their status in Christ, through the initiative of the Father, and in the unity and power of the Spirit:

> There is one body and one Spirit, just as you were called to one hope that belongs to your call, one Lord, one faith, one baptism, one God and Father of us all, who is above all, and through all and in all (Eph 4:4-6).

Turning to John's Gospel, there is evidence of the evangelist's attempt to offer a more co-ordinated account of the fullness of grace and truth now present to the world in Jesus Christ (Jn 1:14). John is conveying a pattern for understanding the divine three in the one mystery of God, clearly influenced by the problems that necessarily arose from the preceding triadic proclamation of the grace of salvation. It is not, therefore, anachronistic to accept that John is already anticipating the doctrinal development of later centuries. If salvation begins with the Father who so loved the world (Jn 3:16), if the Son he gives for the world's salvation is to be confessed as "My Lord and my God" (Jn 20:28), and if he departs to send the "other Paraclete" from the Father (Jn 15:26), then the question could not be long in coming: How are these divine "three" who are demonstrably involved in salvation in Christ related to one another?

Central to the Johannine rhetoric are the exchanges between the Father and the Son in terms of love, life and mutual glorification. In this respect, the whole existence of the Word made flesh is dialogical: his origin is from the Father; his identity is that of being the only Son of the Father; his mission is to do the Father's will, and to reveal him to the world. In so living from and for the Father, he is sent from the Father, receives everything from him, and is one with him. Still, "the Father is greater" (Jn 14:28), the origin and goal of all that Jesus is. No one goes to the Father but by him, but no one can come to Jesus unless drawn by the Father (Jn 6:44). Both the speech of the Son and the silence of the Father who speaks only in this Word, express the character of the transcendent communion into which all believers are drawn. The prayer of Jesus in John 17 is the climax of this kind of rhetoric: ". . . that they may be all one even as you, Father, are in me and I in you, that they also may be in us" (Jn 17:21).

Compared to the clear delineations of Father and Son, the character of the Spirit is not as directly expressed in John's Gospel. On the other hand, the faith's hearing of the Word depends on the gift of the Spirit. For this "other Paraclete", "the Spirit of Truth", whom the Risen Jesus sends, "will teach you all things, and bring to mind all that I have said to you" (Jn 14:26). The Gospel can speak of the Father and the Son because the Spirit gives, and continues to give, an essential testimony (Jn 15:26). The Paraclete guides successive generations of believers into all truth (Jn 16:13). The Spirit is an implicit and pervasive presence in John's Gospel, inspiring the understanding of Christ and guiding its development. A problem seems to have clearly occurred to the evangelist regarding how the triadic overture of Christian faith was to be expressed: how was the presence of the Spirit related to the dialogical relationship existing between the Father and the Son? How did the Spirit figure in the communication taking place between the Father and the Son? At this point the Gospel shows an almost scholastic precision. Rhetorical expression becomes a precise statement of relationships, as Jesus addresses his disciples:

> I have many things to say to you but you cannot bear them now. When the Spirit of truth comes, he will guide you into all truth, for he will not speak on his own authority, but whatever he hears he will speak, for he will declare the things that are to come. He will take what is mine and declare it to you. All that the Father has is mine; therefore I said, he will take what is mine and declare it to you (Jn 16:12-16).

Evidently, the Spirit of Truth is the one who hears and receives what is going on between the Father and the Son in the wholeness of their communication. The Spirit is "of truth" in that he makes this communication open to believers, and draws them into it.

The least that can be said is that John is aware of the problem in the rhetoric of faith. The force of his logic begins to structure a way of thinking about the divine three. It draws its force from a sense of the divine as a field of loving communication which finds its expression in self-surrender to, and for the sake of, the other. The Son lives for the Father. The Father gives everything to the Son. Father and Son give everything over to the activity of the Spirit. The Spirit speaks not on his own authority, but from what he has heard from the Son, and by implication, from the Father—to glorify them both. The phenomenon of the resurrection event thus initiates the dynamics of trinitarian theology.

The Resurrection and Moral Theology

What might be the resurrection effect in moral theology? Given the immense expertise and refined attention to new ethical questions evident in the field of moral theology and Christian ethics, our remarks on the resurrection effect must necessarily be modest. Still, Brian Johnstone, one of the few who have addressed this question,[8] offers a rather disturbing overview. He notes that in neither Protestant nor Catholic versions of Christian ethics is the resurrection a central feature. Even for the eminent Bernard Häring, the cross is the dominant consideration. More recently, in the otherwise valuable works of Charles Curran and Claus Demmer, for example, the resurrection has at most an extrinsic motivational or supporting role. A significant exception is Oliver O'Donovan's *Resurrection and the Moral Order* in which he offers an outline of an evangelical ethics.[9] But even here, Johnstone considers that the resurrection functions as a reinstatement of the moral order of the world, rather than shaping it in a radical fashion. The writings of F.-X. Durrwell have certainly offered an inspiring spiritual vision, but they pretend to no practical ethical, let alone political, application. More recently, N.T. Wright certainly stresses the political importance of resurrection faith in New Testament times, but this does not carry over into contemporary ethical reflection. Moral theology is understandably intent in today's pluralistic world on the articulation and application of universally acceptable ethical norms. To that end, it calls on various versions of the venerable "natural law" tradition—which, in effect, means that the resurrection is quite extrinsic to the context of moral concern. So, the question: Does reflection on the moral life and its global significance remain unaffected by the resurrection event and the hope it inspires? Does the "nature" underpinning "natural law" acknowledge the transformative event of the resurrection? Is it methodologically excluded or deferred, or regarded as of merely motivational significance? On the other hand, the world-transforming event of the resurrection must provoke theology to view the nature of morality in some new way. Receptivity to the focal phenomenon of Christian faith must have some influence in inspiring a distinctive Christian "rationality" in the interpretation, ordering and promotion of the values motivating humanity's future in these increasingly critical times. There is a dilemma to be resolved—and an opportunity yet to be exploited in a thoroughgoing fashion.

We ask, first of all, why the resurrection seems to have affected moral deliberations so faintly. The answer predictably lies in the dominance of an abstract, ahistorical rationality over any sense of particularised reality. The resurrection, despite its cosmic and universal significance, is a very particular phenomenon. A generalised notion of "religious experience" is surely helpful for interfaith exchanges on the need for a global responsibility in issues such as peace, justice and the meaning of life. But something is amiss if the Christian contribution to such dialogue bypasses the originality and uniqueness of the event that gave rise to the Christian tradition itself. We have already argued that a more focused concreteness is made possible by considering the resurrection as a "saturated phenomenon" in Marion's sense. Its various manifestations (as "revelation", "event", "aesthetic form", "flesh", and "face") precede any ontological system, moral law or generalised notion of religious experience. In the phenomenality of the resurrection, the crucified One is disclosed as transformed himself and transforming others, in the power of a self-giving love greater than the death-dealing powers of the world. Such a phenomenon must have its effect, not only on the motivation, but on the method and content of Christian moral responsibility. This may sound like a naïve or fundamentalist simplicity in an incredibly complex world. But there is room for a second, more critical simplicity when theology refocuses its moral deliberations in the light of the resurrection.

No doubt there are many possible responses to the question of how the resurrection might be appreciated as an intrinsic factor in the style, mood and rationality of Christian morality. Besides, theologians working in this area might be apprehensive of negative possibilities at this point, such as a narrowing of a desired moral perspective. Engagement with the values of the secular world in numerous ethical fields might be weakened by what is so unique to the Christian tradition. Admittedly, there is no easy answer. But nor is the situation as simple as it may appear. For example, there is a sense in which the secular world is showing a new, largely unnamed, moral awareness of responsibility to the victims of history. Remarking on this unprecedented contemporary phenomenon, Girard observes, "No historical period, no society we know, has ever spoken of victims . . . you will not find anything anywhere that even remotely resembles our modern concern for victims ... It is the secular face of Christian love".[10] It manifests itself by giving a new hearing to voices from the underside of history, hitherto drowned out by the "success stories" of the powerful. Despite the nihilistic relativism and moral confusions of the age, there is obviously something else at work. It is a powerful factor in any form of social and political awareness. To the degree this is so, the resurrection of the crucified Jesus justifies no retreat from the world, but rather a greater involvement in it.

One of the most noble carriers of a new awareness was the United Nations' *Universal Declaration on Human Rights* (UDHR) in 1948. It gave rise to innumerable commitments to the values of justice in the political process of most of the world's governments.[11] Recognition of the dispossessions suffered by indigenous peoples in the colonial period, claims of poor countries for cancellation of debts, and even the present awakening to ecological values, are all part of the picture. The once marginalised are now within the frame. With the collapse of totalitarian regimes has come a deep suspicion of any self-glorifying version of the history of any particular nation, society or culture. Whether the response is one of authentic compassion or not, the cry of victims cannot be easily dismissed.

As a result, conscience stirs with a refreshed sense of justice. Typically it speaks in the name of a more inclusive common good, in the language of universal rights, and political and economic emancipation. Theologically speaking, this is evidence of a "searching Christology" that will find its fullest meaning in the God revealed in the crucified and risen Victim. It suggests, in a field of mustard seeds, how the gospel slowly permeates the world, sprouting in the stony ground of the violence inherent in any human culture. The reign of God does not lack its signs.

In this context, Michael Ignatieff has made a perceptive observation regarding this extraordinary development in the history of moral conscience:

> Rights are universal because they define the universal interests of the powerless—namely that power be exercised over them in ways that respect their autonomy as [moral] agents ... [Rights] represent a revolutionary creed, since they make a radical demand of all human groups that they serve the interests of the individuals that compose them.[12]

The powerless who effectively had no rights are recognised as having inviolable human rights. Those who in effect possessed no autonomy in the political world begin to enjoy an institutional recognition of their human dignity. The affirmation of human rights is, therefore, a "revolutionary creed". Any human group must now conceive of the common good in a more inclusive way: those who in the past had been left out of political calculation demand now to be acknowledged.

While it is true that the terrible toll of the victims of totalitarian regimes has pricked the conscience of the international community, that conscience has not been uniformly reformed. The moral revolution that was hoped for has been frustrated in innumerable instances. One example of this frustration is the prevalence of a spurious language of victimhood. Claiming "victim status" has now become a familiar manipulative technique in politics. Contributing to this distortion was one aspect of the UDHR itself. As its framers admitted, what was lacking was a fully articulated declaration of responsibilities—on the part of persons, communities and institutions—concerned with the implementation of the basic rights in question. That would be dealt with in a later agenda.[13] With no reasoned grounding of universal human rights in universal responsibility, rights-language can be simply taken over by a consumerist culture. If that is the case, the appeal to rights is no more than a political machination, a useful rhetoric for the exercise of power. It balloons out into an uncontrolled assertion of rights, individual or corporate, against others, without any commitment to the common good or responsibility for the truly powerless. And so it happens that the originally noble conception of human rights for all is trivialised, liable to exploitation by the politically adept few. Shared responsibility for the most vulnerable and powerless is thus compromised. A study by L. C. Keith sought to assess how much belonging to the International Covenant on Civil and Political Rights affected the promotion of human rights.[14] After examining a hundred and seventy eight countries over an eighteen-year period, his conclusions were not optimistic: observable impact was minimal.

Yet somehow hidden in this new awareness is a stirring of conscience. Despite the waning of what was once termed "Christian civilisation", it would seem that the paschal mystery of Christ's death and resurrection has in fact been penetrating human history in a surprising way. Even though the moral and philosophical foundation of human rights remains largely unarticulated, even if a kind of cultural amnesia with regard to the historical sources of social meaning and values is often lamented, the resurrection effect has had its influence. There is a sense, however inarticulate and obscure, that, in the end, the proud are scattered in the conceit of their hearts, the mighty are toppled from their thrones, and the lowly, from the underside of history, are lifted up (Lk 1:52-53).

The moral precariousness of this new conscience with regard to the poor and the powerless provokes a fresh theological reception of the resurrection as the focal Christian phenomenon. For it is the self-disclosure of the truth "that will make you free" (Jn 8:32), the stone rejected by the builders of fortresses against the outsider has been made the chief cornerstone of a home open to all (1 Pet 2:4-8; Mt 21:42; Mk 12:11;

Acts 4:11; cf. Ps 117: 22). A pacific humanity is in-the-making. Domination, exploitation and envy have no place in a culture of peace, while love of the other, forgiveness and reconciliation, solidarity with the suffering are the necessary values. Paul's words have a striking modern relevance: "Bless those who persecute you; bless and do not curse them. . . . do not repay anyone evil for evil, but take thought for what is noble in the sight of all. If it is possible, so far as depends on you, live peaceably with all" (Rom 12:17-19; cf. 14:13). How can we express more exactly the connection of a pacific humanity with the resurrection of the crucified Jesus?

The very gap in the UDHR and the current confusion as to what constitutes the basis of human rights open a door inviting Christian theology to enter. It would mean something like this: Jesus' rising from the dead undermines the history of mutual blaming and victimisation. He freely exposed himself to the violence of cultural forces in order to disrupt, once and for all, the old world order based on the victimisation of others. His resurrection is not a new thought, but an irruptive and communicative event. It has its effect in a human community transformed into the image of the self-giving love of God. Jesus is glorified, not so as to glorify the role of the victim, but to unmask the victimising dynamics latent in all societies. The resurrection of this victim has a disturbing but liberating effect in the human community. It demands to be taken as the decisive influence in human relationships, the inexhaustible inspiration of responsibility for those victimised by suffering and oppression. Those who have suffered as victims and martyrs, and those who have caused such suffering as oppressors and persecutors are alike enfolded in the originary compassion and forgiveness embodied in the risen One.

How Christian moral theology might respond practically to the provocation of the resurrection is a continuing challenge. At issue is a Christian social praxis explicitly focused on the resurrection of the Crucified. Liberation and political theologies, along with the Church's growing body of social teaching, certainly express a Christian solidarity with the weak and the oppressed. The more realistic the understanding and the more practical the application of this sense of Christian solidarity, the more a problem emerges. Any reference to the resurrection can appear as a way of evading the hard, demanding edge of social responsibilities. But need this be so? I would suggest that the resurrection not only does not distract from social responsibilities, it is exactly what a socially and politically concerned Christian morality most needs.

In the self-disclosures of the risen Victim, his disciples receive their mission. They are sent out to work for transformation of the world in the light and in the power of what has already been anticipated in Christ's rising from the dead. However this mission is expressed, it must evidence compassion and responsibility for those who, like the Crucified, have suffered under the death-dealing power of the world. It proclaims a liberation that death is powerless to inhibit. Such a mission finds the source of its energies in the continuing prayer: that the name of the God who raised up Jesus be hallowed, that the kingdom of such a God will come, and that the life-giving will of the Father of Jesus will be done—now on earth, as in the heaven of God's intention "in the beginning". Thus, the "resurrectional" act of God is the source, inspiration and hope of "resurrectional" praxis intent on uplifting the suffering other. It finds expression in the moral imperatives of peace, justice and human dignity.

Jesus' rising from the dead is an expansive event. In the protological and eschatological dimensions of God's saving action, the first and last word is peace and reconciliation. The beginning and the end are not marked with a continuing dialectic of conflict between good and evil. To grasp that is to see that the "other", however malevolent, death-dealing, indifferent—or simply "different"—is not a terminal threat to Christian integrity. All are destined to belong in Christ and to find their reconciliation in him. The "other" can never be sacrificed for the sake of "me" or "us", for "we", in the most comprehensive sense, belong together. The Gospel is clearly quite aware of the contrary perverse option: Caiaphas is prepared to sacrifice Jesus for the stability of the political and religious order (Jn 11:50), while Pilate consigns him to death for reasons of the imperial *pax Romana*.

Political accommodations of that type presume a certain conception of peace. But it is ever fragile and elusive, achievable only through calculations of a balance of power. There is, however, a basic irony in this position: for when is power ever content with a balance? Rivals must remain a threat; and if a threat, there is really no place for them in any future desirable state of affairs. They do not belong with "us" in what is coming to be. In contrast, the resurrection of the crucified Jesus embodies peace as the reconciliatory event which has already occurred.[15] God has acted by vindicating *the* Victim. For the sake of an all-inclusive salvation, Jesus had chosen the way of powerlessness, in contrast to the way of power and domination of others. In the vulnerability of love, he had given himself over to the peace that only God can give. Such love and such peace are the radical subversion of "the way things are" and of the authority of "the powers that be". The inviolable, religiously-sanctioned, social and political order thus has reason to fear. The kind of future that Jesus embodies inspires the conviction that the mighty are to be toppled from their thrones and the lowly and despised raised up (Lk 1:52-53). The event of Christ's resurrection changed this hope from the apparently naïve and impractical idea which made him its chief casualty, to an eschatological vindication of his way of seeing and imagining the world. Consequently, the resurrection event is to be presumed, and, in a profound sense, given into all the labour of peace-making. In this regard, the risen Jesus is peace-in-person. He comes in the trinitarian

vitality of self-giving love, as the way and the truth in which reconciliation is offered to the world. Through his resurrection, the divine persons are disclosed to the world of violence as being from and for each
other in a dynamic of mutual love. Such a divine unity, eternally differentiated and eternally achieved in self-giving love, is the all-encompassing and final truth. Outside and apart from this source and exemplar,
any hope for reconciliation or peace-making activity is deprived of its
ultimate support.

The theological horizon must unfold, therefore, in an open-ness to
the phenomenon of the resurrection. The resurrection of the Crucified
saturates all moral existence. It is the revelation, from beginning to end,
of a communication demanding the re-ordering of all human and religious values. God is revealed in action. The Spirit of the resurrection
counters the idolatrous pretensions of any totalitarian ideology, along
with the violence and victimisation it demands. A new covenant is written into the flesh and blood of the risen victim. In him is disclosed God's
unconditional love for the world—even at the point of maximum evil.
The event of this gift of the new covenant, already realised in Christ and
communicated in his Spirit, renders obsolete the contractual calculations that structure a world against the weak for the advantage of the
powerful. By raising the crucified Victim from the dead, the God of this
covenant exposes the flimsy power-deals made for the purpose of domi-
nating others. The endless dialectic of competitive identities, of the self
asserting itself over the other, is negated at root. An empty tomb becomes a troubling space at the heart of any "order" and "peace" founded
on the domination of the poor and the powerless. This stone, rejected
by the builders of self-serving societies, has become the chief cornerstone for a civilisation of peace and ultimate reconciliation. An alternative form of justice is engendered. The kind of politics intent merely on
restoring the balance of entitlements in a radically diseased and violent
world is called into question. Once the resurrection has occurred, that
"world is passing away" (1 John 2:17). In the new aeon already begun,
justice is newly defined through the vindication of the crucified Victim.
Justice, in such a light, must become the expression of the moral imagination of love. It promotes solidarity with all victims. It realises that
reconciliation of enemies is the only way forward. It dares to see forgiveness as a practical option.

Problems, of course, abound. The political and social seductions of the
death penalty are perennial. New issues arise related to torturing enemies
for the sake of national security. The conditions legitimating war in de-
fence of national or regional interests are the subject of endless delibera-
tion. Is there a point when all such options appear as counsels of des-
peration in a world where nothing has really changed, and no real change
is possible? And is that point found precisely in the resurrection of the
crucified Jesus? Whatever the complexity moral prudence recognises in

the instances just named, that prudence remains questionable if it used to guide human conduct in the world without any recognition of how God has decisively acted within and for it. For the prudence appropriate to a post-resurrectional world is a practical anticipation of eschatological peace. It guides a vision of human community in which the victimisation of some is not the precondition of lasting life for others. The divinely-given victim has unmasked the assumption that making victims is the prelude to peace. His resurrection reveals the ultimate fruitfulness of sharing in his self-giving love.[16] This is to say that the resurrection event inspires the creativity of a new manner of conceiving the common good. Such a new social imagination draws its inspiration, not from some utopian dream, but from the event that changed everything. To meet the challenges involved cannot but be experienced as a terrible risk. The moral life is left with no support other than the way the true God has acted. If that is true, if the source, form and goal of life have been finally revealed in this manner, how can Christian morality not "risk" itself on the belief that what it holds to be true is, as a fundamental fact, really true?

However implicitly Christ's paschal mystery has been at work in the long struggle for emancipation from the oppressions of poverty, power-lessness and degradation, it demands a fresh consideration. In the face of the disillusionment and impotence, all the passionate energies of lib-eration, all the courageous critiques of the way things are, do not finally rely on some mythic symbol or on an ever-deferred future. That future is already inscribed into the reality of history.[17] It is the source of an impetus to something more, and more worthy of God's transformative judgment on human and cosmic history. To this degree, the work of liberation is not first of all the efforts of some courageous few limited human beings concerned to free their fellows, but a sharing in the divine liberative freedom already enacted and at work in the resurrection of Jesus. The compassionate freedom of the transcendent Other, unre-strained by human violence and death, is in action. As a result, it is no more a matter of some, however enlightened and empowered, pitting themselves against recalcitrant others, but of sharing in the self-giving love of the Other whose grace embraces all. In this way, the unknow-able future can be approached only through what has already antici-pated it. The assurance of what is to come and of what is already in-the-making is earthed in the singularity of the resurrection event. The enormous excess of evil, increasingly apparent in its global proportions, is met by another excess, that of love, stronger than any death we know. It has already raised up the Crucified, and made him the source of life to the full (Jn 10:10). At that crucial juncture, the sting of death's power is drawn. The great prophets and martyrs who have given their lives for others are present to the world in the God to whom all are forever alive (Mk 12:18-27; Mt 22:23-33; Lk 20:27-38).[18] The "natural law" built on a communication of global moral values need not be continually mocked by the excess of evil. It is a way of hopeful moral thinking within a history in which the ultimate vindication of human values has occurred in Christ. In a singularly evocative passage, Vatican II's *Gaudium et Spes* points theology in the right direction:

> We know neither the moment of the consummation of the earth or of the human, nor the way the universe will be transformed. The form of this world, distorted by sin, is passing away; and we are taught that God is preparing a new dwelling and a new earth in which righteousness dwells, whose happiness will fill and surpass all the desires for peace arising in human hearts . . .
>
> When we have spread on earth the fruits of our nature and our enterprise—human dignity, fraternal communion, and freedom—according to the command of the Lord and in his Spirit, we will find them once again, cleansed this time from the stain of sin, illuminated and transfigured, when Christ presents to his Father an eternal and universal kingdom . . . Here on earth the kingdom is mysteriously present; when the Lord comes, it will enter into its perfection.[19]

Since, in this vision, it is the values human dignity, community and freedom that have a future, it is "natural" for moral theology to expand its solidarity with all humanity, aspiring to an ultimate good that is not ever at the perverse mercy of evil. Thus, the resurrection event is productive of a universalising, inclusive form of moral reasoning, not as a "second best", but as pertaining to the universal significance of the resurrection itself. "Natural law", in this sense, is the eschatological law of humanity on its path to transformation—and to resurrection in Christ. It remains a mode of ethical thinking within the world of violence and evil. But it sees further. It looks through the recognition of the rights and dignity of all to glimpse the destiny of everyone as called to participate in the communion of eternal life.

The "supernatural" event of the resurrection occurs within a world built on the assumption that the dead stay dead, and that victory belongs to the powerful. Yet it affects the natural moral law, not as an extrinsic motivation, but as an inexhaustibly productive force. It animates moral reasoning, in this respect, as an expression of hope: the values it appeals to and the meaning of personal existence it promotes energise self-transcendence to the point where each one can be a redemptive presence in the community, and each community a creator of a more human future. The last word is not left to death, and to the powers that use the threat of death for their purposes. The resurrection effect is not beholden to an ontology of violence—allowing at best for a balance of power. But it does inspire a patient ontology of peace and of the eternal life in which all that is best in human existence will find its future in the transforming love of God. In such moral thinking, the resurrection is pre-eminently the "God Effect".[20] Understandably, moral theologians and Christian ethicists may well observe a certain disciplina arcani in the conduct of conversations in many areas of ethics today. But this does not mean, nor must it mean, a methodological exclusion of the significance of God's victory over evil in raising Jesus from the tomb. Detached from this event that makes all the difference, Christian moral discourse, however it might attempt to be relevant to a culture that is cut off from its Christian roots, would become irrelevant to what is most fundamental to its vision of the world and its future. At the price of its authenticity, Christian theology cannot pretend that the resurrection has not happened.

Transcultural Openness

As many have been pointing out, our historical present is marked in a special way by the travail of being born into a new stage of history. The change that is taking place provokes trans-cultural consciousness, thereby making imperative a new global integration of human relations—international, inter-religious and intercultural. There is inevitably a worldwide turbulence: previous rigid patterns of division break down, and crises of identity, community and moral responsibility ensue. For example, what Thompson terms the "the over-fed ego"[21] of Western cultural and political domination is being provoked into becoming a more dialogical self. The Northern Hemisphere has become aware that the wide world contains a hemisphere of the South, more populous, more religious in its way, not predominantly white, politically unstable in a post-colonial phase, and certainly poorer.[22] The hitherto unknown or unregarded other cannot be ignored. Hence, there arises the critique of the kind of mono-cultural globalism that is unaware of the vast, differentiated cultural inheritance of the whole of humanity and the critique of the purely economic globalism that serves multinational corporations and leaves the billions to continue to live in poverty.

Such distortions are not the whole story. Something of profound historical importance is taking place. A development of global consciousness is occurring, deeper and broader than any reductively economic description of the phenomenon. Far from occasioning a breakdown in Christian faith, there is no reason why this troubling of former cultural, national and ethnic boundaries should not result in a breakthrough into a new stage of benign co-existence. Indeed, an expansion of global consciousness accords with a fresh appreciation of the transcendent character of the risen Christ. He has risen beyond the containment of any culture or any one stage of history, to be the light of the world in its entirety. This is to say that the risen Jesus is the space, as it were, of both fulfilment and reconciliation in a way which anticipates and provokes

fresh forms of global solidarity. This is not to deny the discomfort occasioned by the collapse of the old boundaries behind which human, or
even Christian, cultural identities functioned in their respective forms of
self-containment. The crisis of particular historical forms of culture is
the pain of a rebirth into another realm of communication, more intense and open compared to anything experienced in the past. The hand
that hurts is the hand that heals. In a new phase of history, larger dimensions of life and new horizons of human selfhood and community are
coming to light, as, in the words of the poet,

> For each age is a dream that is dying,
> Or one that is coming to birth.[23]

Christ is risen, but not as an idol formed by the projections and sup-
posed triumph of any particular culture or religious history. He is given
as the icon of the invisible God, through whom the light of God's universal saving purposes shines. Compared to the historical limits in ancient Palestine, he now belongs to "all nations" and to all times (Mt
28:19), calling for a worship of the one true God "neither on this mountain nor in Jerusalem" (Jn 4:23). Peter found two millennia ago, as he
journeyed from Joppa and then—to the scandal of his Jewish connections—as he entered the house of the pagan Cornelius, that there are no
human limits to the saving will of God (Acts 10:34; cf. 10:1-48). The
resurrection does not mean the glorification of the heritage of Israel,
nor that of the Christian West, nor that of any other culture or location.[24] By entering into our hitherto locked cultural and historical rooms,
the risen One is the luminous space in which the limitless world beyond
is disclosed as the theatre of God's saving purpose. In him, Christian
faith experiences not only the opening of heaven (Jn 1:51), but also the
opening of the world to new proportions.[25]

This transcultural openness of faith in the risen Jesus is not an extrinsic property of Christian existence. His resurrection is more than an
apologetic proof for the truth of Christianity. Nor is it an incitement to
that kind of energetic evangelization that leaves one's own culture
uncriticized and the value of other cultures unrecognised.[26] The resurrection floods Christian consciousness with an expanding sense of universality: "And I, when I am lifted up from the earth, will draw all
people to myself" (Jn 12:32). To this degree, Christ's rising from the
tomb relativises all cultures. It draws each of them out of itself in order
to find itself anew in a universe of grace. If Jesus is the life and light of
"the world", faith in him is necessarily an outreach to all peoples. In
this regard, his departure from the conditions of earthly existence into
the realm of the Father creates a field of new communion with him. It
reaches beyond the exclusions and limitations of the past. In that ever-
new space is found "the advantage" (Jn 16:7) of the Spirit witnessing to

"the many things" that Jesus' disciples could not previously bear (Jn 16:12)—"the things that are to come" (v. 13). Faith thus reaches out to the limitless otherness beyond it. In hearing the words of the risen Jesus, such faith must respond to the original Other from whom he comes: "As the Father has sent me, so I send you" (Jn 20:21).

We have remarked elsewhere[27] that one of the great signs of hope today is the interfaith dialogue taking place on many levels. Those who speak for the deeper places of the heart and the higher reaches of the spirit are playing a part in the emergence of a global human culture. Such a meeting of religions and spiritualities cannot but make the world more hospitable to the values of peace and justice, compassion and human dignity. Eminent missiologists recognise the eschatological or hope-oriented aspect of this dialogue.[28] Engagement in such dialogue is a manifestation of the outreach of the Kingdom of the God who "desires everyone to be saved and to come to the knowledge of the truth" (1 Tim 2:4). But what we wish to emphasise is that this eschatological universality is an effect of the resurrection of the Crucified. That singular event is the effective disclosure of the actuality of God's reign in history and creation. As such, it is the ever-productive impetus to the Church's mission. The risen Jesus reveals himself in the act of sending forth his disciples to all nations and throughout all time.

Nor is it a question of simply adopting a more comprehensive trinitarian framework for interfaith encounters, as has been brilliantly exploited in the writings of Raimundo Panikkar and Jacques Dupuis. For, as we argued above, the phenomenon of the resurrection gave rise to the framework in the first place. For example, Dupuis has carefully clarified the undoubtedly christocentric focus of his approach. Nonetheless, to guard against any narrow and non-trinitarian christomonism, he supplements his theological method with a strongly trinitarian component.[29] Still, the phenomenality of the resurrection is, as we suggested above, the reason for this trinitarian supplement and the theologies that serve it. Yet note Dupuis' words:

> The historic event of Jesus Christ, of itself and of necessity, is particular and circumscribed by the limits of space and time. The human life of Jesus belongs to a particular time and to a precise location; the mystery of the resurrection is itself an event registered punctually in history, even though it introduces the human being of Jesus into a "metahistoric" condition. And, while it is true that, in the glorified state of the risen Christ, the historic salvific event becomes present and actual for all times and in all places, it remains also true that this event does not by itself exhaust—nor can it exhaust—the revelatory and salvific power of the Word of God. While Jesus' human being can never be separated from the person

of the Word of God, neither can the two be identified, as the two natures remain distinct in the personal union.[30]

This is a careful statement, and one must agree with Dupuis that in a genuine sense the resurrection cannot and does not "exhaust" the "revelatory and salvific power of the Word of God". On the other hand, it is not quite clear how faith comes to celebrate this revelatory and salvific power without being receptive to the inexhaustible significance of the resurrection for faith in God's Word and for the theologies that serve it. This event precedes any trinitarian articulation of its meaning. It certainly precedes the Chalcedonian distinctions of nature and person that the above passage refers to. Most of all, the resurrection of Jesus both precedes and inspires the mission of Christian faith to the world, and the theological formulations that guide it.

In conclusion, a more practical possibility: what would be the implications of replacing the usual term "interfaith" with the designation "inter-hope" for describing the inter-religious types of dialogue that are occurring? "Inter-hope" in such a context suggests looking beyond, say, negotiations regarding civil collaboration and democratic freedom, and even beyond theological agreement on a number of themes or doctrines. Set within the horizon of hope and its expectation of an ultimate communion in eternal life, another kind of mutual openness and sympathy comes into play. Inter-hope dialogue evokes the unimaginable "otherness" of eschatological fulfilment. It looks beyond what is, to what is to come. While there is continuity between the present apprehensions of all faiths and eternal life, there is also the discontinuity which only humble adoration dimly discerns. What is hidden will, in the end, be made clear. Dialogue between various religious and spiritual traditions reveals, of course, quite complex differences in eschatological understanding—the future of the individual self, the nature of God, and the meaning of salvation.[31]

Despite the differences and conflicts that have shaped the past of the various religious traditions, the future is what all have in common. At the point where all look forward to a hoped for future, Christian hope, centred in the resurrection of the crucified Jesus, has a vital mediating role. If Christians must never give up hope even for their enemies and persecutors, there is surely a lot that can be said—or left unsaid in the necessary darkness of our present perceptions—regarding the ultimate reconciliation of their friends and partners in dialogue. There is the breadth and length and height and depth of the mystery (Eph 3:18)—dimensions still to be discovered. The love of Christ "surpasses knowledge" (Eph 3:19). It includes all in whom the Spirit of love and hope is moving. Dialogue may reach an impasse, and will certainly pose its problems, but the Christians involved must wait on the unfathomable freedom of the One "who by the power at work within us is able to accomplish abundantly far more than all we can ask or imagine" (Eph 3:20). The mission of dialogue must, in short, wait on its prayers to be answered and for the revelation that has occurred in the resurrection of Christ to keep on being revelation in ways still to be disclosed. If such an attitude is criticized for being too specifically Christian, then at least it will be criticized for the right reasons—namely, for having too much hope in the Other rather than too little—and for all others in our common longing for eternal life. In the light of Christ, these "others" are not identified as individuals on the level of past conflicts and mutual incomprehension. It is not a question of a religious subterfuge, but rather of receptivity to the gift embodied in "the resurrection and the life" that includes all. The other side of such receptivity is the readiness to take the last place in the service of all who together are called to eternal life.

In this chapter we have been touching on how theology can register the resurrection effect in its various topics. In this regard, we selected just three considerations, namely, the Trinity, moral theology and interfaith dialogue. Such instances were meant to illustrate the possibilities of a much more comprehensive project, that of recasting theology and spirituality in the light of the resurrection. If Christ has been raised, a reflective faith is ever being challenged to think "otherwise".

CHAPTER 10

Resurrection as Horizon

The preceding chapters have examined the "resurrection effect" in Christian life and thought. Different perspectives converged on the resurrection of Christ as the originating phenomenon for Christian faith. We first exploited Marion's notion of the saturated phenomenon. That enabled us to present the resurrection event as uniquely revelatory, in the sense of it being the culminating and definitive moment in God's self-revelation. Then, because the resurrection is the world-transforming event in human history, while remaining inherently indefinable, it catches the believer up into the prodigality of its original and unfolding significance. To an aesthetic mode of consciousness, it comes with the attractive and inexhaustible force of a work of art, inviting the receptivity and participation of faith, the ability to see and to sense the world "otherwise". Further, the transformation of the flesh of the Crucified means for him a full-bodied existence at once embracing and transforming our incarnate existence: his body and flesh, in ways that transcend mortal thinking, is the communicative field in which he dwells in his members, and they in him, nourished by his body and blood and breathing his Spirit. In consequence, the phenomenon of the resurrection communicates the experience of being "faced" by Christ throughout all time and space, not only as the form, source and anticipation of eternal life, but as summoning the believer to see him and to respond to him as the Other in the face of all others.

In such a phenomenological context, we moved on to the literary phenomenon of the New Testament itself. Here, we remarked on the creativity and "negativity" of its rhetoric as it strained to word what had occurred but which could never be fully expressed in its eschatological significance. From the resurrection effect in the literary phenomenon of the New Testament, we moved to the resurrection event itself and the multi-dimensionality of its appearance in the experience of faith. These inevitably more general descriptions were re-focused in the particularity of Paul's experience, since, in a remarkable way, he presents himself as the very embodiment of the resurrection effect in his vocation and apostolic mission. Our exposition then grappled with the resurrection as a visual phenomenon. One form of seeing had come to an end with Paul, yet that did not mean that the life of faith was blind. Other forms of gifted "seeing" and sensing belong to the resurrection effect in the history of the Church, as the Spirit works in Christian consciousness to open it to the new creation.

Problems associated with the objective and subjective aspects of the phenomenon then had to be faced. While we pointed out the inadequacy of such distinctions, they retain a relative value by illuminating different aspects of the event that always eludes mundane categories and separations. We emphasised, therefore, the "salvific" character of resurrection, so that polarities of subjectivity and objectivity would be properly located in a God-given field of communication. With that presupposed, we were enabled to bring together the objective and subjective aspects of the resurrection phenomenon in what is hoped to be a coherent and useful manner. The final chapter, necessarily more exploratory and provocative, extended the consideration of the resurrection effect into various theological areas which have often seemed oddly unaffected by the resurrection event. We gave three examples—trinitarian theology, moral theology and the theology of interfaith dialogue.

While I hope that this book will refresh reflective faith with a sense of the resurrection, I sympathise with those readers who might suspect that some cunning amalgam of fundamentalism, revelational positivism and naïve realism has put on a phenomenological mask. That is the risk, but I am convinced that it is a risk worth taking. For what is apparent is that the resurrection, instead of being the determining feature of Christian consciousness and life in the Spirit, easily slips out of focus. It is always *there*—somehow. It might figure as an element of apologetics or a special question in fundamental theology. Presumably it would be a concluding theme in Christology, while being implicit in sacramentology and a determining feature of eschatology. Presumably, too, the resurrection affects the deep motivation in morality, the praxis of liberation, and spirituality as the Church celebrates the various seasons of its liturgical year. It *is* there in different ways; but as I wrote in the introductory chapter, it is somewhat awkwardly located, and even neglected altogether once the "real business" of the theoretical and practical considerations of Christian life gets under way.

Hence, these pages have aimed to sharpen the focus and to redress the balance. Perhaps the point I tried to make seems so obvious as not to need any such statement at all. But it is no harm to restate what I hope is splendidly obvious to Christian faith; and if some readers feel that this is what they always thought and that this book was hardly necessary, I would not be disconsolate. Nonetheless, I remain unconvinced that such is generally the case. And for that reason I have tried a different approach designed to highlight the productive significance of the resurrection, not as a particular part of a theological system nor as an extrinsic motivation, not as a symbol of a new consciousness of the Spirit, but as the phenomenon which saturates our understanding of the scriptures, sacramental celebrations, and the whole life and conduct of ecclesial faith. Receptivity to the phenomenon of the resurrection, openness to the prodigality of its effect, must be both critically and contemplatively recognised as the ongoing and permanent condition for Christian thought and practice. Paradoxically, the postmodern suspicion of philosophically articulated theological systems presents an opportunity to return to this all-meaningful phenomenon with a refreshed sensibility. The Anselmian "faith seeking understanding" must first of all be faith receptive to what has been given, and to what most attracts our seeking. The inexhaustible wonder of the gift embodied in the resurrection of the Crucified demands a continuing effort to explore and understand. Christian thinking is not moving well if it is intent on "proving" the resurrection, when all the time it is more a question of "approving" it as the all-deciding event, and of allowing our thinking to be "proved" and tested by what changed everything.

Not only does this attitude of receptivity provoke a continuing re-reading of the scriptures in the light of the resurrection, it also inspires a re-reading of the theological classics in order to re-appropriate their abiding value. Theological methods have changed; and history presents theologians with different challenges and new questions. For example, one can be disappointed at how little, it would seem, that the systematic theology of St. Thomas Aquinas is affected by the resurrection. I have already made some remarks corrective of such an impression. After all, Aquinas speaks of the resurrection of Christ as the "efficient and exemplary cause of our resurrection".[1] In a sense, everything I have been saying can be found implicit in the sixteen articles of the *Summa*, dealing with its intrinsic meaning of the resurrection, the state of the Christ's risen body, and the manifestation and causality deriving from his rising from the dead.[2] Furthermore, Thomist specialists constantly point to the pervasive character of the resurrection in Thomas' scriptural and theological commentaries.[3] Still, what Aquinas took for granted in the medieval world of Christendom needs now to be more explicitly retrieved in its distinctive originality within the profoundly different world in which faith must now live. In its long history, theology has appealed to various kinds of experiential grounding. Following Augustine, Aquinas interpreted the consciousness of grace as "a kind of experimental knowledge".[4] The Christian contemplative "suffers things divine" (*patiens divina*).[5] The foregoing pages have attempted to show how this experiential aspect of the classic medieval tradition can be profitably re-focused in the resurrection event. It is disclosed as the overbrimming act of divine grace. From it opens the distinctive horizon of Christian faith, hope and love within which moral action and theological thought must move. Faith seeks understanding by first being receptive to what has been given in the particularity of the phenomenon of the resurrection. It is endlessly provocative of theological thought and moral responsibility, but ever inexhaustible in its significance.

When it comes to the theology of the present and the ways in which the resurrection figures, in the course of writing this book on the resurrection and in relying on some of the eminent thinkers concerned, I have the sense of living with a many-sided problem that is not likely to be solved quickly or easily. My frequent citations of the writings of von Balthasar indicate a considerable sympathy for the aesthetic phenomenology of his approach, and an admiration for his extraordinary grasp of the Christian revelatory event as it is disclosed to faith. In his exploration of the multi-faceted phenomenality of the gift of God in Christ, this great Swiss theologian, like Karl Barth before him, evokes the transcendent objectivity of revelation as the self-disclosure of the divine subject. His emphasis is on the uniqueness of the Christian phenomenon even while situating it with unmatched erudition within the history of religious and philosophical thought. Though his vast oeuvre is a commanding elaboration of theological meaning, it contains mythic-dramatic elements that have caused some unease, especially his highly dramatic and seemingly untraditional treatment of Holy Saturday in the *triduum paschale*.[6]

Von Balthasar's contemplative perception of the death and burial of Jesus—his being dead among the dead and descent into hell—seems to break free from the form of the paschal phenomenon as it is presented in both scripture and the liturgical tradition. This is certainly not the case with his treatment of the resurrection, illuminating aspects of which I have already appealed to in the preceding chapters. Still, there is a problem, and it has been perceptively addressed by Robert Doran by comparing the methods of Lonergan and von Balthasar.[7] The theological method of the former is ostensibly the polar opposite of the latter. Where von Balthasar speaks of the particularity of the Christian event in terms of God's self-disclosive act, Lonergan grounds his method in the self-transcending subject. His terms and categories appear to go from the general (shared by all searchers for meaning, truth and goodness) to the particular—expressed in the "outward" word of revelation in Christian tradition.[8] For his part, von Balthasar concentrates on the luminous particularity of biblical events. From that point, his thinking unfolds, using the resources of his erudition, through a variety of concentric circles. It might be said that he is the master in elaborating the aesthetically-given and dramatically-enacted revelatory event. Lonergan, on the other hand, is the master of meaning in all its stages, dimensions, carriers, modes and so on. Doran does not see the two as polar opposites, and I agree. For example, I have made extensive use of many of Lonergan's categories in the course of this work, especially in suggesting how the phenomenon of the resurrection is productive of different dimensions of meaning. In his theological method,[9] Lonergan has little to say about revelation, and even less about the resurrection. Although my presentation of the resurrection as the heart of revelation is more easily aligned to von Balthasar's approach, it has nonetheless been notably strengthened by Lonergan's method. Let me give a brief indication: Doran relates von Balthasar's aesthetics to Lonergan's method by exploiting the categories of "potential meaning" and "conversion"—and, in this case, what Doran terms "psychic" conversion.[10] I would simply state that the phenomenon, however actual as an event, is always the site of "potential meaning", and, indeed, of a limitless potential of meaning. From the shock and confusion of the earliest witnesses, to the risen Jesus himself exegeting the scriptures in the midst of his disciples, to the creation of the New Testament itself and the development of the sacramental forms of the liturgy, and on to the efforts of theology in every age to grasp and explore the significance of all this for thought and praxis, the phenomenon of the resurrection has been a site of "potential" meaning. Moreover, even though I appreciate Doran's specification of "psychic" conversion on the level of imagination and affect as supplementary to the religious, moral and intellectual aspects of conversion shaping the very foundations of theological thinking, my emphasis has been more on receptivity to the resurrection event. It entails a phase of what we might term "phenomenological conversion"—not only to the phenomenon of consciousness itself as Lonergan has so compellingly presented it, but to the resurrection as the focal phenomenon of Christian faith in its "saturating" effect on consciousness. It provokes its own kind of conversion and a self-engagement governed by what is given in the resurrection of the Crucified. Embedded in Lonergan's account of the dynamics of conscious self-transcendence are the "transcendental precepts, Be attentive, Be intelligent, Be reasonable, Be responsible".[11] In this respect, I have endeavoured to stress the necessity of the first, "Be attentive", so that attentiveness is focused on what most demands attention—an event that is not the product of our knowledge and choice, but one that dismantles and abolishes the horizon of what our previous knowing and choosing presupposed. The resurrection introduces a new horizon in which the transformative act of God's love affects every dimension of our consciousness, to transvalue our values and engender new dimensions of meaning in our understanding of God, our selves, and our world.[12]

In the introductory chapter we quoted Wittgenstein: ". . . only *love* can believe in the Resurrection. Or: it is *love* that believes the Resurrection".[13] Such love is given into the heart of our being. It is love for God who is Love in the prodigality of divine self-giving. It brings forth a love that "rejoices in the truth", as "it bears all things, believes all things, hopes all things, endures all things" (1 Cor 13:6-7). It is a love for life in its fullness, as a universal communion and reconciliation. In such love, heart speaks to heart, and the resurrection of the Crucified appears as what is most in accord with love and the reasons of the heart. This is a far more profound disturbance to habitual ways of theological thinking than calling for some new kind of phenomenological method. It raises the question of where theology situates itself—in the Areopagus of modern culture and in the lecture rooms of the university? In places of grief, failure and disgrace? In the hospices of the dying or in the studios of artists? In the world's immense regions of poverty and in the exuberantly religious Southern hemisphere, or in the post-Christian world of the West? The theologian may work in any or all of these situations, for they form an awareness of what we term the postmodern world. It is instructive to imagine how the event of Christ's rising from the tomb would be considered in each of them. In some it would be less awkward and embarrassing than in others. Perhaps we might most appreciate Wittgenstein's point by saying that whatever our cultural or theological location, it will be love—for God, our neighbour, the universe itself—that will feel most deeply the impact of what has been given and what an ultimate love has already disclosed. In a world whose history can be written as an enormous catalogue of horrors, it is timely for Christian believers and thinkers to give a fresh account of the event on which our hope is based: Christ is risen.

Notes

1. "Placing" the Resurrection

[1]See W. J. Sherzer, "Sunday", *New Catholic Encyclopedia* 13 (Palatine, IL: Jack Heraty and Associates, Inc., 1981), 797-799, and John Paul II's Apostolic Letter, *Dies Domini* (1998).

[2]The concluding words of Gerald O'Collins's magisterial article, "The Resurrection: The State of the Questions", in Stephen T. Davis, Daniel Kendall, SJ, and Gerald O'Collins, SJ, eds., *The Resurrection: An Interdisciplinary Symposium on the Resurrection of Jesus* (New York: Oxford University Press, 1997), 5-28.

[3]The case of Aquinas' treatment of the resurrection is more complex than at first appears to anyone reading the *Summa* apart from its contextualisation in the scriptural commentaries. Still, the overall systematic structure of Aquinas' *Summa* would seem to overwhelm the significance of *Christus resurgens*, specifically treated only in questions 53-56 of the *Pars Tertia*.

[4]I find myself in broad agreement with Anthony J. Godzieba, Lieven Boeve and Michele Saracino, "Resurrection—Interruption—Transformation: Incarnation as Hermeneutical Strategy: A Symposium", *Theological Studies* 67 (2006): 777-815. As will appear, my differences from this approach lie in not seeing the resurrection as an addendum to the incarnation, but as its defining moment.

[5]Karl Rahner, "Dogmatic Questions on Easter", *Theological Investigations IV*, trans. Kevin Smyth, (Baltimore, MD: Helicon Press, 1966), 121-133.

[6]François-Xavier Durrwell, *The Resurrection: A Biblical Study*, trans. Rosemary Sheed (London and New York: Sheed and Ward, 1960), xxiii.

[7]F.-X. Durrwell, *The Resurrection* (London: Sheed and Ward, 1960). The main points of Durrwell, *The Resurrection*, are conveniently summarised in his more recent work, *Christ Our Passover: The Indispensable Role of the Resurrection in Our Salvation*, trans. John F. Craghan (Liguori, Missouri: Liguori Publications, 2004).

[8]N. T. Wright, *The Resurrection of the Son of God* (Minneapolis, MN: Fortress Press, 2003).

[9]Robert B. Stewart, ed., *The Resurrection of Jesus: John Dominic Crossan and N.T. Wright in Dialogue* (Minneapolis, MN: Fortress Press, 2006), 18.

[10]Brian V. Johnstone, CSsR, "Transformation Ethics: The Moral Implications of the Resurrection", in Davis et al., eds., *The Resurrection: An Interdisciplinary Symposium on the Resurrection of Jesus*, 339-360.

[11]Kenan Osborne, OFM, *Christian Sacraments in a Postmodern World: A Theology for the Third Millennium* (Mahwah, NJ: Paulist, 1999); David N. Power, *Sacrament: The Language of God's Giving* (New York: Crossroad, 1999).

[12]Kenan Osborne, *The Resurrection of Jesus: New Considerations for Its Theological Interpretation* (New York: Paulist Press, 1997).

[13]The extreme case is instanced in John Hick, *The Metaphor of God Incarnate* (London: SCM, 1993), 24, and Sallie McFague, *Models of God: Theology for an Ecological, Nuclear Age* (Philadelphia: Fortress Press, 1987), 59. More moderately, Peter Carnley, *The Structure of Resurrection Belief* (Oxford: Clarendon, 1987).

[14]This may be the reason why the *Cambridge Companion to Liberation Theology* (Christopher Rowland, ed. [Cambridge: Cambridge University Press, 1999])

has no mention of the resurrection in its index! Some clear references, however, are to be found in Ignacio Ellacuría, and Jon Sobrino, eds., *Mysterium Liberationis: Fundamental Concepts of Liberation Theology* (Maryknoll, NY: Orbis Books, 1993), 184-186, 436-437. Still, see Gerald O'Collins, SJ, "The Resurrection: The State of the Questions" in Davis et al., *The Resurrection: An Interdisciplinary Symposium on the Resurrection of Jesus*, 5-28. He writes, ". . . one must admit, a little sadly, how little the theologians of that school have reflected on Christ's resurrection" (26).

[15]As will be clear, I depend on von Balthasar in many other places and instances, where the resurrection is given its due. It is just that he seems to lose all sense of proportion when it comes to Holy Saturday. For a vigorous critique of von Balthasar's Holy Saturday theology, see Alyssa H. Pitstick, *Lux in Tenebris: The Traditional Catholic Doctrine of Christ's Descent into Hell and the Theological Opinion of Hans Urs von Balthasar* (Grand Rapids, MI: Eerdmans, 2006).

[16]From a different but converging point of view, see Marianne Sawicki, *Seeing the Lord: Resurrection and Early Christian Practices* (Minneapolis, MN: Fortress Press, 1994), especially her spirited remarks, 314-335.

[17]For a critical appreciation, see Anne Hunt, "With the Risen Lord: Francois-Xavier Durrwell, CSsR (1912-2005)", *Australian EJournal of Theology*, Pentecost 2006 Special Edition, http://dlibrary.acu.edu.au/research/theology/ejournal/aejt_hunt.htm

[18]Pheme Perkins, *Resurrection: New Testament Witness and Contemporary Reflection* (Garden City, NY: Doubleday, 1984).

[19]Xavier Léon-Dufour, *Resurrection and the Message of Easter* (London: Geoffrey Chapman, 1974).

[20]For Pannenberg's proleptic theology in the light of the resurrection, see Christiaan Mostert, *God and the Future: Wolfhart Pannenberg's Eschatological Doctrine of God* (Edinburgh: T & T Clark, 2002), especially 43-54.

[21]Gerald O'Collins, *Jesus Risen: The Resurrection—What actually happened and what does it mean?* (London: Darton, Longman and Todd, 1987). O'Collins' work has been seminal. See Davis et al., eds., *The Resurrection: An Interdisciplinary Symposium*, and Daniel Kendall, SJ, and Stephen T. Davis, eds., *The Convergence of Theology: A Festschrift Honoring Gerald O'Collins, SJ* (New York: Paulist Press, 2001).

[22]Francis Schüssler-Fiorenza, *Foundational Theology: Jesus and the Church* (New York: Crossroad, 1984), 5-55.

[23]N. T. Wright, *The Resurrection of the Son of God* (Minneapolis, MN: Fortress Press, 2003)—constantly referred to in what follows.

[24]Richard Swinburne, *The Resurrection of God Incarnate* (Oxford: Clarendon Press, 2003).

[25]See Richard Swinburne, *Revelation: From Metaphor to Analogy* (Oxford: Clarendon, 1992), 110-112, 145, 219.

[26]Raymund Schwager, *Jesus in the Drama of Salvation: Toward a Biblical Doctrine of Redemption*, trans. James G. Williams and Paul Haddon (New York: Crossroad, 1999).

[27]James Alison, *Raising Abel: The Recovery of the Eschatological Imagination* (New York: Crossroad, 1996); *The Joy of Being Wrong: Original Sin through Easter Eyes* (New York: Crossroad, 1998); and the earlier summary work, *Knowing Jesus* (London: SPCK, 1993).

[28]Gil Bailie, *Violence Unveiled: Humanity at the Crossroads* (New York: Crossroad, 1997). See especially, chapter 12, "It is Accomplished", 217-233, for a profound reflection on Christ in the Gospel of John.

[29]William Desmond, "Is There Metaphysics after Critique?", *International Philosophical Quarterly* (2004): 221-241.

[30]Hans Urs von Balthasar, *The Glory of the Lord: A Theological Aesthetics*, vol. I: *Seeing the Form*, ed. Joseph Fessio and John Riches, trans. Erasmo Leiva-Merikakis (New York: Crossroad, 1983), 228.

[31]Von Balthasar, *The Glory of the Lord*, I, 22.

[32]Von Balthasar, *The Glory of the Lord*, I, 238-239.

[33]J.H. Newman, "On the Introduction of Rationalistic Principles into Revealed Religion", *Essays, Critical and Historical 1* (London: Longmans and Green, 1890), 34-35.

[34]Karl Rahner, "The Experience of God Today", *Theological Investigations XI*, trans. David Bourke (London: Darton, Longman and Todd, 1974), 149-165.

[35]Rahner, "The Experience of God Today", 164.

[36]Rahner, "The Experience of God Today", 165.

[37]Bernard J. F. Lonergan, S.J., *Method in Theology* (London: Darton, Longman and Todd, 1972).

[38]Lonergan, *Method in Theology*, 107, 120-123.

[39]Lonergan, *Method in Theology*, 105-106. Cf. also 340-343.

[40]Lonergan, *Method in Theology*, 267-270.

[41]Lonergan, *Method in Theology*, 106.

[42]Lonergan, *Method in Theology*, 112-113.

[43]Lonergan, *Method in Theology*, 283-293.

[44]Lonergan, *Method in Theology*, 112-113.

[45]Lonergan, *Method in Theology*, 113.

[46]Lonergan, *Method in Theology*, 113.

[47]Kevin Hart, *The Trespass of the Sign: Deconstruction, Theology and Philosophy* (New York: Fordham University Press, 2000), 273-298.

[48]See Kevin Hart's excellent exposition, *Postmodernism: A Beginner's Guide* (Oxford: Oneworld Publications, 2004), especially chapter 6, "Postmodern Religion", 107-128.

[49]Hart, *The Trespass of the Sign*, 296.

[50]Hart, *The Trespass of the Sign*, 296.

[51]*Christus autem resurgens non rediit ad vitam communiter hominibus notam, sed ad vitam quandan immortalem et Deo conformem* (*STh* 3, q. 55, a. 2).

[52]Wright, *The Resurrection of the Son of God*, 477, 606-612, 678-679.

[53]Robyn Horner, *Rethinking God as Gift: Marion, Derrida and the Limits of Phenomenology* (New York: Fordham University Press, 2001), in reference to Levinas, 73; to Derrida, 79, 221, 231-2, 236; to Marion, 144-5, 149, 157, 166.

[54]Lonergan, *Method in Theology*, 6-13, 101-104.

[55]For a comprehensive treatment, see Richard Bauckham, *Jesus and Eyewitnesses: The Gospels as Eyewitness Testimony* (Grand Rapids, MI: Eerdmans, 2006), especially 114-153; 472-508.

[56]Jean-Luc Marion, *God without Being: Hors-Texte*, trans. Thomas A. Carlson (Chicago: University of Chicago Press, 1991).

[57]*STh* 1, q. 20, a. 2. Note that *STh* is used as the abbreviation for St. Thomas Aquinas's *Summa Theologiae* throughout this volume. For further elaboration of Aquinas's approach, see Anthony J. Kelly, "A Multidimensional Disclosure: Aspects of Aquinas' Theological Intentionality", *The Thomist* 67/3 (July 2003), 335-374.

[58]*STh* 1, q. 20, a. 2.

[59]*STh* 1, q. 1, a. 13, objection 1.

[60]*STh* 1, q. 12, a. 13, ad 1.

[61]*STh* 1, q. 32, a. 1, ad 2 .

[62]*STh* 1, q. 43, a. 5, ad 2.

[63]*STh* 2-2, q. 1, a. 2, ad 1.

[64]*Actus credentis non terminatur ad enuntiabile sed ad rem: non enim formamus enuntiabilia nisi ut per ea de rebus cognitionem habeamus, sicut in scientia et in fide* (*STh* 2-2, q. 1. a. 2 ad 1).

[65]Lonergan, *Method in Theology*, 231.

[66]See Jean Mouroux, in *The Meaning of Man*, trans. A. Downes (New York:

Image Books, 1961), 256, n. 33. He is citing J. Delacroix, *Psychologie de l'Art*.

[67]See Robert Sokolowski, *Introduction to Phenomenology* (Cambridge: University of Cambridge Press, 2000), 8-33, 64-65, 185-186.

[68]Hart, *Postmodernism*, 107-128.

[69]Hart, *Postmodernism*, 111-115.

[70]L. Wittgenstein, *Culture and Value*, trans. Peter Winch (Chicago: University of Chicago Press, 1980), 83. Sarah Coakley, " 'Not With the Eye Only': The Resurrection Epistemology and Gender", *Reflections 5* (2001): 1-15, connects Wittgenstein to the premodern theological tradition of "spiritual senses", as an alternative to the modern extremes of "Lockean" empiricism and the history-transcendent emphasis of the early Barth.

2. A Phenomenological Approach to the Resurrection

[1]These "authorities" are scripture, oral apostolic tradition, the Catholic Church, the councils, the Roman Church, the Church Fathers, theologians, human reason, philosophy, and history. The phenomenon of the resurrection is, however, the locus or hermeneutical space in which all such *loci* are most fully justified and appreciated.

[2]For a general approach to phenomenology, its methods, and terms, see Robert Sokolowski, *Introduction to Phenomenology* (Cambridge: Cambridge University Press, 2000), and for some theological applications, see his *Christian Faith and Human Understanding: Studies on the Eucharist, Trinity and the Human Person* (Washington, DC: The Catholic University of America Press, 2006).

[3]See Ian Leask, "The Dative Subject and the 'Principle of Principles' ", in *Givenness and God: Questions of Jean-Luc Marion*, ed. Ian Leask and Eion Cassidy (New York: Fordham University Press, 2005), 182-189.

[4]John Henry Newman, *Discourses Addressed to Mixed Congregations* (London: Burns and Oates, 1881), 309. For further citation and insightful commentary, see Mark A. McIntosh, *Discernment and Truth: The Spirituality and Theology of Knowledge* (New York: Crossroad, 2004), 184-186.

[5]Marion's phenomenology follows in the wake of Husserl's original efforts to return "to the things themselves", *zu den Sachen selbst* (Husserl). Along with Husserl and Heidegger and most others, he is engaged in a critical reversal of Descartes' egological subjectivism. However, Marion considers that neither of these two sufficiently breaks free from the limits of the imposition of the ego or the self in their concerns to respect the "given-ness" of the phenomena. They are still considered too much as projections of the self, either as objects constituted by consciousness or in terms of being. His emphasis, therefore, can be termed "donatology" (i.e., a critical receptivity to what is given, beyond the limits prescribed by the imposition of the self). See Robyn Horner, *Rethinking God as Gift: Marion, Derrida and the Limits of Phenomenology* (New York: Fordham University Press, 2001).

[6]Jean-Luc Marion's influential trilogy, *Reduction and Givenness: Investigations of Husserl, Heidegger, and Phenomenology*, trans. Thomas A. Carlson (Evanston, IL: Northwestern University Press, 1998); *Being Given: Toward a Phenomenology of Givenness*, trans. Jeffrey L. Kosky (Stanford, CA: Stanford University Press, 2002), 236-241; *In Excess: Studies of Saturated Phenomena*, trans. Robyn Horner and Vincent Barraud (New York: Fordham University Press, 2002). For further elaboration and background, see *God without Being: Hors-Texte*, trans. Thomas A. Carlson (Chicago, IL: University of Chicago Press, 1991); "*Le possible et la revelation*", in *Eros and Eris: Contribution to a Hermeneutical Phenomenology: Liber Amicorum for Adriann Peperzak*, ed. P. van Tongeren, P. Sars, C. Bremmer and K. Boey (Dordrecht: Kluwer Academic, 1992), 217-231; "The Saturated Phenomenon", *Philosophy Today* 40 (1996): 103-124 ; "They Recognised Him; and He Became Invisible to Them", *Modern Theology* 18 (2002): 145-152; *Le phénomène érotique:*

Six meditations (Paris: Grasset, 2003). I am much indebted to Shane Mackinlay, *Interpreting Excess: The Implicit Hermeneutics of Jean-Luc Marion's Saturated Phenomena* (New York: Fordham University Press, 2008); also his "Phenomenality in the Middle: Marion, Romano, and the Hermeneutics of the Event", in *Givenness and God: Questions of Jean-Luc Marion*, ed. Ian Leask and Eion Cassidy (New York: Fordham University Press, 2005), 167-181.

[7]Marion, *Being Given*, 216.

[8]A phrase given currency by Sokolowski. See his *Christian Faith and Human Understanding*, 36, 39, 48-50.

[9]Marion, *Being Given*, 261.

[10]Marion, *Being Given*, 216-217.

[11]Marion, *Being Given*, 264-265.

[12]Marion, *Being Given*, 289; *In Excess*, 33, 42.

[13]In some ways, as his critics point out, this emphasis on the sheer self-givingness of the phenomena is so extreme, so one-sided, that the conscious subject seems to have no role at all in responding to and interpreting what is being given. But need subject and object be so adversarially opposed? I do not think so, as we shall explain later in reference to the multiple dimensions of meaning the phenomenon provokes.

[14]Marion, *Being Given*, 234-236.

[15]Marion, *Being Given*, 5.

[16]Dominique Janicaud et al., *Phenomenology and "The Theological Turn": The French Debate*, trans. Bernard G. Prusak (New York: Fordham University Press, 2000).

[17]Marion, *"Le possible et la revelation"*, 228.

[18]For a critical appreciation of Marion's contribution, see Brian Robinette, "A Gift to Theology? Jean-Luc Marion's 'Saturated Phenomenon' in Christological Perspective", *Heythrop Journal* 48/1 (January, 2007): 86-108.

[19]Marion, *"Le possible et la revelation"*, 231; *Being Given*, 242.

[20]Marion, *Being Given*, 367.

[21]Marion, *Being Given*, 235-236.

[22]Marion, "The Saturated Phenomenon", 103.

[23]Marion, *"Le possible et la revelation"*, 232.

[24]Marion, *Being Given*, 236.

[25]Marion, *Being Given*, 238.

[26]Marion, *Being Given*, 239.

[27]Marion, *Being Given*, 240.

[28]Marion, "They Recognised Him", 148.

[29]Marion, "They Recognised Him", 149.

[30]Marion, "They Recognised Him", 151-152.

[31]For a theological phenomenology of voice, see Sergio Gaburro, *La Voce della Rivelazione: Fenomenologia della Voce per una Teologia della Rivelazione* (Milano: Edizioni San Paolo, 2005).

[32]This account makes no pretense of giving a critical treatment of Marion's work in this area. I do, however, find in it a number of evocative starting points, taking us in the direction of the phenomenon of the resurrection.

[33]Marion, *Being Given*, 140, 165, 172.

[34]Marion, *Being Given*, 170-172.

[35]Marion, *Being Given*, 201.

[36]The phrase "Evential Hermeneutics", while truer to the French text, does not travel so well in English.

[37]Claude Romano, *L'événement et le monde. Épithée: Essais Philosophiques* (Paris: Presses Universitaires de France, 1998), 60-69.

[38]Romano, *L'événement et le monde*, 72-96.

[39]Marion, *Being Given*, 203.

[40]Marion, *God without Being*, 9-14; *In Excess*, 72.

[41]Medard Kehl, "Hans Urs von Balthasar: A Portrait", in Medard Kehl and Werner

Löser, eds., trans. Robert J. Daly, SJ, and Fred Lawrence, *The von Balthasar Reader* (Edinburgh: T. & T. Clark, 1985), 47-48.

[42]Hans Urs von Balthasar, *The Glory of the Lord: A Theological Aesthetics*, vol. I: *Seeing the Form*, ed. Joseph Fessio and John Riches, trans. Erasmo Leiva-Merikakis (New York: Crossroad, 1983), 467.

[43]David Bentley Hart, *The Beauty of the Infinite: The Aesthetics of Christian Truth* (Grand Rapids, MI: Eerdmans, 2003).

[44]Hart, *The Beauty of the Infinite*, 15-28.

[45]Hart, *The Beauty of the Infinite*, 15-16.

[46]Hart, *The Beauty of the Infinite*, 334.

[47]Hart, *The Beauty of the Infinite*, 334.

[48]Hart, *The Beauty of the Infinite*, 334.

[49]Marion, *Le phénomène érotique*, 185.

[50]Marion, *Le phénomène érotique*, 170.

[51]Marion, *In Excess*, 100; *Le phénomène érotique*, 170, 180-181.

[52]Marion, *Being Given*, 239.

[53]Anthony Godzieba, " 'Stay with us' (Lk 24:29)—'Come, Lord Jesus' (Rev 22:20): Incarnation, Eschatology, and Theology's Sweet Predicament", *Theological Studies* 67 (2006): 787.

[54]Michel Henry, *Incarnation: Une philosophie de la chair* (Paris: Seuil, 2000), 350-352.

[55]Hans Urs von Balthasar, *The Glory of the Lord: A Theological Aesthetics*, vol. VII: *The New Covenant*, trans. Brian McNeil, CRV (Edinburgh: T & T Clark, 1989), 308-9.

[56]See Michael Sheldon, *Orwell: The Authorised Biography* (London: Minerva, 1992), 343.

[57]Emmanuel Levinas, *Ethics and Infinity: Conversations with Philippe Nemo*, trans. Richard A. Cohen (Pittsburgh, PA: Duquesne University Press, 1985), 85.

[58]Marion, *Being Given*, 216; *God without Being*, 19.

[59]Marion, *Being Given*, 232.

[60]Marion, *In Excess*, 124.

[61]For a seminal article, see Karl Rahner, "The Concept of Mystery in Catholic Theology", *Theological Investigations IV*, trans. Kevin Smyth (Baltimore, MD: Helicon Press, 1966), 36-73.

3. The Resurrection and the Phenomenon of the New Testament

[1]James D. G. Dunn, *Christianity in the Making*, vol. 1, *Jesus Remembered* (Grand Rapids, MI: Eerdmans, 2003), 828-862.

[2]See equivalent confessions in Acts 10:40; Rom 4:23-25; 8:11; 10:9; Gal 1:1-2; Eph 1:20; Col 2:12; 1 Pet 1:21; Heb 13:20.

[3]Hans Urs von Balthasar, *The Glory of the Lord: A Theological Aesthetics*, vol. VII: *The New Covenant*, trans. Brian McNeil, CRV (Edinburgh: T & T Clark, 1989), 325.

[4]Von Balthasar, *The Glory of the Lord*, VII, 325.

[5]D. Moody Smith, "When Did the Gospels Become Scripture?", *JBL* 119 (2000): 3-20.

[6]See Francis J. Moloney, SDB, "The Gospel of John as Scripture", *The Catholic Biblical Quarterly* 67 (2005): 455-468.

[7]On the impossible "depaschalisation" of the New Testament, see Von Balthasar, *The Glory of the Lord*, VII, 321-322—even if we concede, with whatever explanation, that there is no mention of the resurrection in some half dozen New Testament writings (2 Thessalonians, Titus, Philemon, 3 John, 2 Peter, Jude and James).

[8]Von Balthasar, *The Glory of the Lord*, VII, 323.

[9]Von Balthasar, *The Glory of the Lord*, VII, 322-323. Note also James Alison's insightful interpretation of the post-resurrectional consciousness of the disciples in

his *The Joy of Being Wrong: Original Sin through Easter Eyes* (New York: Crossroad, 1998), 70-77.

[10]Brendan Byrne, SJ, "Peter as Resurrection Witness in the Lucan Narrative", in Daniel Kendall, SJ, and Stephen T. David, eds., *The Convergence of Theology: A Festschrift Honoring Gerald O'Collins, SJ* (New York: Paulist Press, 2001), 19-33.

[11]Byrne, "Peter as Resurrection Witness in the Lucan Narrative", 29.

[12]Von Balthasar, *The Glory of the Lord*, VII, 329-333.

[13]See Francis Schüssler-Fiorenza, *Foundational Theology: Jesus and the Church* (New York: Crossroad, 1984), 29-33; and "The Resurrection of Jesus and Roman Catholic Fundamental Theology", in Stephen T. Davis, Daniel Kendall, SJ, and Gerald O'Collins, SJ, eds., *The Resurrection: An Interdisciplinary Symposium on the Resurrection of Jesus* (New York: Oxford University Press, 1997), 225.

[14]Anthony J. Kelly, "The Historical Jesus and Human Subjectivity", in Matthew C. Ogilvie and William J. Dannaher, eds., *Australian Lonergan Workshop II* (Drummoyne, NSW: Novum Organum Press, 2003), 151-179.

[15]See especially B. F. Meyer, *The Aims of Jesus* (London: SCM, 1979) and *Critical Realism and the New Testament* (Allison Park: Pickwick, 1989); Larry Hurtado, *Lord Jesus Christ: Devotion to Jesus in Earliest Christianity* (Grand Rapids, MI: Eerdmans, 2003), N. T. Wright, *The Resurrection of the Son of God* (Minneapolis, MN: Fortress Press, 2003) and James D. G. Dunn, *Christianity in the Making*, vol. 1, *Jesus Remembered* (Grand Rapids, MI: Eerdmans, 2003).

[16]Von Balthasar, *The Glory of the Lord*, VII, 362-363.

[17]Hans Urs von Balthasar, *Mysterium Paschale: The Mystery of Easter*, trans., and introduction by Aidan Nichols, OP (Edinburgh: T&T Clark, 1990), 246.

[18]A particularly intriguing case: see Byrne, "Peter as Resurrection Witness in the Lucan Narrative", 19-33.

[19]Wright, *The Resurrection of the Son of God*, 585-615.

[20]Wright, *The Resurrection of the Son of God*, 646.

[21]Von Balthasar, *The Glory of the Lord*, VII, 159.

[22]Von Balthasar, *The Glory of the Lord*, VII, 266-268.

[23]See Christopher Morse, *Not Every Spirit. A Dogmatics of Christian Disbelief* (Valley Forge, PA: Trinity Press International, 1994).

[24]See the criticism of the self-referential and amorphous spirituality recently impugned in Jeremy Carette and Robert King, *Selling Spirituality: The Silent Takeover of Religion* (London: Routledge, 2005).

[25]See Hart, *The Trespass of the Sign*, and my "Blessed Negativities: The Contribution of Deconstruction to Theology", *Australian EJournal of Theology* 2 (February, 2004).

[26]Robyn Horner, *Rethinking God as Gift: Marion, Derrida and the Limits of Phenomenology* (New York: Fordham University Press, 2001).

[27]It would take us too far afield to survey all the Old Testament in this regard. Here I refer mainly to an excellent article by Walter Brueggemann, "Faith at the *Nullpunkt*", in *The End of the World and the Ends of God*, ed. Polkinghorne and Welker, 143-154. Good general references are Zachary Hayes, *Visions of a Future: A Study of Christian Eschatology* (Wilmington, DE: Michael Glazier, 1989), 15-42, and Philip S. Johnston, *Shades of Sheol: Death and Afterlife in the Old Testament* (Downers Grove, IL: InterVarsity Press, 2002).

[28]Brueggemann, "Faith at the *Nullpunkt*", 150.

4. The Resurrection Event

[1]James D. G. Dunn, *Christianity in the Making*, vol. 1, *Jesus Remembered* (Grand Rapids, MI: Eerdmans, 2003), 826.

[2]Pheme Perkins, *Resurrection: New Testament Witness and Contemporary Reflection* (Garden City, NY: Doubleday, 1984), 18.

³This is well brought out in Bertold Klappert, *Diskussion um Kreuz und Auferstehung* (Wuppertal: Aussaat Verlag, 1967). For constructive criticism, see Gerald O'Collins, "Christ's Resurrection as a Mystery of Love", *Heythrop Journal* 25 (1984): 39-50.

⁴For the excess of love, see Hans Urs von Balthasar, *Love Alone*, trans. and ed. Alexander Dru (New York: Herder and Herder, 1969).

⁵For some sixteen possible connotations of "resurrection", see James H. Charlesworth, with C.D. Elledge, J. L. Crenshaw, H. Boers, and W. W. Willis Jr, *Resurrection: The Origin and Future of a Biblical Doctrine* (New York: T & T Clark, 2006), 2-17.

⁶G. Martelet, *L'au-delà retrouvé: Christologie des fins dernières* (Paris: Desclée, 1975) provides an elegant theological model.

⁷See James Alison, *The Joy of Being Wrong: Original Sin through Easter Eyes* (New York: Crossroad, 1988), 72-77.

⁸See, for instance, "Priest and Poet, *Theological Investigations III*, trans. Karl-H. and Boniface Kruger, OFM (Baltimore, MD: Helicon Press, 1967), 294-317.

⁹For example, Jn 1:18; 3:16, 35; 4:23, 34; 5:18-21, 26-28, 30, 36-37; 6:32-33, 37-40, 44-45, 57, 65; 7:16.

¹⁰Anthony Godzieba, " 'Stay with us' (Lk 24:29)—'Come, Lord Jesus' (Rev 22:20): Incarnation, Eschatology, and Theology's Sweet Predicament", *Theological Studies* 67 (2006): 777-815. Godzieba articulates a crucial point: "I want to argue here that Christ's resurrection points us towards a fully incarnational theology, and that only a theology with a fully incarnational and sacramental imagination discloses the deeper implications of the resurrectional *inclusion* in which faith is lived" (785).

¹¹See Jn 1:18; 3:16; 8:19, 38; 10:17, 30; 12:45, 50; 14:7, 10-11; 16:28.

¹²See Anthony J. Kelly, CSsR, and Francis J. Moloney, SDB, *Experiencing God in the Gospel of John* (New York: Paulist, 2003), 29-42.

¹³Raymond Brown, *The Virginal Conception and Bodily Resurrection of Jesus* (New York: Paulist, 1973), 128.

¹⁴Hans Urs von Balthasar, *The Glory of the Lord: A Theological Aesthetics*, vol. VII: *The New Covenant*, trans. Brian McNeil, CRV (Edinburgh: T & T Clark, 1989), 252-255.

¹⁵Von Balthasar, *The Glory of the Lord*, VII, 262.

¹⁶William L. Craig, "John Dominic Crossan on the Resurrection of Jesus," in Stephen T. Davis, Daniel Kendall, SJ, and Gerald O'Collins, SJ, eds., *The Resurrection: An Interdisciplinary Symposium on the Resurrection of Jesus* (New York: Oxford University Press, 1997), 265-270.

¹⁷Jn 13:14, 34-35; 15:12-13; 1 John 2:7-11; 3:10-18; 4:7-8, 11, 20; 5:1-2, 16; 2 John 1:5; 3 John 5-8.

¹⁸William Henn, OFM Cap, "The Church as Easter Witness in the Thought of Gerald O'Collins, SJ", in Daniel Kendall, SJ, and Stephen T. Davis, eds., *The Convergence of Theology: A Festschrift Honoring Gerald O'Collins, SJ* (New York: Paulist Press, 2001)

¹⁹Von Balthasar, *The Glory of the Lord*, VII, 151.

²⁰For the realism of communion, see Phillip F. Esler, *New Testament Theology: Communion and Community* (Minneapolis, MN: Fortress, 2005), especially 229-254.

²¹Brian E. Daley, *The Hope of the Early Church* (Cambridge: Cambridge University Press, 1991), 224.

²²See Jaroslav Pelikan, *The Light of the World: A Basic Image in Early Christian Thought* (New York: Harper and Brothers, 1962).

²³Von Balthasar, *The Glory of the Lord*, VII, 289.

²⁴Von Balthasar, *The Glory of the Lord*, VII, 284-287.

²⁵Von Balthasar, *The Glory of the Lord*, VII, 115.

²⁶See Joseph Sittler, in Steven Bouma-Prediger and Peter Bakken, eds., *Evocations of Grace* (Grand Rapids, MI: Eerdmans, 2000), 92-116.

[27]See *STh* 1, q. 38, a. 2.

[28]Here I am using Lonergan's four dimensions of meaning as found in his *Method in Theology* (London: Darton, Longman and Todd, 1972), 76-81.

[29]Robert B. Stewart, ed., *The Resurrection of Jesus: John Dominic Crossan and N.T. Wright in Dialogue* (Minneapolis, MN: Fortress Press, 2006).

5. Paul and the Resurrection Effect

[1]Eric Voegelin, *Order and History*, vol. 4, *The Ecumenic Age* (Baton Rouge, LA: Louisiana State University Press, 1974), 239-271.

[2]Voegelin, *The Ecumenic Age*, 242.

[3]Voegelin, *The Ecumenic Age*, 242-243.

[4]Voegelin, *The Ecumenic Age*, 246.

[5]Voegelin, *The Ecumenic Age*, 252-253.

[6]Voegelin, *The Ecumenic Age*, 253.

[7]I have noticed it, for instance, in the writings of Wright, Crossan, Hurtado, Byrne and Martelet, perhaps because it has been given general theological currency through the influence of Teilhard de Chardin. Note its evolutionary provenance—with implications of prior biological and genetic dynamics. Hence, a critical awareness of this kind of analogy is called for.

[8]Voegelin, *The Ecumenic Age*, 255.

[9]Voegelin, *The Ecumenic Age*, 260-266.

[10]Voegelin, *The Ecumenic Age*, 265-266.

[11]This section and the following section are much indebted to N. T. Wright's, *The Resurrection of the Son of God* (Minneapolis, MN: Fortress Press, 2003), especially 275-398.

[12]Hans Urs von Balthasar, *The Glory of the Lord: A Theological Aesthetics*, vol. VII: *The New Covenant*, trans. Brian McNeil, CRV (Edinburgh: T & T Clark, 1989), 358.

[13]Cf. Jerome Murphy-O'Connor, "What Paul Knew about Jesus", *Scripture Bulletin* 12/11, 1981, 35-40); *Paul: His Story* (Oxford: OUP, 2004); *Paul: A Critical Life* (Oxford: Clarendon Press, 1996).

[14]Von Balthasar, *The Glory of the Lord*, VII, 362-363.

[15]David Stanley, "Pauline Allusions to the Sayings of Jesus", *Catholic Biblical Quarterly* 23 (1961): 34.

[16]See Wright, *The Resurrection of the Son of God*, 312-374.

[17]Phillip F. Esler, *New Testament Theology: Communion and Community* (Minneapolis, MN: Fortress, 2005), 229-254.

[18]Wright, *The Resurrection of the Son of God*, 312-374.

[19]Wright, *The Resurrection of the Son of God*, 330-331.

[20]See Wright, *The Resurrection of the Son of God*, 339-340.

[21]Wright, *The Resurrection of the Son of God*, 350-354.

[22]Von Balthasar, *The Glory of the Lord*, VII, 280.

[23]A valuable reference here is Brendan Byrne, SJ, "Christ's Pre-Existence in Pauline Soteriology", *TS* 58 (1997): 308-330 who attempts to answer the problem posed in K.-J. Kuschel, *Born Before All Time: The Dispute over Christ's Origin*, trans. John Bowden (London: SCM, 1992). See also Jan Lambrecht, "The Identity of Christ Jesus (Philippians 2, 6-11)", in Veronica Koperski, ed., *Understanding What One Reads: New Testament Essays* (Leuven: Peeters, 2003), 245-262. For useful general commentary, Raymond F. Collins, *First Corinthians*, Sacra Pagina Series, vol. 7 (Collegeville, MN: The Liturgical Press, 1999).

[24]Byrne, "Christ's Pre-existence in Pauline Soteriology", 311.

[25]Byrne, "Christ's Pre-existence in Pauline Soteriology", 311.

[26]Larry W. Hurtado, *Lord Jesus Christ: Devotion to Jesus in Earliest Christianity* (Grand Rapids, MI: Eerdmans, 2003), especially, for the present context, 98-134.

[27]Byrne, "Christ's Pre-existence in Pauline Soteriology", 313.

[28]Texts such as Phil 2:6-8, 2 Cor 8:9 and Rom 5:15-17 are of the utmost significance.

[29]Byrne, "Christ's Pre-existence in Pauline Soteriology", 319.

[30]Byrne, "Christ's Pre-existence in Pauline Soteriology", 317.

[31]Byrne, "Christ's Pre-existence in Pauline Soteriology", 316.

[32]Larry Hurtado, "A Case Study in Early Christian Devotion to Jesus: Philippians 2:6-11", in *How on Earth Did Jesus Become a God? Historical Questions about Earliest Devotion to Jesus* (Grand Rapids, MI: Eerdmans, 2005), 83-107, especially 93-94.

[33]Hurtado depends to a large extent on Takeshi Nagata, *Philippians 2:5-11: A Case Study in the Shaping of Early Christology*. PhD thesis, Princeton Theological Seminary, 1981, available from UMI Dissertation Services.

[34]God's exaltation of Jesus to God's right hand and his raising of Jesus from the dead must never be separated. See Hurtado, "A Case Study in Early Christian Devotion to Jesus: Philippians 2:6-11", especially 93-94.

[35]Byrne, "Christ's Pre-existence in Pauline Soteriology", 321.

[36]Byrne, "Christ's Pre-existence in Pauline Soteriology", 325. See Byrne's careful exegesis of Rom 5:15-17, 322-328.

[37]Byrne, "Christ's Pre-existence in Pauline Soteriology", 330.

[38]Byrne, "Christ's Pre-existence in Pauline Soteriology", 330.

[39]This can be usefully compared to Hendrikus Boers, "The Meaning of Christ's Resurrection in Paul", in Charlesworth *et al.*, *Resurrection: The Origin and Future of a Biblical Doctrine*, 104-137.

[40]Von Balthasar, *The Glory of the Lord*, VII, 363.

6. Resurrection: The Visual Phenomenon

[1]For a full discussion, see Richard Bauckham, *Jesus and the Eyewitnesses: The Gospels as Eyewitness Testimony* (Grand Rapids, MI: Eerdmans, 2006), especially 358-411.

[2]See Cajetan's commentary on *STh* 2a-2ae, q. 171, a. 5, Leonine ed. X, 374b. Full text is cited by Hans Urs von Balthasar, *The Glory of the Lord: A Theological Aesthetics*, vol. I: *Seeing the Form*, ed. Joseph Fessio and John Riches, trans. Erasmo Leiva-Merikakis (New York: Crossroad, 1983), 308.

[3]*STh* 3, q. 55, a. 2 ad 1.

[4]Admittedly, this does not seem so apparent in the case of Paul—though his seeing was obviously subsequent to his hearing of the Word of God in the sacred scriptures of Israel, and, it might be, his hearing of the testimony of the early Christians he so vigorously persecuted.

[5]Hans Urs von Balthasar, *The Glory of the Lord: A Theological Aesthetics*, vol. VII: *The New Covenant*, trans. Brian McNeil, CRV (Edinburgh: T & T Clark, 1989), 273.

[6]Von Balthasar, *The Glory of the Lord*, VII, 274-5.

[7]Von Balthasar, *The Glory of the Lord*, I, 308-309, 343-345; *The Glory of the Lord*, VII, 277.

[8]For a sense of the developing traditions, see Brendan Byrne, SJ, "Peter as Resurrection Witness in the Lukan Narrative", in Daniel Kendall, SJ and Stephen T. Davis, eds., *The Convergence of Theology: A Festschrift Honoring Gerald O'Collins, SJ* (New York: Paulist Press, 2001), 9-33.

[9]Byrne, "Peter as Resurrection Witness in the Lucan Narrative", 29.

[10]See *STh* 3, q. 55, a. 1, ad 3.

[11]Sarah Coakley, " 'Not With the Eye Only': The Resurrection Epistemology and Gender", *Reflections* 5 (2001): 1-15.

¹²See L. Alcoff and E. Potter, eds., *Feminist Epistemologies* (New York: Routledge, 1993).

¹³N. T. Wright, *The Resurrection of the Son of God* (Minneapolis, MN: Fortress Press, 2003), 209.

¹⁴Von Balthasar, *The Glory of the Lord*, VII, 354.

¹⁵Hans W. Frei, *The Identity of Jesus Christ: The Hermeneutical Bases of Dogmatic Theology* (Philadelphia: Fortress Press, 1975), 145.

¹⁶Von Balthasar, *The Glory of the Lord*, VII, 119-121.

¹⁷G. Bornkamm, cited in Von Balthasar, *The Glory of the Lord*, VII, 120.

¹⁸Stephen T. Davis, " 'Seeing' the Risen Jesus", in *The Resurrection: An Interdisciplinary Symposium on the Resurrection of Jesus* (New York: Oxford University Press, 1997), 126-147.

¹⁹Cf. 1 Cor 9:1; Mk 16:7; Jn 20:25; Mt 28:17; Lk 24:34, 39-46; Jn 20:14, 18; 1 Cor 15:5-8.

²⁰Von Balthasar, *The Glory of the Lord*, VII, 356.

²¹Von Balthasar, *The Glory of the Lord*, VII, 360-361.

²²See Jn 2:22; 12:38; 13:18; 15:25; 17:12; 19:17-22; 19:36-37; 20:9.

²³Von Balthasar, *The Glory of the Lord*, VII, 295, and Anthony J. Kelly, CSsR, and Francis J. Moloney, SDB, *Experiencing God in the Gospel of John* (New York: Paulist, 2003), 297-305.

²⁴See Denis Edwards, *Breath of Life: A Theology of Creator Spirit* (Maryknoll, NY: Orbis Books, 2004), 171-179.

²⁵Thomas Aquinas, *Postilla super Psalmos*, 33, 8 (my translation).

²⁶For a valuable exploration of this affective dimension, see Thomas Ryan, SM, "Revisiting Affective Knowledge and Connaturality in Aquinas", *Theological Studies* 66 (2005): 49-68.

²⁷Von Balthasar, *The Glory of the Lord*, I, 365-380.

²⁸Augustine, *Confessions*, X, 6, 8. From John E. Rotelle, O.S.A., ed., *The Confessions. The Works of Saint Augustine: A Translation for the 21st Century* (New York: New City Publishing, 2000), 242.

²⁹Von Balthasar, *The Glory of the Lord*, VII, 288.

³⁰Von Balthasar, *The Glory of the Lord*, VII, 288.

³¹See my "The Gifts of the Spirit: Aquinas in the Modern Context", *The Thomist* 38 (1974): 193-231. Many years ago when I attempted to transpose St. Thomas's theology of the gifts into "the modern context", I did not realise the rapid onset of "postmodernity". Nonetheless, the various contexts I considered, e.g., Lonergan's intentionality analysis, Macquarrie's existential theology, Heideggerian *Gelassenheit*, and the intercultural phenomenologies of the self are still valuable resources in the postmodern situation. Needless to say, I have come to recognise the need for a more inclusive language!

³²Von Balthasar, *The Glory of the Lord*, I, 244, 294; *The Glory of the Lord*, VII, 326.

³³*III Sent* d. 34, q. 1 a. 1; *STh* 1-2, 70, 4.

³⁴*STh* 1-2, q. 68, a. 1.

³⁵*STh* 1-2, q. 68, a. 2.

³⁶In the activity of the theological virtues is found the radical condition for the operation of the gifts. The movement of the Spirit is recognized in charity: "faith is about what is not seen, hope is concerned with what is not possessed, but the love of charity concerns the one who is already possessed, for the beloved is somehow within the lover, and also the lover is affectively attracted to be united with the beloved" (*STh* 1-2, 66, 5).

³⁷*STh* 2-2, q. 45, a. 1-6.

³⁸*STh* 2-2, 45, 2. Compare with John Macquarrie, "The Seven Gifts of the Holy Spirit", *Studies in Christian Existentialism* (London: SCM, 1965), 246-273.

[39]*STh* 2-2, q. 19, a. 1-12.

[40]*STh* 2-2, q. 8, a. 1-8.

[41]*STh* 2-2, q. 9, a. 1-4.

[42]Cf. *ST* 2-2, q. 52, a. 1-4.

[43]Cf. *STh* 2-2, q. 139, a. 1.

[44]*Ad Romanos*, VIII, lect. 3.

[45]Von Balthasar, *The Glory of the Lord*, VII, 288, note 3.

[46]Letter to William Sotheby, in E. L. Griggs, ed., *Collected Letters of Samuel Taylor Coleridge*, vol. 2 (Oxford: Oxford University Press, 1960), 810.

[47]Cf. Jn 5:22; 7:7; 8:24; 9:39; 12:31.

[48]Jn 5:16-18, 39-40, 45-47; 7:12, 18, 20-24, 48-49; 8:58-59; 9:16, 24; 10:24-38; 11:48-50; 16:2.

[49]Note, here, that appearances of the Risen Jesus are distinct from the Lukan account of Pentecost. See Wright, *The Resurrection of the Son of God*, 324-325.

[50]For an excellent treatment of discernment, see Mark A. McIntosh, *Discernment and Truth: The Spirituality and Theology of Knowledge* (New York: Crossroad, 2004).

[51]R. S. Thomas, "Suddenly" in *Laboratories of the Spirit* (London: Macmillan, 1975), 32. For a keen reflection on the whole poem, see Coakley, " 'Not With the Eye Only': The Resurrection Epistemology and Gender", *Reflections* 5 (2001): 14-15.

7. Subjectivity, Objectivity and the Resurrection

[1]A fuller treatment would demand the recognition of the inter-subjectivity occurring between Christ and the disciples, and even the "inter-objectivity" in the accounts of the appearances/disappearances: it happened here, not there; to these disciples, not those; in relation to the emptiness of this tomb, not another, and so forth.

[2]For our present purposes, I emply the term "disciples" in a restrictive sense. It designates the persons or groups to whom the risen Lord had revealed himself in a unique way. Such appearances constitute the distinctiveness of the apostolic witness (1 Cor 9:1; 15:3-11) within the economy of revelation and for the ongoing life of the Church.

[3]See James D. G. Dunn, *Christianity in the Making*, vol. 1, *Jesus Remembered* (Grand Rapids, MI: Eerdmans, 2003), 872-874; N. T. Wright, *The Resurrection of the Son of God* (Minneapolis, MN: Fortress Press, 2003), 323, 381-382. I recognize that Wright does not make much of the Greek verb in question, or put much stock on the objective-subjective polarity. Still, I think that even his magnificent exposition might profit from the distinctions here employed.

[4]Bernard Lonergan, *Method in Theology* (London: Darton, Longman and Todd, 1972), 265, 292.

[5]Jean-Luc Marion, *In Excess: Studies of Saturated Phenomena*, trans. Robyn Horner and Vincent Barraud (New York: Fordham University Press, 2002). For a nicely sketched theological comment on Marion in this regard, see Robyn Horner, *Jean-Luc Marion: A Theo-Logical Introduction* (Burlington, VT: Ashgate, 2005).

8. The Salvific Realism of the Resurrection

[1]Chapters 2-4 in N. T. Wright, *The Resurrection of the Son of God* (Minneapolis, MN: Fortress Press, 2003), offer an invaluable survey of the different views.

[2]Wright, *The Resurrection of the Son of God*, 131-140; 415-429.

[3]See Jean-Luc Marion, *Being Given: Toward a Phenomenology of Givenness*, trans. Jeffrey L. Kosky (Stanford, CA: Stanford University Press, 2002), 236-241.

[4]For a remarkably clear and fresh account of the resurrection as a divinely gratuitous act, see James Alison, *Knowing Jesus* (London: SPCK, 1993), 3-32.

[5]James D. G. Dunn, *Jesus Remembered* (Grand Rapids, MI: Eerdmans, 2003), 875-876.

[6]F.-X. Durrwell, *The Resurrection: A Biblical Study*, trans. Rosemary Sheed (London and New York: Sheed and Ward, 1960) remains a valuable resource.

[7]See the massive study, N. T. Wright, *The Resurrection of the Son of God*, especially 312-361.

[8]See Wright, *The Resurrection of the Son of God*, for its useful summary and conclusion, "Belief, Event and Meaning", 683-739.

[9]See Wright, *The Resurrection of the Son of God*, 322-329.

[10]See Robyn Horner, *Rethinking God as Gift: Marion, Derrida and the Limits of Phenomenology* (New York: Fordham University Press, 2001), 241-248.

[11]Dunn, *Jesus Remembered*, 874-875.

[12]Wright, *The Resurrection of the Son of God*, 605, 607.

[13]Cf. Wright, *The Resurrection of the Son of God*, 652.

[14]*STh* 3, q. 54. a. 4.

[15]Anne Hunt, *The Trinity and the Paschal Mystery: A Development in Recent Catholic Theology* (Collegeville, MN: The Liturgical Press, 1997), especially the chapter on von Balthasar, "Love Alone Is Credible", 57-89.

[16]Anthony J. Kelly, CSsR, and Francis J. Moloney, SDB, *Experiencing God in the Gospel of John* (New York: Paulist, 2003), 380-382.

[17]See Wright, *The Resurrection of the Son of God*, 607-608.

[18]Wright, *The Resurrection of the Son of God*, 607-608.

[19]Wright, *The Resurrection of the Son of God*, 737.

[20]David Bentley Hart, *The Beauty of the Infinite: The Aesthetics of Christian Truth* (Grand Rapids, MI: Eerdmans, 2003), 334.

[21]Hart, *The Beauty of the Infinite*, 334.

[22]Hart, *The Beauty of the Infinite*, 334-335.

[23]Hart, *The Beauty of the Infinite*, 335.

[24]Hart, *The Beauty of the Infinite*, 394.

[25]Hart, *The Beauty of the Infinite*, 394.

[26]Hart, *The Beauty of the Infinite*, 394.

[27]Alan E. Lewis, *Between Cross and Resurrection: A Theology of Holy Saturday* (Grand Rapids, MI: Eerdmans, 2001), especially 133-163.

[28]*STh* 3, q. 54, a. 1.

[29]*STh* 3, q. 51, a. 3.

[30]For the divinely willed economy of what "must" (*dei*) take place, see Wright, *The Resurrection of the Son of God*, 651-652.

[31]The resurrection accounts are not about the future resurrection of the disciples, but an instigation to the immediate task of mission to the world: see Wright, *The Resurrection of the Son of God*, 603-4.

[32]See G. Martelet, *The Risen Christ and the Eucharistic World*, trans. René Hague (New York: Seabury Press, 1976), 93.

[33]James Alison, *The Joy of Being Wrong: Original Sin through Easter Eyes* (New York: Crossroad, 1998), notes, ". . . simultaneous presence in the Gospels of two sorts of understanding: the incomprehension or miscomprehension of the disciples, and at the same time, the clear comprehension of Jesus of what was to come to pass. This presence of two understandings in the same texts was made possible by the texts themselves having been written *after* the resurrection, when the apostolic group was able to understand, for the first time, what Jesus had really been about and at the same time to understand that, unlike themselves, *he* had understood what was going on all along" (78).

[34]Larry W. Hurtado, *Lord Jesus Christ: Devotion to Jesus in Earliest Christianity*

(Grand Rapids, MI: Eerdmans, 2003), provides strong documentation for this throughout the New Testament.

[35]For an evocation of the disciples' experience, see Sebastian Moore, *The Fire and the Rose Are One* (London: Darton, Longman and Todd, 1980), 80-87.

[36]See my *Eschatology and Hope* (Maryknoll, NY: Orbis Books, 2006).

[37]Here we are relying on Lonergan's sketch of these four dimensions of meaning in *Method in Theology* (London: Longman, Darton and Todd, 1972), 76-81. See also his "Dimensions of Meaning", *Collection: Collected Works of Bernard Lonergan*, vol. 4, eds. Frederick E. Crowe and Robert M. Doran (Toronto: University of Toronto Press, 1993) 232-243. See my "Dimensions of Meaning: Theology and Exegesis", in Rekha M. Chennattu and Mary M. Coloe, eds., *Transcending Boundaries: Contemporary Readings of the New Testament* (Rome: LAS, 2005), 41-56.

[38]Alison is relying on the cultural anthropology of René Girard which, through the writings of Gil Bailie, R. Schwager and Alison himself is of growing influence. See, for example the journal, *Colloquium on Violence and Religion* (*COV&R*), and the home page of the University of Innsbruck devoted to Girard's mimetic theory: http://theol.uibk.ac.at/cover/. Our remarks pretend to no critical appreciation of Girard. Suffice it to say that, despite some debatable issues (e.g., the status of founding-murder in human culture), Girard's writings continue to provide refreshing perspectives for biblical exegesis, the theology of redemption and the analysis of Human Rights Theory. Alison's oft-repeated phrase, "the intelligence of the victim", intends to connote a Girardian anthropology, but seems too general as a technical term: at least it needs to be properly understood in terms of the self-revelation of God, union with the salvific will of God, surrender to the "law of the cross", the creativity of God-given love, its triumph over evil, and the values that are preserved in the new creation (cf. Vatican II, G&S, #39).

[39]See Bonnie B. Thurston and Judith M. Ryan, *Philippians & Philemon. Sacra Pagina* 10, ed. Daniel J. Harrington, S.J. (Collegeville, MN: Liturgical Press, 2005), 80, note 5.

[40]See William M. Thompson, *The Struggle for Theology's Soul: Contesting Scripture in Christology* (New York: Crossroad, 1996), 44-46.

[41]Wright, *The Resurrection of the Son of God*, 320-321.

[42]Josef Ratzinger, *Eschatology: Death and Eternal Life*, trans. M. Walstein (Washington, DC: The Catholic University of America Press, 1988), 234.

[43]See Kelly and Moloney, *Experiencing God in the Gospel of John*, 111-113.

[44]R. Girard, *A Theatre of Envy: William Shakespeare* (Oxford: Oxford University Press, 2004), 341-42.

9. Extensions of the Resurrection Effect

[1]I am not hereby denying the critical hermeneutical role of divine "Be-ing" for a proper appreciation of the transcendent nature of the gift and the love that it manifests. See Anthony J. Kelly, "A Multidimensional Disclosure: Aspects of Aquinas' Theological Intentionality", *The Thomist* 67/3 (July 2003), 335-374.

[2]*STh* 1, 27-43.

[3]For a spirited defense of the trinitarian psychological analogy, see Neil Ormerod, *The Trinity: Retrieving the Western Tradition* (Milwaukee, WI: Marquette University Press, 2005).

[4]For a perceptive treatment of the different approaches, see Anne Hunt, "The Psychological Analogy and the Paschal Mystery in Trinitarian Theology", *Theological Studies* 59 (1998): 197-218.

[5]Robert Doran, "The Starting Point of Systematic Theology", *Theological Stud-*

ies 67 (2006): 750-776, presents a profound argument for a trinitarian "starting point" for systematics, with special emphasis on the divine missions particularly as related to a "phenomenology of grace" (770). As will be evident, I would argue that the "starting point" is more basically related to the phenomenon of the resurrection as determining "the unified field structure" (753-757) of theological creativity. Once this is recognized, there is much in Doran's approach with which I cannot but agree. See especially his *What is Systematic Theology?* (Toronto: University of Toronto Press, 2005).

[6]Anne Hunt, *The Trinity and the Paschal Mystery: A Development in Recent Catholic Theology* (Collegeville, MN: The Liturgical Press, 1997).

[7]James Alison, *The Joy of Being Wrong: Original Sin through Easter Eyes* (New York: Crossroad, 1998), 213-219.

[8]Brian V. Johnstone, CSsR, "Transformation Ethics: The Moral Implications of the Resurrection", in Stephen T. Davis, David Kendall, SJ, and Gerald O'Collins, SJ, eds., *The Resurrection: An Interdisciplinary Symposium on the Resurrection of Jesus* (New York: Oxford University Press, 1997), 339-360.

[9]Oliver O'Donovan, *Resurrection and the Moral Order: An Outline for Evangelical Ethics* (Grand Rapids, MI: Eerdmans, 1986).

[10]René Girard, *I See Satan Fall Like Lightning* (Maryknoll, NY: Orbis Books, 2001), 161.

[11]For a major study, see Peter Stork, *Human Rights in Crisis: A Cultural Critique* (Saarbrücken: VDM Verlag Dr Müller, 2007).

[12]Michael Ignatieff, "Attack on Human Rights", *Foreign Affairs* 80/6 (December 2001), 102-116. For a major study, see Michael Ignatieff, *Human Rights as Politics and Idolatry* (Princeton: Princeton University Press, 2001).

[13]See Mary Ann Glendon, *A World Made New: Eleanor Roosevelt and the Universal Declaration of Human Rights* (New York: Random House, 2001), 36.

[14]L. C. Keith, "The United Nations Covenant on Civil and Political Rights: Does It Make a Difference in Human Rights Behavior?" *Journal for Peace Research* 36, no. 1 (1999): 95-118.

[15]See William Bole, Drew Anderson SJ, and Robert Hennemeyer, *Forgiveness in International Politics* (Washington, DC: United States Conference of Catholic Bishops, 2004).

[16]Johnstone notes that for Aquinas war is treated in the context of charity, not justice! (cf. *STh* 2-2, q. 39).

[17]Denis Edwards, "Resurrection and the Costs of Evolution: A Dialogue with Rahner on Non-Interventionist Theology", *Theological Studies* 67 (2006): 816-833—especially 827-833.

[18]See James Alison, *Raising Abel: The Recovery of the Eschatological Imagination* (New York: Crossroad, 1996), 31-41, for a profound exegesis of this text.

[19]*Gaudium et Spes*, "The Pastoral Constitution on the Church in the Modern World", par. 39, in *Documents of Vatican II, New Revised Edition*, ed. Austin P. Flannery OP (Grand Rapids, MI: Eerdmans, 1984), 938.

[20]Kevin Hart, *The Trespass of the Sign: Deconstruction, Theology and Philosophy* (New York: Fordham University Press, 2000), 273-298.

[21]William M. Thompson, "The Risen Christ, Transcultural Consciousness, and the Encounter of the World Religions", *Theological Studies* 37/3 (1976): 381-409.

[22]For an informative and challenging reflection, see Philip Jenkins, "Believing in the Global South", *First Things* 168 (December 2006): 12-18.

[23]Arthur O'Shaughnessy, "Ode" in Louis Untermeyer, ed., *Albatross Book of Verse* (London: Collins, 1966), 480.

[24]David Burrell, *Faith and Freedom: An Interfaith Perspective* (Oxford: Blackwell, 2004) points to the medieval experience of interfaith communication as a model,

and in some measure an antidote for the "monocultural attitude of *certainty* in which we know we are right" (255).

²⁵See William M. Thompson, *Jesus, Lord and Savior: A Theopathic Christology and Soteriology* (New York: Paulist, 1980), especially chapter 9, "Exploring the Christ-Experience IV: Thomas Merton's Transcultural Christ", 250-276.

²⁶On the inadequacies of the standard "inclusivist-exclusivist-pluralist" distinctions, see Lieven Boeve, "Resurrection: Saving Particularity: Theological-Epistemological Considerations of Incarnation and Truth", *Theological Studies* 67 (2006): 795-808.

²⁷Anthony J. Kelly, *Eschatology and Hope* (Maryknoll, NY: Orbis Books, 2006), 15-17.

²⁸Standard references here are: Stephen B. Bevans and Roger P. Schroeder, *Constants in Context: A Theology of Mission for Today* (Maryknoll, NY: Orbis Books, 2004). See also the much-discussed Jacques Dupuis, *Toward a Christian Theology of Religious Pluralism* (Maryknoll, NY: Orbis Books, 2001) and his more succinct, *Christianity and the Religions: From Confrontation to Dialogue*, trans. Phillip Berryman (Maryknoll, NY: Orbis Books, 2002).

²⁹Dupuis, *Christianity and the Religions,* 90-95; 123ff.; 185-187.

³⁰Dupuis, *Christianity and the Religions,* 159.

³¹On the relevance of John 4 to this question, see Anthony J. Kelly and Francis J. Moloney, *Experiencing God in the Gospel of John* (New York: Paulist, 2003), 97-114. See also Keith Ward, "Cosmology and Religious Ideas about the End of the World", in George F. R. Ellis, ed., *The Far-Future Universe: Eschatology from a Cosmic Perspective* (London: Templeton Foundation, 2002), 235-248. For any early attempt at a more global theology, see N. Smart and S. Konstantine, *Christian Systematic Theology in a World Context* (London: Marshall Pickering, 1991).

10. Resurrection as Horizon

¹*STh* 3, q. 56, a. 1, ad 3.

²*STh* 3, qq. 53-56.

³An excellent indication of this is Jean-Pierre Torrell, OP, *St. Thomas Aquinas: Spiritual Master*, trans. Robert Royal (Washington, DC: The Catholic University of America Press, 2003), especially 7-8, 132-136, 141-143, 256-257. See also, for a variety of topics and different approaches, Matthew Dauphinais and Matthew Levering, eds., *Reading John with St. Thomas Aquinas* (Washington, DC: The Catholic University of America Press, 2005), especially Pim Valkenberg, "Aquinas and Christ's Resurrection: The Influence of the *Lectura super Ioannem* 20-21" (277-289).

⁴*STh* 1, q. 43, a. 5 ad 2. See John Dedek, "*Quasi-Experimentalis Cognitio*: An Historical Approach to the Meaning of St Thomas", *Theological Studies* 22 (1961), 363-370.

⁵*STh* 1, q.1, a. 6 ad 3.

⁶Alyssa H. Pitstick, Lux in Tenebris:*TheTraditional Catholic Doctrine of Christ's Descent into Hell and the Theological Opinion of Hans Urs von Balthasar* (Grand Rapids, MI: Eerdmans, 2006).

⁷Robert Doran, SJ, "Lonergan and Balthasar: Methodological Considerations", *Theological Studies* 58 (1997): 61-84.

⁸Bernard J. F. Lonergan, S.J., *Method in Theology* (London: Darton, Longman and Todd, 1972), 112-113.

⁹See Neil Ormerod, *Method, Meaning and Revelation* (Lanham, MD: University of America Press, 2000) for a thorough treatment of this topic—which includes a refutation of my previous critical position on Lonergan's method.

[10]Doran, "Lonergan and Balthasar: Methodological Considerations", 78-83.

[11]Lonergan, *Method in Theology*, 53.

[12]Here, I am deliberately rephrasing Lonergan's beautiful description of the gift of radical love. See Lonergan, *Method in Theology*, 106.

[13]L. Wittgenstein, *Culture and Value*, trans. Peter Winch (Chicago: University of Chicago Press, 1980), 83.

Select Bibliography

Alison, James. *Knowing Jesus*. London: SPCK, 1993.

———. *Raising Abel: The Recovery of the Eschatological Imagination*. New York: Crossroad, 1996.

———. *The Joy of Being Wrong: Original Sin through Easter Eyes*. New York: Crossroad, 1998.

Bailie, Gil. *Violence Unveiled: Humanity at the Crossroads*. New York: Crossroad, 1997.

Bauckham, Richard. *Jesus and the Eyewitnesses: The Gospels as Eyewitness Testimony*. Grand Rapids, MI: Eerdmans, 2006.

Boeve, L. and L. Leijssen, eds. *Sacramental Presence in a Postmodern Context*. Leuven: Leuven University Press, 1991.

Charlesworth, James H. with C.D. Elledge, J. L. Crenshaw, H. Boers, and W. W. Willis Jr. *Resurrection: The Origin and Future of a Biblical Doctrine*. New York: T & T Clark, 2006.

Chauvet, L.-M., *Symbol and Sacrament: A Sacramental Reinterpretation of Christian Existence*. Trans. Patrick Madigan and Madeleine Beaumont. Collegeville, MN: The Liturgical Press, 1995.

———. *The Sacraments: The Word of God at the Mercy of the Body*. Collegeville, MN: The Liturgical Press, 2001.

Coakley, Sarah. " 'Not With the Eye Only': The Resurrection Epistemology and Gender". *Reflections* 5 (2001): 1-15.

Davis, Stephen T., Daniel Kendall, SJ, and Gerald O'Collins, SJ, eds. *The Resurrection: An Interdisciplinary Symposium on the Resurrection of Jesus*. New York: Oxford University Press, 1997.

Dunn, James D. G. *Christianity in the Making*, vol. 1: *Jesus Remembered*. Grand Rapids, MI: Eerdmans, 2003.

Durrwell, F.-X. *The Resurrection: A Biblical Study*. Trans. Rosemary Sheed. London and New York: Sheed and Ward, 1960.

Ellacuría, Ignacio and Jon Sobrino, eds. *Mysterium Liberationis: Fundamental Concepts of Liberation Theology*. Maryknoll, NY: Orbis Books, 1993.

Esler, Phillip F. *New Testament Theology: Communion and Community*. Minneapolis, MN: Fortress Press, 2005.

Gaburro, Sergio. *La Voce della Rivelazione: Fenomenologia della Voce per una Teologia della Rivelazione*. Milano: Edizioni San Paolo, 2005.

Glendon, Mary Ann. *A World Made New: Eleanor Roosvelt and the Universal Declaration of Human Rights*. New York: Random House, 2001.

Godzieba, Anthony J., Lieven Boeve and Michele Saracino. "Resurrection—Interruption—Transformation: Incarnation as Hermeneutical Strategy: A Symposium", *Theological Studies* 67 (2006):777-815.

Hart, David Bentley. *The Beauty of the Infinite: The Aesthetics of Christian Truth*. Grand Rapids, MI: Eerdmans, 2003.

Hart, Kevin. *The Trespass of the Sign: Deconstruction, Theology and Philosophy*. New York: Fordham University Press, 2000.

———. *Postmodernism: A Beginner's Guide*. London: Oneworld Publications, 2004.
Henry, Michel. *Incarnation: Une philosophie de la chair*. Paris: Seuil, 2000.
Hidber, Bruno. "Evil: Questioning and Challenging Theology Again and Again", *Studia Moralia* 44/1 (January-June 2006): 93-120.
Horner, Robyn. *Rethinking God as Gift: Marion, Derrida and the Limits of Phenomenology*. New York: Fordham University Press, 2001.
———. *Jean-Luc Marion: A Theo-Logical Introduction*. Burlington, VT: Ashgate, 2005.
Hunt, Anne. *The Trinity and the Paschal Mystery: A Development in Recent Catholic Theology*. Collegeville, MN: The Liturgical Press, 1997.
———. "The Psychological Analogy and the Paschal Mystery in Trinitarian Theology", *Theological Studies* 59 (1998): 197-218.
———. *Trinity: Nexus of the Mysteries of Christian Faith*. Maryknoll, NY: Orbis Books, 2005.
———. "With the Risen Lord: Francois-Xavier Durrwell CSsR (1912-2005)", *Australian E-Journal of Theology*, Pentecost 2006 Special Edition http://dlibrary.acu.edu.au/research/theology/ejournal/aejt_hunt.htm
Hurtado, Larry W. *Lord Jesus Christ: Devotion to Jesus in Earliest Christianity*. Grand Rapids, MI: Eerdmans, 2003.
Ignatieff, Michael. "Attack on Human Rights", *Foreign Affairs* 80/6 (December 2001): 102-116.
———. *Human Rights as Politics and Idolatry*. Princeton: Princeton University Press, 2001.
Janicaud, Dominique et al. *Phenomenology and "The Theological Turn": The French Debate*. Trans. Bernard G. Prusak, New York: Fordham University Press, 2000.
Kelly, Anthony and Francis J. Moloney. *Experiencing God in the Gospel of John*. New York: Paulist, 2003.
Kelly, Anthony J. *Trinity of Love: A Theology of the Christian God*. Wilmington, DE: Michael Glazier, 1989.
———. "Spirituality and Church", *Australasian Catholic Record* 78/3 (July 2001): 309-320.
———. "The Historical Jesus and Human Subjectivity", in Matthew C. Ogilvie and William J. Dannaher, eds., *Australian Lonergan Workshop II*. Drummoyne, NSW: Novum Organum Press, 2003, 151-179.
———. "A Multidimensional Disclosure: Aspects of Aquinas' Theological Intentionality", *The Thomist* 67/3, July 2003, 335-374.
———. "Dimensions of Meaning: Theology and Exegesis", in Rekha M. Chennattu and Mary M. Coloe, eds., *Transcending Boundaries: Contemporary Readings of the New Testament*. Rome: LAS, 2005, 41-56.
———. *Eschatology and Hope*. Maryknoll, NY: Orbis Books, 2006.
Kendall, Daniel, SJ, and Stephen T. Davis, eds. *The Convergence of Theology: A Festschrift Honoring Gerald O'Collins, SJ*. New York: Paulist Press, 2001.
Kessler, Thomas. *Peter as the First Witness to the Risen Lord: An Historical and Theological Investigation*. Rome: Editrice Pontificia Università Gregoriana, 1998.
Leask, Ian and Eion Cassidy, eds. *Givenness and God: Questions of Jean-Luc Marion*. New York: Fordham University Press, 2005.
Léon-Dufour, Xavier. *Resurrection and the Message of Easter*. London: Geoffrey Chapman, 1974.
Levinas, E.. "The Trace of the Other", in *Deconstruction in Context*, Mark C. Taylor, ed. Chicago: University of Chicago Press, 1986, 345-359.
Lonergan, Bernard. *Method in Theology*. London: Darton, Longman and Todd, 1972.
———. "Dimensions of Meaning", *Collection: Collected Works of Bernard Lonergan*, vol. 4, Frederick E. Crowe and Robert M. Doran, eds. Toronto: University of Toronto Press, 1993, 232-243.

Mackinlay, Shane. *Interpreting Excess: The Implicit Hermeneutics of Jean-Luc Marion's Saturated Phenomena*. New York: Fordham University Press, 2008.
Marion, Jean-Luc. *God without Being: Hors-Texte*. Trans. Thomas A. Carlson. Chicago: University of Chicago Press, 1991.
———. "The Saturated Phenomenon." Trans. Thomas A. Carlson, *Phenomenology and the "Theological Turn": The French Debate*, Dominique Janicaud et al. New York: Fordham University Press, 2000, 176-216.
———. *The Idol and Distance: Five Studies*. Trans. Thomas A. Carlson. New York: Fordham University Press, 2001.
———. *In Excess: Studies of Saturated Phenomena*. Trans. Robyn Horner and Vincent Barraud. New York: Fordham University Press, 2002.
———. *The Crossing of the Visible*. Trans. James K. A. Smith. Stanford: Stanford University Press, 2004.
Matera, Frank J. "Christ in the Theologies of Paul and John: Diverse Unity of New Testament Theology", *Theological Studies* 67/2 (June 2006): 237-256.
McIntosh, Mark A. *Discernment and Truth: The Spirituality and Theology of Knowledge*. New York: Crossroad, 2004.
Meyer, B. F. *The Aims of Jesus*. London: SCM, 1979.
———. *Critical Realism and the New Testament*. Allison Park: Pickwick, 1989.
Moore, Sebastian. *The Fire and the Rose Are One*. London: Darton, Longman and Todd, 1980.
Morse, Christopher. *Not Every Spirit: A Dogmatics of Christian Disbelief*. Valley Forge, PA: Trinity Press International, 1994.
Mostert, Christiaan. *God and the Future: Wolfhart Pannenberg's Eschatological Doctrine of God*. Edinburgh: T & T Clark, 2002.
O'Collins, G. *Jesus Risen: The Resurrection—What actually happened and what does it mean?* London: Darton, Longman and Todd, 1987.
———. "Peter as Easter Witness", *Heythrop Journal* 22 (1981), 1-18.
Osborne, Kenan. *The Resurrection of Jesus: New Considerations for Its Theological Interpretation*. New York: Paulist Press, 1997.
Pannenberg, Wolfhart. *Jesus—God and Man*. Trans. Lewis L. Wilkins and Duane A. Priebe. London: SCM Press, 1976.
Perkins, P. *Resurrection: New Testament Witness and Contemporary Reflection*. Garden City, NY: Doubleday, 1984.
Pitstick, Alyssa H. *Lux in Tenebris: The Traditional Catholic Doctrine of Christ's Descent into Hell and the Theological Opinion of Hans Urs von Balthasar*. Grand Rapids, MI: Eerdmans, 2006.
Polkinghorne, J. C. and M. Welker, eds. *The End of the World and the Ends of God*. Harrisburg, PA: Trinity Press International, 2000.
Rahner, Karl. "The Concept of Mystery in Catholic Theology", *Theological Investigations IV*. Kevin Smyth, Baltimore, MD: Helicon Press, 1966, 36-73.
———. *Theological Investigations III: Theology of the Spiritual Life*. Trans. Karl-H. and Boniface Kruger. Baltimore, MD: Helicon Press, 1967, 294-317.
———. "The Experience of God Today", *Theological Investigations XI*. Trans. David Bourke. London: Darton, Longman and Todd, 1974, 149-165.
Ratzinger, Joseph. *Eschatology: Death and Eternal Life*. Trans. M. Walstein. Washington, DC: The Catholic University of America Press, 1988.
Robinette, Brian. "A Gift to Theology? Jean-Luc Marion's 'Saturated Phenomenon' in Christological Perspective", *Heythrop Journal* 48/1 (January, 2007): 86-108.
Romano, Claude. *L'événement et le monde*. Paris: Presses Universitaires de France, 1998.
———. *L'événement et le temps*. Paris: Presses Universitaires de France, 1999.
Sawicki, Maryanne. *Seeing the Lord: Resurrection and Early Christian Practices*. Minneapolis, MN: Fortress Press, 1994.

Schüssler-Fiorenza, Francis. *Foundational Theology: Jesus and the Church*. New York: Crossroad, 1984.

Schwager, Raymund. *Jesus in the Drama of Salvation: Toward a Biblical Doctrine of Redemption*. Trans. James G. Williams and Paul Haddon. New York: Crossroad, 1999.

Sokolowski, Robert. *Introduction to Phenomenology*. Cambridge: Cambridge University Press, 2000.

———. *Christian Faith and Human Understanding: Studies on the Eucharist, Trinity and the Human Person*. Washington, DC: The Catholic University of America Press, 2006.

Stewart, Robert B., ed. *The Resurrection of Jesus. John Dominic Crossan and N.T. Wright in Dialogue*. Minneapolis MN: Fortress Press, 2006.

Stork, Peter. *Human Rights in Crisis: A Cultural Critique*. Saarbrücken: VDM Verlag Dr Müller, 2007.

———. *Human Rights in Crisis: Is There no Answer to Human Violence? A Cultural Critique in Conversation with René Girard and Raymund Schwager*. PhD diss., Australian Catholic University.

Thiel, John E. "For What May We Hope? Thoughts on the Eschatological Imagination", *Theological Studies* 67/3 (September 2006): 517-541.

Thompson, William. *Jesus, Lord and Savior: A Theopathic Christology and Soteriology*. New York: Paulist, 1980.

———. *The Struggle for Theology's Soul: Contesting Scripture in Christology*. New York: Crossroad, 1996.

Voegelin, Eric. *Order and History*, vol. 4:*The Ecumenic Age*. Baton Rouge, LA: Louisiana State University Press, 1974.

Von Balthasar, Hans Urs. Mysterium Paschale: *The Mystery of Easter*. Translated with an introduction by Aidan Nichols, OP. Edinburgh: T&T Clark, 1990.

———. *The Glory of the Lord: A Theological Aesthetics,* vol. I: *Seeing the Form*. Trans. Erasmo Leiva-Merikakis. Joseph Fessio, SJ and John Riches, eds. New York: Crossroad, 1983.

———. *The Glory of the Lord: A Theological Aesthetics,* vol. VII: *The New Covenant*. Trans. Brian McNeil, CRV. Edinburgh: T & T Clark, 1989.

Wittgenstein, Ludwig, *Culture and Value*. Trans. Peter Winch. Chicago: Chicago University Press, 1980.

Wright, N. T. *The Resurrection of the Son of God*. Minneapolis, MN: Fortress Press, 2003.

Subject and Name Index